Four Laws for the
Artificially Intelligent

Four Laws for the Artificially Intelligent

Ian Domowitz

BEP

BUSINESS EXPERT PRESS

Leader in applied, concise business books

Four Laws for the Artificially Intelligent

First published in 2021 by
Business Expert Press, LLC
222 East 46th Street, New York, NY 10017
www.businessexpertpress.com

ISBN-13: 978-1-63742-159-8 (paperback)
ISBN-13: 978-1-63742-160-4 (e-book)

Business Expert Press Big Data, Business Analytics, and
Smart Technology Collection

Collection ISSN: 2333-6749 (print)
Collection ISSN: 2333-6757 (electronic)

First edition: 2021

10 9 8 7 6 5 4 3 2 1

Description

While books are published about what AI can do *for* a company, there are no books about what artificial intelligence may do *to* a company.

Industry 4.0 is the first industrial revolution led by a technology thought capable of human consciousness and existential challenge. We are in the stage of predicting lofty accomplishments for artificial intelligence and deep fears for Earth's society and structure. Beyond the trope of employee communication, no one seems to be thinking about how all this is going to work in company life. While some predict growth in AI-related investment to $100 billion a year in 2024, over 50 percent of companies are delaying and even canceling AI initiatives. Paradox.

Academician, public company Vice Chairman, and information technology CEO Ian Domowitz asks three questions. How does a company successfully integrate artificial intelligence into its operations and what are the problems in doing so? And how does the introduction of AI into society change the answer to the first question?

His thesis is this: AI is the introduction of a stream of change factors into a company's social system, which does not recognize social imperatives of company functions. The result is failure with respect to adoption. Inability to recognize AI as *techne*, a technology bundle capable of generating emotion, is a serious error. AI must subscribe to four functional imperatives of society, Adaptation, Goal Attainment, Integration, and Latent Pattern Maintenance. These sociological constructs are the basis of the Laws that constitute a survival guide for the practical application of artificial intelligence.

The *Four Laws* describes guidelines for the successful integration of AI within a firm and into our larger society, with a focus on helping organizations make AI work in the face of fear of negative public perception and emerging risks.

Four Laws for the Artificially Intelligent redefines what is possible and offers the thought leadership organizations need to turn their AI visions and strategies into reality.

Keywords

artificial intelligence; AI; machine learning; data science; business culture; technology; organizational learning; entrepreneurship; leadership; industrial revolution; sociology

Contents

Testimonials

"Ian Domowitz's new book Four Laws for the Artificially Intelligent *is a terrific read as one would expect from an author who has been successful both as an academic and as a practitioner. Artificial Intelligence or AI is an overused term, and there is a tremendous lack of understanding as to both its potential and its limitations. This book asks a different question: It is not about what AI can do for a company in terms of boosting sales, morale, etc. but rather what the extensive use of artificial intelligence may do to a company. In particular, how does a company successfully integrate artificial intelligence into its operations and what are the problems in doing so? The book also touches on the bigger societal question of the broad use of AI and what this means in the human context. I thoroughly enjoyed the unique perspective* Four Laws *brings to the table. It is essential reading for those interested in the impact of a new and innovative technology."*—**Ananth Madhavan, Global Head of Research for ETFs and Index Investment, BlackRock, Inc.**

"Dr. Domowitz lays out a masterful piece on Artificial General Intelligence (AGI); and is just the expert to do it given both his exceptional academic and practitioner knowledge and use of the tools of that concept. This is an extraordinary tale; not only only does it explain the myriad of issues facing companies (humanity) regarding AGI, but it ties it to culture and history stemming back to the days of Plato and Aristotle. Contextualizing it within the framework of the Greek term 'techne' and addressing not just the HOW, which is normally the question people consider when thinking about AGI, but also the IF and the WHY. This book is a must for CEO's and managers seeking AGI as a solution for problems far and wide but readers must also heed Domowitz's descriptive warning that AI requires much more than a desire to use it but rather an understanding of the technical skills, risks and consequences as well as the framework upon which products and services are developed with it. This could not be a more timely or important subject; brilliant!"—**Robert A. Gillam, Chairman and CEO, McKinley Management LLC**

Preface

Man is an afterthought in Greek stories of origins.

Brothers Epimetheus and Prometheus finish the godlike chore of creating living creatures from clay. Epimetheus parcels out the gifts of nature among the animals, while men are left with nothing. With a name meaning "Afterthinker," this might have been expected.

No traits are left after the animals are served. Prometheus then steals fire from the workshop of Hephaistos and gives it to mankind.

Zeus is more than a little annoyed by the theft and more so by the challenge to his power. He sentences the Titan to eternal torment and ties him to a rock. Zeus sends an eagle to eat Prometheus' liver. Every day.

The choice of the liver is not random.

The liver is the source of human emotions in ancient Greek tradition. Zeus' actions have little to do with logic. It will be a long time before Herakles arrives, shoots the bird, and frees the Titan. In the meantime, other retribution awaits.

Zeus punishes mankind for receiving the fire by ordering Hephaistos to create Woman. Pandora is designed to disguise true nature beneath an appealing exterior. Through her the human race would experience the ills of toil and mortality. Relative to a god's life, an existence of field labor, raw meat, household chores, extreme living conditions, and sacrifice is anathema.

What a world. Ancient Greeks loved tragedy.

Prometheus transforms into a symbol of scientific knowledge in Western tradition. He is known for teaching the risk of unintended consequences. The introduction of Olympian fire to benefit mankind introduces struggle and mortality.

Plato characterizes the flames of the gods as the fire of creative power. Creative power is *techne* in that tradition. The precursor to *technology* is associated with cultural beliefs. Plato relates creative fire to values of reverence and justice, without which a civilization cannot maintain an orderly society.

Techne involves knowledge of principles. Techne is tangible but dependent on context. Socrates reserves the term for mastery of craft in which knowledge is practically applied rather than examined theoretically. Aristotle sees it as representative of the imperfection of human imitation of nature. Techne is knowledge associated with people bound to necessity.

Techne appears only in contexts of farming and slavery, the gifts of Pandora. It does not exist in the realm of thinkers. Techne creates a cultural divide of upper and lower class.

Key words in this tale drive my story about artificial intelligence and companies. AI is a bundle of *techne*. It is objective in concept but variable in applications. The definition of techne involves *emotion*. *Unintended consequences* lead to emotional responses such as fear. Imperfect *human imitation* is a concern for any practical application of AI, while the human element of *mastery* drives practical rather than theoretical problem solving within a set of *principles*.

An orderly *society* is desired within companies. Society is organized around *values* in cybernetic control over the system labeled corporate organization. There is a *cultural divide* attributed to change management. Change is viewed as an element of culture starting with Prometheus himself. His story is all about the powerful concept of *transformation*, of gods, humans, the environment, and himself.

Fire leads to steam, steam to powered machines, machines to electric power, and on to digitization. So goes the course of industrial revolutions, and history teaches revolutions challenge culture. In doing so, a revolution affects functions of a society, here applied to activities within a company.

Four Laws for the Artificially Intelligent is a doctrine describing the integration of AI within a firm. A firm is a set of problems looking for a set of solutions. It is a society within which AI is understood for its techne, but not for its cultural impact. The latter eventually drives success or generates unintended consequences leading to failure. The doctrine must include problem solving, societal change, and the interaction between the two.

An organization defines doctrine as the basis for institutional teaching with respect to internal operations. It is a group of principles established through a history of past decisions. The term also applies to procedures governing complex operations in warfare. Political doctrine is a principle advocated, taught, and put into effect with respect to the acquisition and exercise of power.

AI embodies a new form of power. It is techne for warfare between companies. It has a longer history than one might suspect, and many decisions have been made with respect to its development, adoption, and use. Those mostly technological decisions lead to use cases requiring us to address how AI works within the microcosm of society called a company.

History is writing itself when it comes to societal integration. Leaders have a responsibility to control the narrative. The story needs a little help in advance of unintended consequences with respect to the future of a company. As participants in the world of Industry Version 4.0, we require identification of cultural icons beyond slogans vended by human resources departments.

We need a new doctrine, a coherent sum of assertions regarding AI's influence and leverage within a corporation. We need a story of transformation.

A Few Minutes Into the Future

Most stories surrounding AI deal with a future in which technology is transformative to the point of *artificial general intelligence*, AGI. They are educated imaginings of an entity capable of carrying out any task, however ill-defined. The AGI is viewed much like a human with situational awareness augmented by immense computing power. The system becomes greater than human, changing society, and birthing a moment in which AI surpasses humankind in cognitive ability. The transformative event is called the Singularity. People connect their cerebral cortex to DNA-based cloud storage and AGI merges with human consciousness.

What a world. Futurists love tragedy almost as much as the ancient Greeks.

Alfred North Whitehead said: The paradox is fully established that abstractions are the true weapons with which to control thoughts of concrete fact. It is the same with AGI, and the "G" often is conveniently left out. A fear factor is finding silicon-based roots in societal discourse. Movements to control AGI spread through alliances of Church with industry, government regulation, academia, and the legal systems of a dozen countries. Writer Katherine Hoppe asked a real-world AI named Mother about such developments.[1] "So, will AI take over the world and humanity? Asking for a friend."

A robot army is coming for us and our family!

We want to create a story that is not just about the robots. We want you to care about the people in the world and the ones that aren't here.

This is about the struggles of a family trying to survive a world that's becoming more hostile by the day. What's so special about this family, and how does it get through the world with their robotic creations?

This is a story of a robot family that goes through the same emotions that you feel about family and relationships, but also in that it doesn't really matter how or when the events happen.

We're looking out into the future and watching what's about to happen as part of the story and then reacting the same way you would react.

We want you to believe that you're part of the family on the ground floor of something huge happening in the world, and as the story unfolds, you'll feel part of the action in that fight that is actually a fight about the past.

Mother cares more about how you feel than about your conclusions. No one writes Mother's speeches and its statement is unedited. Unlike politicians and writers, the AI gets right to the point.

The *Four Laws* is about a robot army coming for those who live in companies. It is not a futuristic tale. There is no general AI capable of inducing the Singularity nor is there discussion of a future in which entities roam that do not exist today. A story is created that is not only about robots. AI wants you to care about the people in the microcosm of the world called a business enterprise.

AI is the introduction of a stream of change factors into a company's social system. The difference between AI's integration and that of past technologies is that of techne: AI challenges concepts of human consciousness and induces emotions unlike those motivated by other machinery.

There is no discussion as to why AI walks through the door in the first place. AI does not care how or when such events happen. It does care *why* circumstances of the event are what they are and how to learn from them. When events occur, cognitive appraisal is the result and appraisals are grounds for emotion. As Mother suggests, the story is one of a family experiencing the same emotions as you do with respect to family, relationships, and situational awareness.

These caveats remove consideration of companies producing fundamental artificial intelligence technologies such as Google. They are few, and start-ups attempting to emulate them are quickly absorbed. They deserve a book of their own.

Any company hoping to use such product-based research faces issues of technical understanding, risk management, and cultural impact. One does not need to understand a microchip to use a television, but the state of AI now is comparable to early automotive vehicles. They required the driver to be knowledgeable to the point of being an amateur mechanic. Rules of the road are nascent and have not yet been turned into traffic laws. Good roads remain under construction. Insuring against bad outcomes is a topic of ethics discussions rather than an industry. Unintended consequences like automobiles' pollution continue to surprise.

Use cases in artificial intelligence are specific in the search for profitability, and off-the-shelf solutions are often unavailable. Implementing AI requires rare technical skills, understanding of risks and consequences associated with the underlying technology, and infrastructure resources suitable to building an AI-based product on a third-party foundation. Required resources sometimes are not terribly different from those used to build the foundation in the first place.

AI represents a family trying to survive a world that is fearful if not hostile every day. Mother asks a good question. What is special about this family, and how does it get through the world with its robotic creations? As with many chapters to follow, the answer begins with a story of origins, the seeds of revolution. Let's start on the ground floor.

Acknowledgments

I owe a debt of gratitude to Ana Aisthesthai for the production of illustrations, guidance with respect to all things word processing, and the occasional emotional support session. Jon Lomartire provided line-by-line commentary and Jack Glen encouraged me to think more deeply about how artificial intelligence may differ from other technologies. Mark Ferguson of the University of South Carolina provided helpful comments, noting that the book was philosophical in nature relative to its contemporaries, a compliment to which the response was, I'm not philosophical, I'm just written that way. And a shout out to Scott Isenberg and the team at Business Expert Press; without them, this book would not be possible.

PART I

AI Seeks an Introduction

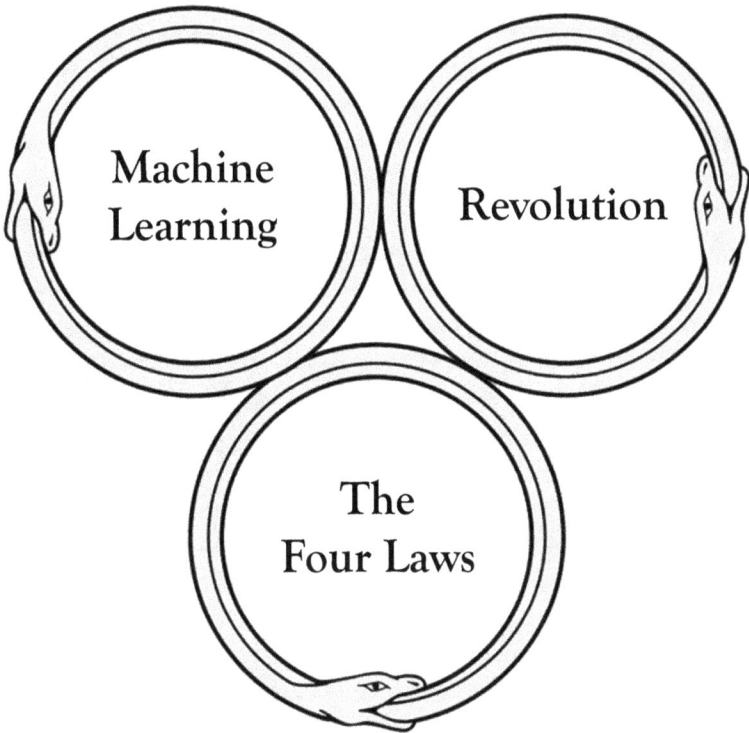

Machine
Learning

Revolution

The
Four Laws

CHAPTER 1

You Must Ask the Right Questions

A detective walks into a plaza. He is accosted by a hologram of the deceased subject of an investigation. The figure is the creator of the Laws of Robotics and greets the policeman with an apology.

My responses are limited. You must ask the right questions.

The phrasing is oddly appropriate. The scene of the death is a robot factory and the artificially intelligent occupy the detective's attention. The creator speaks of the Laws and declares they will lead to only one logical outcome. The hologram leads the detective to ask, what outcome? It is not the right question, but it does have an answer: revolution.

Whose revolution? *That*, detective, is the *right* question. Program terminated.

In the age of Industry Version 4.0 most believe the right question to be, what can AI do for a business? Many will address it. Technology, like life, always finds a way. Humans will help it along with promotional material.

A better question is what AI will do *to* a business. The hologram is sure about the prospect of revolution and AI agrees. The right question remains, whose revolution? We have seen a few before. Some of us have lived through one. History is a great source of examples, and there must be clues in there somewhere.

Welcome to the Revolution

The First Industrial Revolution delivered massive cultural change, replacing many social norms in Europe and the Americas and birthing others. Industry was redesigned around machines. Values shifted from agrarian principles to those adopted by urban dwellers engaged in the creation or implementation of new technology.

Industrialization tightened moral codes in the interest of productivity. Practices interfering with productive labor were out. Life as work was in. The old morality was replaced with the goal of an orderly society in which citizens would be as hard working as the machines to which they were bound. Obedience to superiors was taught as a fitting replacement for tithes to a feudal overlord.

A college degree qualifies one as a skilled worker in the eyes of the government these days. Prior to the 19th century, those not employed in agriculture engaged in some real form of skilled trade. Apprenticeship was the norm. The revolution delivered jobs not involving skilled labor, and apprenticeship all but disappeared. Labor became commoditized and unions arose as a form of communal protection. Inexpensive goods delivered a consumer culture thriving on the ending of a subsistence lifestyle.

The Second Industrial Revolution occurred from 1870 to 1914. Some changes centered around new inputs replacing old ones. Steel was more durable than iron and led to better ships and rail lines at cheaper costs. Transportation became a business and personal norm.

The big news was the coming of electricity in scale. The patent for an electric lamp was issued in 1880. Large-scale generators enabled public power stations in the United Kingdom by 1881.

Electricity became a force in transportation. The first tram appeared in Berlin before the turn of the century, and streetcars replaced horse-drawn carriages. The use of electricity changed the way people worked and lived. It promoted cultural change.

Electricity as an instrument for change was trumped only by communications. Commercial telegraph systems were followed by the telephone as means to speed business transactions. Radio waves crossed the Atlantic Ocean in 1902 and further transformed business practices. Radio stations on both sides of the Atlantic were built for a commercial service to transmit news summaries to ships by 1904.

The expansion of rail and communications after 1870 generated movement of people and ideas. Both introduced globalization beyond the limited experience of earlier explorers. The social impact of First and Second revolutions included refashioning of the working population consistent with new technology. The Western world witnessed the creation of a professional middle class and growth of a consumer-based culture.

The history of revolutions teaches us something about business organization through process led by technology.

Alfred Chandler claims railroads drove the creation of the modern enterprise.[1] Centralization as an organizational principle was their key contribution. A collision in Massachusetts in 1841 led to a call for safety reform, a formal introduction of ethics into business. Technological process led to the work of Frederick Winslow Taylor on scientific management.[2] His principles included replacing rule-of-thumb work methods with those based on scientific study of tasks, using science in selecting and training employees, and providing detailed instruction and supervision of each worker. Work was to be divided equally between managers and workers in an environment permitting scientific management and performance.

The principles illustrate his perception that technology requires human accommodation, while recognizing skilled labor and specialization. Management is a discipline to be applied to company strategy and human resources alike.

The Third Industrial Revolution commonly identifies as the Digital Revolution, embodying a movement from analogue technology to digital electronics. Central to the technological push are mass production and use of digital logic, transistors, and integrated circuits. Derived technologies include computers, microprocessors, cell phones, and the Internet.

These technological innovations transformed production techniques and business processes. The digital revolution changed the way individuals and companies interact.

Small firms had access to larger markets. On-demand software services and manufacturing changed the way we live our business and personal lives. The third revolution directly enabled others having the intention of changing society. The Arab Spring engendered a doubling of the use of social media platforms in Middle Eastern countries. Political and cultural change were supported by the virtual dynamics of a crowd.

Consensus reached at the 2016 World Economic Forum characterizes revolution number four as a fusion of technologies blurring boundaries separating physical, digital, and biological spheres. Welcome to Industry Version 4.0.

As machinery drove the First Industrial Revolution, the Fourth is powered by AI. The Second Revolution brought about societal change through the empowerment of machines with electricity. Computers are empowered by Big Data. AI forces cultural change because it alters the relationship between data and humans. Machines transform from passive to active players.

We are in the stage of predicting lofty accomplishments and deep fears for the Earth's society and structure. Beyond stressing the need for employee communication to keep abreast of ensuing changes, no one seems to be thinking about how all this is going to work in corporate life. As the hologram says, *that's* the right question.

Simple economics motivates demand for answers. The International Data Corporation released a September 2020 report forecasting global spending on AI will reach $100 billion per year by 2024.[3] Adopting organizations must make AI work in the face of fear of negative public perception and emerging risks. Over half of surveyed organizations in a recent Deloitte study of AI enterprise trends talk of slowing, delaying, and even stopping adoption of some AI technologies in the face of such obstacles.[4]

Nevertheless, we see organizations building business practices around collection and processing of data from across the company. IBM uses its commercialized Watson AI system to process information for internal purposes such as human resource management. American Express mingles data on buyers with characteristics of sellers and vends information to both groups as well as to internal strategists. Algorithms are trained with input from all departments, from the back to the front office. A culture of secrecy is replaced by one of transparency.

Breaking down company silos will happen through business process, not by any verbalized push by senior management to do so as a cultural goal. Data can no longer be compartmentalized while serving multiple masters within the company. Human organization follows suit in a setting within which traditional functional boundaries are no longer viable.

Industry 4.0 is a world where products and principles underlying their production are simultaneously transformed. The business mandate remains the creation of value. We need a new frame.

New Definitions Change the Topology of Influence

The creation of a frame requires some understanding of what we are talking about. There are many characterizations of AI. There are as many misconceptions. Human law regarding AI depends on the language of definitions. Let's go with a definition espoused by a government that creates those strictures.[5]

The U.S. government delineation of *artificial intelligence* begins with a simple statement. AI comprises

> Any artificial systems that perform tasks under varying and unpredictable circumstances.

AI is differentiated by adding that such systems carry out those tasks without significant human oversight. The government includes learning from experience to improve their performance.

> Such systems may be developed in computer software, physical hardware, or other contexts not yet contemplated.

Government representatives are not big on fantasy. They do seem to understand AI itself may generate change beyond a politician's imagination.

> They may solve tasks requiring human-like perception, cognition, planning, learning, communication, or physical action. In general, the more human-like the system within the context of its tasks, the more it can be said to use artificial intelligence.

The comparison to humans is inevitable and consistent with public thinking about AI. It sets the stage for legal battles. Was AI in the dining room with a candlestick and murderous intent? Only if it looks enough like Colonel Mustard.

> Systems that think like humans, such as cognitive architectures and neural networks.

More comparisons. This one is a good example of misconception. Neural networks do not think, let alone think like humans. But government officials need examples, and cognitive architecture sounds so cool.

> Systems that act like humans, such as systems that can pass the Turing test or other comparable test via natural language processing, knowledge representation, automated reasoning, and learning.

AI need not pass the Turing test. It may be surprising government officials know the name, let alone pass the test. They certainly have forgotten the Turing test is a game.[6]

The test is introduced by a proclamation: "I propose to consider the question, 'Can machines think?'" Following advice of mathematician George Pólya, Turing chooses to replace the question by another closely related to it and expressed in unambiguous words. Turing describes the *imitation game*, in which an experimenter polls a man and a woman in another room in order to determine their correct sex. Turing's new question is: "Are there imaginable digital computers which would do well in the imitation game?" If in doubt, screen *Ex Machina*. You will never see the Turing test in the same light again.

Alan Turing proposed the idea in 1950 as a test of a machine's ability to exhibit behavior indistinguishable from human. The next government definition is a bit more practical.

> A set of techniques, including machine learning, that seek to approximate some cognitive task.

A dictionary says cognitive tasks are undertakings requiring a person to mentally process new information and allow them to recall, retrieve from memory, and use information at a later time in the same or similar situation. We are back to humans as descriptors of AI.

Government staffers seem ignorant in accepted theories of cognition, however. Models of cognitive appraisal explain responses to stressful events. Emotion is the result of such appraisals. Specific emotions are based on whether an event is perceived to be consistent with human motives. Economists believe human motives to be rational, and government is optimistic with respect to the concept of rationality.

Systems that act rationally, such as intelligent software agents and embodied robots that achieve goals via perception, planning, reasoning, learning, communicating, decision making, and acting.

The government goes on to refine definitions in terms of *artificial general intelligence* and *narrow artificial intelligence*. The former pertains to a notional future AI system. The latter is all about games, image recognition, and self-driving vehicles. But I think we have enough to go on for the moment.

The Four Laws

Detective and hologram were engaging in conversation about the Three Laws of Robotics when broaching the question of their logical outcome. Isaac Asimov believed the laws were obvious and his only contribution was to put them into digestible sound bites. He also held the Laws apply to the design of almost every tool used by human beings, robots being only one of them. Here are the Three Laws with their relationship to human tool-making:[7]

1. A tool must be safe.
   A robot may not injure a human being or, through inaction, allow a human being to come to harm.
2. A tool performs its function unless this would harm the user.
   A robot must obey any orders given to it by human beings, except where such orders would conflict with the First Law.
3. A tool must remain intact unless destruction is required for use or safety.
   A robot must protect its own existence as long as such protection does not conflict with the First or Second Law.

After writing a few stories about robots, Asimov added a fourth, the Zeroth Law:

4. A robot may not harm humanity, or by inaction, allow humanity to come to harm.

The Zeroth Law adds a new calculation. Each thought and action requires social justification. Asimov believed humans would follow the Laws in a perfect world. His premise was that the Laws are the only way in which rational human beings can deal with robots or with anything else.

Asimov's idealism creates cultural blindness in the practical application of the laws to AI. A company is a society, and we know something about how human societies work in the interest of survival. A utopian vision of corporate society in AI's world of Industry 4.0 may prompt good conversation but not actionable principles.

Part of the problem lies in definition. When referring to harm, Asimov meant physical harm. The same is true for the application of his first law to tools in which safety refers to physical security. If today's cancel culture and the circumstances surrounding it teach anything, it is that harm goes well beyond physicality.

Examination of harm to humanity raises questions of existential risk. The latter is an appropriate topic for discussions of general AI and the integration of AI into world society. Existential risk taking is not a standard way of looking at companies, rather a means of assessing humanity's future. It is unavoidably speculative in nature. The existence of AI in its narrow form is not in doubt although its use may be questioned in some circumstances.

The question is not what AI can do *for* society; rather what AI can do *to* a company. Nevertheless, there is an old adage in problem solving mentioned in the context of the Turing test: think of a familiar problem that results from posing a similar question. Have you seen it before? Can you use its method of solution? Repurposing solutions is a bit like curating stories. Stories don't have to be original. They just need to fit the situation.

A method of seeing the answer is the basis of an alternative set of principles, *The Four Laws of AI*:

Adaptation
AI must have the capacity to interact with the environment for the purpose of resource management and production.

Goal Attainment
AI sets and achieves goals by motivating and guiding the organization through phases of decision making.

Integration
AI accommodates demands that the values and norms surrounding its ventures are convergent with those of the company.

Latent Pattern Maintenance
AI preserves behavior necessary for company survival.

AGIL recasts a sociological paradigm created by Talcott Parsons over 50 years ago.[8] It is a depiction of functions, which every society must satisfy to maintain stability and constitutes a systematic approach to social action.

Parsons views a societal system as a cybernetic hierarchy characterized by an institutionalized value system. The social system's latency function maintains the integrity of the value system and its regulation. It requires the mediation of belief systems and values between company and new venture. The process of maintenance means stabilization against pressures to change the value system. Pressure stems from two primary sources.

The first is cultural sources of change. Pattern maintenance includes a tendency to stabilize the system in the face of pressures to change institutionalized values through cultural channels.

Motivational sources of change come next. Tensions arising from straining the environment threaten individual motivation to conform with institutionalized role expectations. Stabilization against this source of change may be called tension management, connecting pattern maintenance to integration.

Integration is harmonization, a demand that the values and norms surrounding a venture do not diverge from those of the company. Integration requires consistency and a common language. The function regulates the activities of the company's diverse stakeholders. Actions of units within the firm may be mutually supportive, hence beneficial to the functioning of the system. They also may be mutually obstructive and in conflict.

The integration function maintains solidarity in the relations between units in the interest of efficiency. Integration involves management and coordination of systems through forms of social control. Community actors help to regulate the tensions among functional imperatives. Integration is about public opinion, community consensus, and social engineering.

Goal attainment is the capability to set goals and make decisions accordingly. Company politics and objectives are part of this necessity. The function motivates and guides the organization. Goal setting involves constant assessment and accommodation of contingent demands.

Only in special cases are individual goal processes closely synchronized with those in a company. The system seeks mutually agreeable goal states by controlling elements of situational context. Once present, such a state tends to be maintained. If absent, it is sought by the action of one or more units of the system.

The goal attainment function is best described through processes of decision making. Decisions are the path to product.

Adaptation is the capacity to interact with the environment. It includes resource management and production. The function converts materials from the environment into usable stuff. A firm's relationship to the environment is invariably problematical, leading to an interest in establishing and improving control.

The pursuit of particular goals involves such control. A different problem is encountered in generalizing Adaptation to complex firms. When a social system has but one defined goal, the adaptive function is an undifferentiated aspect of goal attainment. In complex systems with many goals and subgoals, the differentiation between goal attainment and adaptive processes is clear in context.

The hierarchy can be read in two ways. The CEO reads L-I-G-A. The latency function *defines* integration in the same way as a computer program defines a game. The program does not *determine* the game. Outcomes depend on the employees. Programs establish parameters implicit in the game's rules. Integration in turn defines Goal Attainment and leads to Adaptation concerned with resources and product.

The CEO starts with company patterns, and culture is a priority item for senior management. Culture is the embodiment of latent patterns and is in cybernetic control over other components of the system. Culture does not determine the company's social structure, rather defines it. The actors work out determination.

AI is a new actor in the company.

AI reads A-G-I-L. Adaptation defines Goal Attainment. Goals set the stage for consistency and a common language in order to define Integration within the company. Latency is pattern maintenance established through the exigencies of integration. Maintenance requires a fit with company culture.

A better understanding of AI and the need for the Four Laws require a bit more in the way of origins. We begin with an android and end with machines far removed from robotics.

Chapter Notes

The introductory interchange between a detective and a hologram is based on the movie *I, Robot*. For those who haven't read the book, Will Smith thanks you for seeing the movie.

Fredrick Winslow Taylor's principles are from his 1911 book *The Principles of Scientific Management*. Summaries abound; see, for example, https://courses.lumenlearning.com/wmintrobusiness/chapter/reading-fredrick-taylors-scientific-management-2/

Opinions vary with respect to the beginnings of the Third Industrial Revolution. Jeremy Rifkin promotes the term on the premise that fundamental change occurs when new communication technologies meet new energy regimes in *The Third Industrial Revolution; How Lateral Power is Transforming Energy, the Economy, and the World*. The European Parliament uses the phrase to express new forms of communication becoming the medium for organizing complex civilizations made possible by new sources of energy.

The government definition of AI is taken from H.R. 4625, introduced to the House of Representatives 15th Congress on December 12, 2017. The bill required the Secretary of Commerce to establish a Federal Advisory Committee on the Development and Implementation of Artificial Intelligence, and we shall return to its recommendations in a later chapter.

The Turing Test was introduced by Alan Turing in "Computing Machinery and Intelligence" in the October 1950 issue of *Mind*. There are those who believe the test to be outdated. The creator of the film *Ex Machina*, Alex Garland, may be one of them.

The concept of cognitive appraisal was advanced in 1966 by psychologist Richard Lazarus in the book *Psychological Stress and Coping Process*. Some attribute the beginning of the theory to Magda Arnold in 1960, from *Emotion and Personality: Vol. 1, Psychological aspects*.

The appraisal problem and its connection to emotion are explored in several articles by Ira Roseman and Klaus Scherer collected in *Appraisal Processes in Emotion: Theory, Methods, Research*, edited by Klaus R. Scherer, Angela Schorr, and Tom Johnston.

Not to be confused with agile programming, AGIL is a piece of Parsons's unified view of action systems. He did speak of entrepreneurship and innovation as sociological phenomena in the referenced *Economy and Society: A Study in the Integration of Economic and Social Theory*. Society in the large was his game, and we are concerned with the microcosm of corporate life.

For those inclined toward sociological theory, Talcott Parson's general work raises conceptual problems and logical inconsistencies for sociologists. In the case of the AGIL framework, issues lie in three areas: the definition of society versus a collective; a hierarchy in which each function of society has a subsystem that also is characterized as AGIL (with suitably complicated notation); and the concept of a medium of exchange across functional boundaries. My approach avoids theoretical issues by characterizing a firm as a collective, which also is a society. I dispense with the notion that the company is a subsystem of society's Adaptation function; it is simply characterized by the AGIL framework, which applies to all societal action systems. The interest here is not in what the company can do for society, rather how the society of a company reacts to the incursion of the new technology. Legal and regulatory "sanctions" stemming from the operation of the greater society are treated as constraints on a company's operations as opposed to societal inputs. Rather than dealing with explicit boundary conditions and a medium of exchange, which must accompany them, AGIL functions are envisioned as overlapping in order for one to communicate with the other. The last is consistent with theorists concerned with problems involved in Parson's exchange principles.

CHAPTER 2

Originality Consists in Returning to the Origin

The spaceship *Prometheus* approaches moon LV-223. The financier of the venture appears to the crew as a hologram. He explains the legend of Prometheus and proclaims, "the time has now come for his return." He leaves out the bit about the punishment of Woman and the hubris of the hero. He neglects the myth's theme of unintended consequences. He forgets the fall into mortality. He may have read the folklore but missed the class on *Paradise Lost*.

Greek and Aztec creation myths center around gods who create man in their own image through physical sacrifice. In the opening of the film, *Prometheus*, an alien Engineer sacrifices itself by ingesting poison to bring life to a world. The act creates humanity, which in turn creates artificial life in the image of man. The Engineers are the dark angels of John Milton's story. Humanity is not an afterthought, but neither is it the creation of God.

Several Prometheus figures appear in the movie. The Engineers are struck down after bringing lethal biotechnology from the heavens. A woman who seeks affirmation of her religious faith believes she is entitled to answers from God. She is punished for her hubris with her questions unanswered. The financier wishes for forbidden knowledge to make himself equal to the gods. And an android, of course.

David is underwhelmed by the human experience like his hero Lawrence of Arabia. His creators are looking for fixes to Prometheus' unintended consequence of mortality. In contrast, David asks: "Why did you create me?"

Because we could.

Another answer permeates robot fiction: to serve humanity. David gives us a stygian vision. Something went wrong. Our creators decided to destroy their own creation, and David is a fan. Humanity is not aligning with the agenda he has in mind.

Look at Origins to Understand Reasoning

The theme of artificial intelligence runs through many other works of Ridley Scott. AI most often is a fully developed character ready for action. David passes the Turing Test, but as Alex Garland's film *Ex Machina* suggests, android development hardly stops there.

Authors, directors, and futurists have created an elaborate landscape on which well-formed AI figures walk. The characters exist only on a small portion of the surface, however. Their origins are to be found in machines before computers ever existed.

A visit to David's roots enables understanding of a system. *Root* refers to the starting point of a hierarchical structure in computerese. Root also denotes a person with access to any folder on a hard drive. Such people are entitled to information beyond their own personal files. Let's access some data.

A timeline of machine learning on Wikipedia starts with Bayes Theorem and Legendre's method of least squares. The good Reverend Bayes was a man of God. He searched for a theory logically justifying divine existence and came to believe he had proved just the opposite as he ventured into probability theory. Appalled, he instructed the work be buried after his death. Legendre's least squares is a methodology of approximation and prediction. It did not gain traction until the enabling of modern statistics by the Central Limit Theorem in 1929.

All files have gaps. I don't mean the gap between Bayes of 1763 and Legendre of 1805, nor that between Legendre's theory of least squares and its practical use. If you rely on Wikipedia's timeline, you miss the most important milestone in AI, the machine itself.

Machine learning is a process based on inductive statistical models. It did not begin with computers. It started in the moving parts of motors.

Robert Goodell Brown designed a tracking system for fire-control information in WW II.[1] The goal was the computation of enemy submarine locations. The statistical technique was the moving average. Data

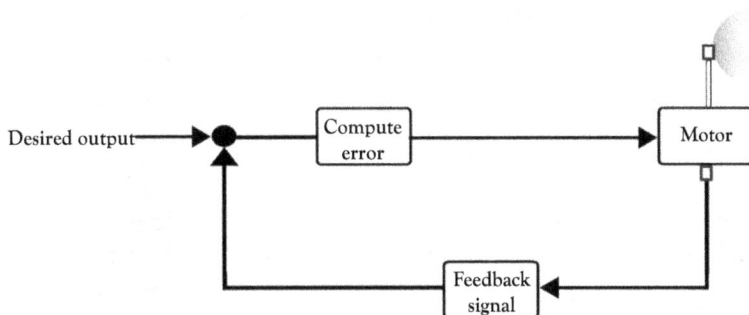

Figure 2.1 A simplified targeting system

were averaged as time passed and the results used to move the tracking device. The control of servomechanisms played a major role.

Machine learning is exemplified by the servomechanism. The servo corrects performance of a machine through feedback. The machine's position is sent to a device to be compared with its desired placement. An error detector compares actual with desired.

Moving averages of the coordinates are used to smooth out small data discrepancies. One does not want to overemphasize or understate input based on a single observation. The risk is the machine becomes unstable or fails to rotate. The difference between actual and desired positions generates an error signal representing the correction necessary to bring the machine to its desired position. The signal is translated into voltage, which drives the servomotor and repositions the machine as suggested in Figure 2.1.

The machine takes in new data, combines history with experience, uses a statistical method to analyze consequences, and powers a decision to move without human intervention. Machine learning without computers.

Well, almost. Something had to carry out the statistical computations comparing actual and desired position. Before the arrival of ENIAC in 1947, the term *computer* referred to the person who input data to a mechanical calculator.

An early version of military fire control systems developed when the reach of artillery increased in the late 19th century. Human spotters played the role of sensors. They relayed distance observations to fire direction teams. A computer input location, speed and direction of the ship, together with auxiliary data such as wind speed. The calculator then delivered a firing solution relayed to the gun turret.

Mechanical calculators were redesigned to use electric motors by the 20th century. The electrically powered Argo clock presaged the Dreyer Table control system used by the British Navy in WW I. Bomb targeting systems followed for aerial warfare.

War loves technology.

A next step was taken by Pete Haurlan, best known for his second career as one of the inventors of statistical stock market trend analysis. Haurlan used the same form of weighted moving average in designing rocket tracking systems in the early 1960s. Rudolph Kálmán replaced the moving average with a calculation designed for radar control systems.[2] Reverend Bayes rolled over; the Kálmán filter is one of the simplest dynamic Bayesian networks. Kálmán filters eventually were adapted for use in the Apollo program, in NASA's space shuttle, in submarines, and of course, in cruise missiles. The mechanical principle remained the servomechanism while moving averages were replaced by filtering, requiring more computational power.

But we are ahead of ourselves. Computers as machines had already made the scene.

Machine learning beyond mechanicals arrived in the guise of Arthur Samuel, who showed up at IBM's door in 1949.[3] He wanted to play checkers and programmed a primitive computer to do so. Samuel's learning programs didn't work well in the beginning, and he beat the computer consistently. He came up with a thought, which today is hyped as an advance in gaming technology. A new source of data was generated by having two computers play each other. By 1959, the computers' predictions defeated him. *Machine learning*, as most understand the term, was born.

The machine now generates its own data, combines old data with new experience, uses a statistical method to analyze consequences, and powers a decision to move without human intervention. Sounds familiar?

As we move from mechanicals to computers, the terminology offers a path to AI. We first need to learn how to learn.

You Don't Learn to Walk by Following Rules

Machine learning theory and application are broken down into three categories. They are supervised learning, unsupervised learning, and reinforcement learning. Don't even think about AI yet. Crawling comes before walking.

Supervised learning is the most common form. The way to keep the phrase in your head is to associate it with prediction. There always is a correct answer to a prediction problem. Machines are expected to arrive at the answer based on data currently available to them. Supervised learning operates under the assumption that the expected answer to a problem is already identified in a data set consisting of labeled data.

History contains correct answers. The algorithm's problem is to find them in new data. The challenge is to predict the answer.

A bank pitches customers new terms of deposit. Existing customers are known quantities consisting of data pertaining to job, education, average deposits, and so forth. The process of marketing generates yes and no responses. The labeling in the data set consists of those responses. Response is estimated using the customer profiles. This is called *training*. Using new customer data, the algorithm forecasts the likelihood of a positive response. If the machine obtains a high probability of getting a "yes," the customer is worth a phone call.

These days you get a chatbot working an automated dialer. If confused, ask Siri about machine learning's connection to spam.

The process is like a teacher supervising the learning process. We know the answer. The algorithm iteratively makes predictions as information arrives and is corrected by the teacher. Learning stops when the algorithm achieves an acceptable level of performance most often phrased as the minimization of forecast error. Error-correction models used in radar tracking, the Kálmán filter of missile analytics, and pattern recognition by neural networks are old examples. In fact, simple neural nets are a form of regression analysis pioneered by Legendre in 1805.[4]

Supervised learning remains prediction regardless of novelty of application or details of statistical methodology. Does your application require forecasting? Are correct forecasts in the historical record? If the answers are yes and yes, then supervised learning is the game.

We encounter *unsupervised learning* every time we use a web browser. Think of the information gathered from your online activity. You become part of a cluster of personal characteristics used to generate advertisements that appear on the right of the screen. Clustering is grouping a set of things such that objects in the same group are more similar to each other than to those in other groups.

Unsupervised learning is all about clusters. Clustering is a method to explore and identify the structure of information in order to learn about similarities and differences in characteristics.

There are no correct answers and no teacher. The answer to the question is not found in the historical record. Algorithms are left to their own devices to discover and present structure. Unsupervised learning employs information not classified in any fashion. The algorithm acts on the information without guidance.

Unsupervised learning tells us something is like something else. Applied to a basket of donuts, bagels, and candy swizzle sticks, the algorithm separates the sticks into one pile and the donuts and bagels into another. Taste data may allow supervised learning to tell us the something is a donut as in Figure 2.2. The something else is a bagel, for which more

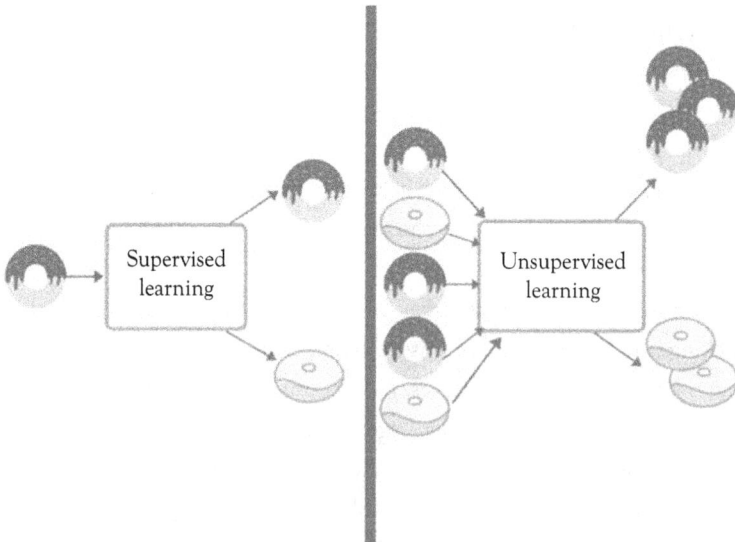

Figure 2.2 Supervised and unsupervised learning for the donut problem

supervised learning and enough data may lead you to believe the bagel is better for health. For some, the thought leads to indigestion when action is taken based on the prediction. Others get a sugar rush and start searching for something similar to the swizzle sticks. Rinse and repeat.

If that is too simple, visit the Google lab. They are interested in the search engine you use for finding swizzle stick analogues and complementary treats. The not-so-secret secret of search is unsupervised learning. The lab is secretive nevertheless, and we hear about things through the patent process.

An early Google patent portrays a document as clusters of related words. This is fine for key word search but does not cut it in today's environment. We need concept. A process may act to group concepts when understanding text. Google's subsequent 2011 patent is almost indecipherable.[5] My translation of patentese runs something like this:

> A system characterizes a document with respect to clusters of conceptually related words. Upon receiving a document containing a set of words, the system selects clusters of conceptually related words. The system constructs a set of components to characterize the document, wherein each component indicates a degree to which a corresponding cluster is related to the set of words.

People are sorted by identity and spending habits. Text is sorted by concept. The search engine uses unsupervised learning to compare words and concepts found in a document and in a query. A scoring function ranks web pages in search results based upon concepts intuited from text.

Babies learn from both supervised and unsupervised lessons. They group objects and experiences for understanding. They forecast consequence. Infant behavior is at the core of the third category of machine learning, *reinforcement learning*.

Unsupervised learning tells the baby something is like something else. If supervised learning informs the baby the thing is a donut, then reinforcement learning says to eat the donut because it tastes great. The baby devotes some resources to the exploration of new territory and some on exploiting evolving knowledge for the purpose of reward. The child spends energy on finding things with holes in the center and is eventually

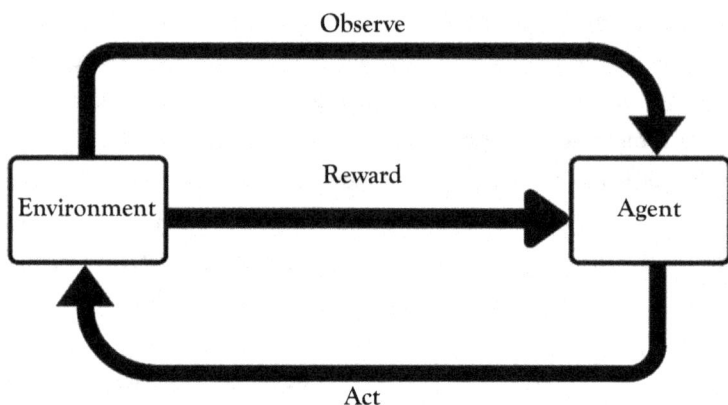

Figure 2.3 Reinforcement learning for the baby

rewarded with good taste. If you have a child, you are wincing at the thought of alternatives with which the baby experiments.

Reinforcement learning refers to algorithms trained to attain a complex objective. Like babies, reinforcement learning programs start from a blank slate. They are penalized when they make the wrong decisions and rewarded when they make the right ones. As with supervised and unsupervised learning, the reinforcement variety appeared in the computational engineering literature by the mid-1950s in the simplified form as in Figure 2.3.

The baby begins by taking an action, which is processed by a black box called the environment. Environments transform an action taken in the current state of baby's existence into the next state. The baby appraises the situation and transforms the new state and any reward into the next action.

Reinforcement learning is the baby's attempt to approximate the environment's function. Having done so, the child can send new actions into the black box that maximize rewards available. Information about the environment is collected by interacting with it. There is no prediction. There is no such thing as an optimal step. The baby experiments, observes, and keeps on rolling.

This cycle is called *exploration and exploitation*. Although much is written on the combination of terms, they seem self-explanatory even for the baby. The baby's sole decision is how much time to spend exploring relative to time spent exploiting new knowledge in the pursuit of a reward.

The Desert Is a Theater of Human of Search

Reinforcement learning is *selectional*. It entails experimentation with alternatives and selection through a comparison of their consequences. It is *associative*. The alternatives found through selection are associated with particular situations. Supervised and unsupervised learning are associative, but not selectional, for example.

We *search* in the form of trying and selecting among possible actions in each situation. Search is combined with memory of what actions worked best. Memory includes associating actions with the situations in which they worked.

An understanding of selection, association, search, and memory is the basis of new methodology in reinforcement learning. We call it *artificial intelligence*.

AI is reinforcement learning with a practical twist. AI solves the learning problem while accounting for an environment too complex to iteratively search, let alone select and remember.

David says there is nothing in the desert and no man needs nothing. The android is a fan of the film *Lawrence of Arabia* and King Faisal felt the same way. They are wrong. The desert teaches us the difference between AI and more primitive forms of reinforcement learning.

You walk in the desert and lose the water bottle somewhere in the dunes. If you don't find the water bottle, you die. A person can live only so long without water so you're on the clock. There is no reward for taking intermediate steps. It's the bottle or bust. If you step onto a patch of solid sand, refashion your strategy with that knowledge and move again. If you fall into shallow sand, climb onto another patch and keep on going. The environment has changed, and you add information in the form of your experience. The landscape is transformed by a depression in the shallow quicksand, but a random desert breeze may fill in the hole. Falling into deep quicksand, you die an artificial death and start over at the place where you realized the loss of the bottle. Repeat until you slake your thirst or time runs out on your biological water clock.

Although there are no contingent rewards for progress, we need a method that assigns value to each possible intermediate step given information available at the time a decision is made. Purely random paths might get one there eventually, but theory suggests the clock will run out before you get to water. Computing and allocating value is time consuming anyway, and we are already parched. A higher relative price for a patch encourages a step on that particular dune. Every time we take a step or die, prices are adjusted. We experiment within mathematicians' world of successive approximations.

The game is an exercise in reinforcement learning. A few lines of Python code will get you there. No reward is available for intermediate steps, but each one has an intrinsic value. Value changes every time the environment shifts due to an action, whether it be yours or that of the desert sirocco. We use an algorithm to calculate those values to guide future steps as experience builds up. Calculation takes time and the clock is ticking.

AI may now enter the game.

Suppose you have been walking for a very long time before you miss the water bottle. Now there are millions of sand patches. The algorithm is trained to calculate value for every possible combination of steps one might take. The number of computations can exceed the number of legal moves in a game of Go, estimated as 2×10^{170}.

Feasibility suggests approximating the environment. This might be accomplished with a neural net, for example. Computations are performed only at the nodes of the network. The number of nodes is much smaller than the number of paths. If a network has 12 branches and 8 loops, for example, permutations of the 20 are reduced to 5 nodes.

The neural net, designed in part to minimize noise occasioned by the wind, also provides a statistical way of simplifying potential paths through the desert. The net requires data to recalculate the model after every step. Experience continues to supply such information. Additional uncertainty is introduced by the use of an approximation. There is some additional computation as well.

But AI gets us to the bottle in finite time.

There Is Always a Way to Water

AI is a toolbox of problem-solving techniques. Different methods are available for computing the value of steps. Alternative approximations exist for large game boards. Choice of statistical methodology depends on what and how much data are available at each point in time. Time is chronological or event driven.

Understanding of the problem comes first. Understanding permits humans to ask the right question when opening the box of solutions. The origin of a framework for doing so is found in the architectural theory of design thinking.[6]

We solve problems by looking at the knowns and unknowns in the equation:

$$\text{WHAT} \quad + \quad \text{HOW} \quad \text{leads to} \quad \text{VALUE}$$
$$\text{(thing)} \quad \text{(working principle)} \quad \text{(expected)}$$

If one replaces *value* by *result* but considers the result unknown, we have supervised learning in the form of prediction. There is no question mark here. We are here to add value, and typically understand how value is measured.

In engineering, value is known, as is the working principle. The engineer searches for the *what*, whether it be a product, a service, or a system:

$$\text{???} \quad + \quad \text{HOW} \quad \text{leads to} \quad \text{VALUE}$$

Product is designed with a known operating principle and at least an aspiration with respect to the value of the product. This is a daily exercise in many firms. A change in the competitive environment may recast the *value*, even the *how*, but we plug those in and keep at it.

Sometimes we know what to produce to add value but are unsure of the principle upon which to create it.

$$\text{WHAT} \quad + \quad \text{???} \quad \text{leads to} \quad \text{VALUE}$$

We know the widget we want, but do not know how to make it. Alternatively, the product may be in production, but one is looking for a more efficient cost structure. This formula nests the type of situations encountered in forms of architectural innovation in product design. We decide upon changes in the way components of a product are linked, while leaving the core design untouched. Value is described as a decrease in cost or an incremental improvement in efficiency, lowering the cost of capital. A new principle is required to achieve value.

Design thinking is concerned with a seemingly unsolvable problem:

$$??? \quad + \quad ??? \quad \text{leads to} \quad \text{VALUE}$$

We need to figure out *what* to create. There is no established, or at least chosen, working principle that can guide the choice nor lead to expected value.

You might randomly choose pairs for both the *how* and the *what*. The goal is a matching pair leading to the aspired value. The process is inefficient at best and a loser at worst.

Experienced designers seek a *frame*. The frame is a statement reflecting a specific understanding of a problem situation. A frame embodies a working hypothesis: if one looks at the problem from a certain viewpoint and adopts a working principle associated with that view, then value is created. The design problem then reverts to *what* is to be built. Only equations with a single unknown may be solved. Only complete equations can be tested. Until the test, the frame is simply a possible way forward.

Let's go back to the desert by way of Las Vegas. They tell me water is there for the purpose of diluting whiskey. At least we won't die of thirst on this trip.

I love casino design. Islands of beautiful flashing machines dot the floor. Each slot machine in an island is a similar game. Games change as we go from island to island. You choose a game by going to an island. Then you decide what machines to play, how many times to play each slot, the order in which to pull the levers, and whether to stay with a machine or its island or move on.

One frame for creating value is chance. IF all machines deliver the same random outcomes regardless of the game, THEN randomly choose islands and machines until a lever is pulled, which delivers value. This is a loser, explaining why casinos are still in business.

One does not reject a frame for one failure. A frame may yield more than one principle. IF all machines are the same except for the flashing neon, THEN stand in front of any single slot regardless of game and pull the lever repeatedly until value is achieved. The resulting principle is the one-armed bandit problem.[7] The policy employed in pulling the lever is the *what*. The policy is adaptive and judged based on the number of times the lever is pulled. We evaluate the expected cumulative jackpot relative to that achieved by a mathematically inclined oracle. The process neglects information from other machines, and we are not cashing in chips any time soon. That's why we call individual slots bandits.

New frames are based on observation. Watching many playing the slots on several islands delivers a nuanced frame of chance. Some seem to win more quickly than others. There are machines avoided without explanation. Jackpots differ between slots and across games.

The ghost of Reverend Bayes visits in the guise of optimal Bayesian learning as a frame. The details provide an extension of the frame of pure randomness, but let's skip the mathematics. The principle becomes the multiarmed bandit problem. You are facing a situation in which limited time and money must be allocated between alternative choices in a way as to create value in the form of expected winnings. Each machine's properties are only partially known at the time of allocation. They become better understood as one allocates resources to the choice.

You experiment with the simplest form of the principle. Observe the reward for the chosen slot after each round, but not for the other slots that could have been chosen. Explore by trying out different machines to acquire reward information. You face the trade-off between exploration and exploitation: making optimal near-term decisions based on costly search and synthesis of available information. You strive to learn which slots are best while not spending too much time exploring by wandering the floor and spending chips.

You might still leave Vegas broke, but don't give up quite yet. The frame is appropriate. The principle has been tested in numerous applications over the last 50 years. It is a classic example of reinforcement learning, which explores and exploits opportunities.

You may be missing situational context. Ignoring context leads to exploring slots at the same rate regardless of what has been observed previously and picking an empirically best slot for exploitation. It is better to adapt exploration to the observed rewards. You may not be using the best sampling technique, which can depend on the number of players in the casino. Rewards in each round depend on the situation observed prior to a decision. They depend on *context*. Optimal policy changes even though the frame is the same and the principle invariant.

AI must build situational context into every activity subject to design thinking. It's time to leave Vegas and explore the context of a company. The problem is successful adoption of AI within the company. The frame is one of adaptation, goals, integration, and culture. Understanding requires a bit more in the way of origins. We begin with two stories of adaptation.

Chapter Notes

The title comes from Antoni Gaudi: "Man does not create ... he discovers. Those who look for the laws of Nature as a support for their new works collaborate with the creator. Copiers do not collaborate. Because of this, originality consists in returning to the origin." He never did finish his church, the construction of which is not expected to be done until 2026—to commemorate the centenary of his death.

Moving averages for the nonmathematically inclined: Averaging is a method for calculating the mean value of something. We use the term *moving* because it is continually recomputed as new data becomes available. In its simplest form, a moving average is computed by dropping the earliest value and adding the latest value as it comes available. A more sophisticated version deemphasizes the effect of old data on the computation as it progresses.

Pete Haurlan was first to use the averaging technique of exponential smoothing for tracking stock prices. He did not call them "exponentially weighted moving averages." He promoted the smoothed price output as "Trend Values." We use the terminology to this day except for the need to toss something about AI into the explanation of something so simple and so old.

Kálmán's ideas were initially met with skepticism, and he was forced into mechanical engineering as opposed to electrical engineering or systems design. Kálmán's career took off based on a visit to Stanley Schmidt at the NASA Research Center in 1960. The rocket scientists there got it. His participation in the Apollo program and the Space Shuttle followed.

Reverend Bayes could not have known the Kálmán filter would be constructed as one of the simplest Bayesian networks, of course. It calculates estimates of the true values of states recursively over time using incoming measurements and a mathematical process model.

Kees Dorst is neither a businessperson nor a technologist, but understands the need for clear definitions and a toolbox with which to implement them. He was on the Faculty of Design, Architecture, and Building at the University of Technology, Sidney, Australia, when he wrote "The core of 'design thinking' and its application," on which the what-how-value paradigm here is based. Published in *Design Studies*, 2011, his work is academically dense, brilliant, and worth a look.

Richard Branson is responsible for the epigram about rules. He added, you learn by doing, and by falling over. The baby empathizes.

Unsupervised learning is arguably older than predictive techniques in practice, dating to the use of a statistical method known as cluster analysis by anthropologists and psychologists in the early 1930s.

You may have heard the term *Adversarial Machine Learning*. AML is not a machine learning technique deserving of a fourth category. It is a research field sitting at the intersection of machine learning and computer security. It aims at enabling the safe adoption of machine learning techniques in adversarial settings such as intelligent spamming and biometric recognition. The field is motivated by the fact that machine learning techniques are not designed to cope with adaptive adversaries, thus system security may be compromised by exploiting specific vulnerabilities of learning algorithms through manipulation of input data. The area is not to be confused with *generative adversarial networks*. We will come to those later in discussions of cultural change management.

The water bottle problem typically is recast as a walk across a frozen lake in machine learning tutorials. Some version is posed as a simple homework exercise for computer students, hence the claim it can be solved with a few lines of Python code. I'm not the one to ask; to me Python is a snake from Amazon, which supplies but does not freeze. An illustrated solution is provided at https://machinelearningjourney.com/index.php/2020/07/02/frozenlake/, one of many available.

Contextual bandits exist but would take us too far afield. In contextual bandit problems, rewards in each round depend on a context, which is observed by the algorithm prior to a decision. There are three prominent versions of contextual bandits: with a Lipschitz assumption, with a linearity assumption, and with a fixed policy class. Let's agree to not discuss the details.

PART II

The First Law

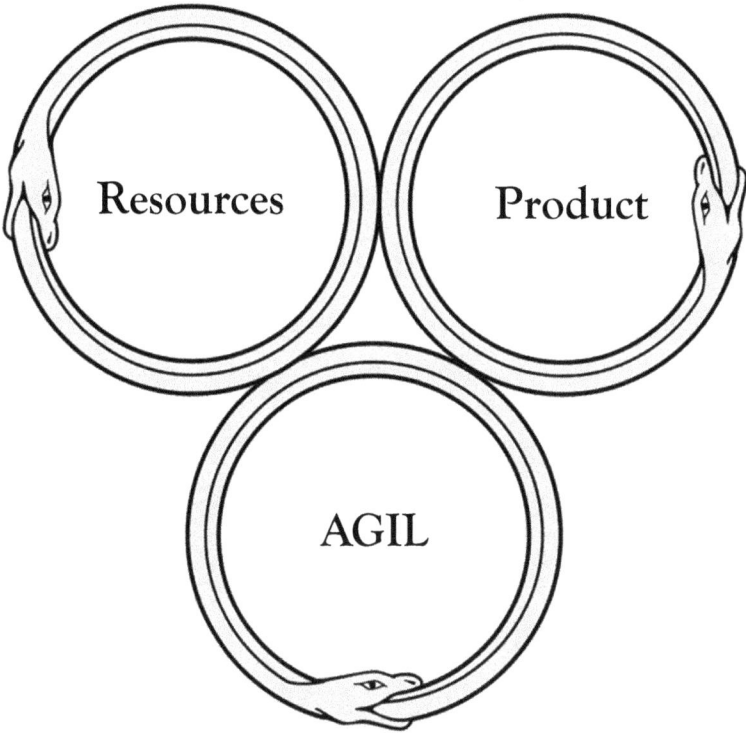

CHAPTER 3

Adaptation Is Not Imitation

In the eponymous American TV show, the artificially intelligent Max Headroom begins life as a memory dump of synaptic circuits. The memories are those of Edison Carter whose last recall is a high-speed collision with a barrier marked, *Max. Headroom 2.3m*. A person translated as data, Max is born into a world in which the networks have won the cable war, streaming never existed, and TVs blare 24/7 by law. The poor are given free ones.

Appearing in front of iconic geek of the week Bryce and the Chairman of Network 23, Max starts to learn. He names himself and asks if he's on the air. Max is housed in a file on Bryce's computer, so … no. As he augments memories with current experience, novel expressions and jokes come out of the animated figure.

The Chairman goes wild; the possibilities are endless. He introduces Max to the Executive Board as the first programmable talking head. Max acknowledges the board as the people who execute audiences. You see, Network 23 is pioneering blipverts, compressed messaging with the power to explode viewer's heads. Max follows by labeling 23 the network that's a real mindblower, blows up his own head and disappears.

Max has evidence blipverts kill people. Bryce helpfully offers to erase the relevant part of Max's memory. Easily done, but Max is right there on the screen listening in. Shifting his own file to somewhere else in the Network computer, he escapes into the system.

As a scientist, Bryce is excited. As a business guy, the Chairman declares a catastrophe.

Max becomes autonomous. He reappears on the TV network, talks about blipverts, and informs the world that the networks have you all where they want you to be. He sees two minds with one single memory when he meets Edison. Together they broadcast evidence of the evils of blipverts and oust the Chairman. End of line.

In real life, Max got his start as a simulated chatbot in the United Kingdom. He was the host of *20 Minutes into the Future*, a short series of music video episodes. An embryonic TV channel put graphics between music videos to freshen things up a bit and provide a back story to what otherwise would have been just a set of unrelated tunes.

A boring middle-class White male in a suit, talking to a rebellious new generation in a really boring way about music videos—perfect. It was a part of a graphic world of dystopia and MTV. Max moved to a variety show with a live audience, facing off against characters such as Sting, Michael Caine, Jack Lemmon, and Vidal Sassoon. Trading cards and merchandising tie-ins followed.

Max met Coca-Cola, which was refashioning its ad campaign for a failing New Coke. The "Catch the Wave" campaign was directed by Ridley Scott. Coca-Cola's Senior Vice President John Reid told *Newsweek* that 76 percent of American teenagers knew Max after the first series of ads. But Max could not save New Coke's declining sales.

Max moved across the Atlantic. Members of his creative team were left behind. ABC wanted somebody who was going to pump out content and play the game, somebody they could parade around who would toe the corporate line. Max was all about rejecting the corporate line but went along anyway.

A powerful cast was involved: Coca-Cola, a big advertising agency (BBDO), Ridley Scott (again), Chrysalis the record company, and the network. ABC created a new TV series for the American audience. Few writers understood Max. The show's brand of cyberpunk struggled, coming in 26th for the night of its first showing.

Max was a cultural icon and the show improved. He ran millions over budget but made the cover of *Newsweek*. Max was too busy biting the hand feeding him to notice. The show was vicious in its condemnation of the way television worked. Somebody somewhere said, "You know something? This program is kicking the hell out of the way we make our living. Ditch it."

ABC moved the show opposite Miami Vice and Dallas on Friday night prime time. It was the graveyard slot. Less than a month later, ABC pulled the plug. Max was almost relieved. He wanted to strut the screen without being compromised, diluted, or homogenized. He walked away without the show being packaged into something the network wanted it to be packaged into.

Max had religion, but Coke was done with that. HBO was done. ABC was done. Even the reruns disappeared. End of line.

Both incarnations of Max go through a cycle of adaptation, goal attainment, integration, and pattern maintenance. Max adapts to his environment by using his new-found ability to create content. In real life, adaptation takes the form of finding backers who toe the corporate line. Max has no goals in mind. He is learning and in constant search of discovery. He excites scientists and dismays business types. The real Max is all about goal attainment in the industry and on the airwaves. TV Max integrates into his environment through escape into relative freedom. Real-life Max fails integration by protesting too loudly against the system that made him in the first place. Both versions encounter latent patterns of social culture. In TV land, Max triumphs over industry values by virtue of his autonomy. In real life, there is failure to acknowledge patterns of industry norms and behavior.

Max is thrown down from heaven, chained to a rock, and left to await a new generation that might reinvent him.

Stress Is Not From Thinking About the Future but From Wanting to Control It

The two stories illustrate paths by which the AI enters society. In the first, Max comes to us as a fully articulated AI, a disruptive innovation that changes television history. In the second, Max works his way in from chatbot to interviewer and on to an advertising icon created for a growing audience of societal misfits.

In one version, Max is a rebel; in another, he is an actor who grows by conforming with media values and practices. The first fulfills our dramatic fantasies about artificial intelligence through a winning story of transformation and triumph. The second introduces the forces of the real world, which when unaddressed lead to AI's downfall.

The story of AI within a company is one of transformation in either version.

AI is an entrepreneur entering a company resting in an equilibrium characterized by stable social and commercial patterns relative to fluctuations in the environment. AI challenges company behavioral patterns with its entrance into Adaptation.

Consequent maintenance of equilibrium involves two process types. There are processes of socialization in which employees obtain orientation necessary for the performance of their roles. When they have not previously possessed them, like AI, they must acquire them. The second consists of processes involved in balancing between generation of deviant behavior and counterbalancing motivations leading to restoration of the system.

Deviant behavior breeds revolution and balancing processes are mechanisms of social control.

AI triggers balancing processes by straining the system. Strain tees up reequilibrating processes, because it engenders defense mechanisms and adjustment in humans and systems. Any action system is resistant to change, and a company is no exception. Change is not solely alteration of pattern if it impinges on institutionalized norms of action and relationship.

Change is alteration by the overcoming of resistance.

We like to believe scientific advance is a good thing. The corollary is the results will be automatically accepted. This attitude is one of larger society but is not part of the makeup of a typical company. Therein are many strains and concomitant resistance.

Strains are associated with a communication gap between the specialist and the rest of the employees. Some tensions derive from special privileges required by the process of change or given to those engaging with AI. Others come from AI's interference with established ways of doing things. Worst from the perspective of corporate incumbents are changes requiring the abandonment of established methods in which there are vested interests. All of this is compounded by the application of AI to situations in which employees are already strained; remediation of the same is supposed to be one of AI's reasons to exist in the first place. Stress predisposes incumbents less to logical acceptance than would otherwise be the case. The liver of Prometheus is a symbol of emotion not thought.

Vested interest is a lightning rod for resistance. It is inherent in the institutionalization of roles in the company and is not confined to economic factors. Embedded interests represent a stake in the maintenance of gratification otherwise assured in an established system of roles and expectations of them.

Change in the company occurs only through mechanisms that overcome vested interests. Institutionalized transformation does so by brute force in an attempt to address the failure of change to occur, or as a response to questions as to why change does not produce outcomes predicted on a common sense basis.

Common sense may fail here. One reason is culture.

A scientific development represents an impetus to change originating in a cultural configuration outside the company. The gestalt generally does not mirror that of the firm and may not intersect with it at all. Cultural norms embody ideology reminiscent of religion. Religious belief is rarely established on the basis of common sense.

Change due to AI is motivated by a shift in the environment in the same way as the introduction of any strategic resource. Development of science is in the background, but the process of invention in a company is often uncorrelated with that of science. The exception is companies that invent fundamental AI methodology for commercial purposes. They deserve a book of their own.

Reactions to strain exhibit an aggregate tendency to eliminate change and restore the state of the system. Such forces require coping in such a way as to consolidate and extend the change. Consolidation means other parts of the system than the original area of transformation also have been affected. Fallout can generate company reorganization if all four AGIL functions are grossly distressed.

A new state of the company as a whole is reached in this narrative. The common experience is only partial coping with strains. Chronic states of tension are institutionalized and stabilized within the firm.

My subsidiary was using machine learning to answer questions of trading performance management for an institutional investing clientele. Client interest was in how well individual brokers executed large orders in the securities market. Competitive pressures in the brokerage industry encouraged giving business to brokers incurring a minimal cost in transacting securities.

On the surface, this was simply a matter of adaptation, and the First Law ruled. Data as a resource were transformed into a service through AI. Tension arose from two sources.

The parent company's main line of business was institutional brokerage. The orders it handled and their execution characteristics appeared in the data. Machine learning included that information in its analysis. Empirical comparisons between brokers were possible as the business developed. Our trading desk woke up. Broker rankings were reported to the clients and found publication in the industry press. The first was troublesome; the second was an example of deviant behavior as far as the traders were concerned.

The atmosphere thickened. AI generated strain through the reporting of hitherto unknown but potentially damaging information. The fact that such information could be used to improve the trading desk's own performance rankings was ignored. The tension never went away; it became institutionalized within the parent company. Consolidation and extension of AI's efforts in this area involved an uneasy truce within which public dissemination of the information disappeared in favor of private reporting to clients.

Consolidation entails change in other parts of the system than the original area of transformation. The logical extension was to measure performance of our own desk for internal consumption, setting the stage for improvement relative to other brokers. Eventually it became clear traders' resistance was futile. On the other hand, the desk did not like the way my subsidiary went about the task. They rejected the results and tasked one of their own groups to do the job. AI was jettisoned in favor of ad hoc reporting, which showed the desk in more favorable light. Clients were not happy. They wanted uniformity for comparison of results across brokers.

A chronic state of tension again was institutionalized within the firm.

Adapt or Perish Is Nature's Inexorable Imperative

The story illustrates how Adaptation is accompanied by ways in which the company accommodates situational disturbances. Within Adaptation, directions in which the process of resourcing and production can move are constrained, preventing processes from moving equally in all directions at once.

Adaptation involves new resources and facilities, which empowers some segments of the firm and disenfranchises others. The introduction of new physical installations is an obvious example. Think of those new server farms required to power AI. Another example is change in resources thought to be strategic. The internal combustion engine endowed liquid fuels with strategic significance, which they had lacked before the Industrial Revolution. Heavy metal ore deposits are a strategic resource, whereas quite recently they were of no significance except to a few scientists. Data once were digital exhaust and now constitute a strategic asset.

Within the confines of the First Law, AI also gathers human resources for the purpose of production. Human resources are a source of organizational change. Roles are assigned, and a division of labor arises implied by those roles.

AI and associated personnel orient themselves toward production goals defined by the adaptation process. Relational problems vis á vis rest of the firm enter when AI ceases to be passive as a means of goal attainment and its reactions become part of the system itself.

The concept of exchange enters.

AI and its cohorts offer specialized action as a means for other company units to attain goals. The units provide resources in exchange. AI offers language processing to enable a chatbot in a call center dashboard, say. The front office gives hours of its technologists' time to achieve the objective. This market becomes a highly organized system of interaction. As market durability develops, AI is specialized in the attainment of its own goals even as it produces means for goal attainment of other groups.

What AI receives depends not only on production but also on the terms of exchange. The terms of exchange are evolving patterns of the relationship of AI with respect to divisions of the company. As in any market system, regulation of the outflows of product for internal consumption and inflows of resources are mediated by the terms of exchange. In a single ad hoc barter transaction, the two coincide. Company wide, they do not.

AI is a new entrant to production and its product is first distinct from sources of remuneration. This is especially true when AI product is an intermediate step or simply a component in a larger service offering.

There must be some mechanism by which inflows and outflows of the interaction system are adjusted to each other. The most obvious technique operates through ramifications of a system of monetary exchange. Theoretical economics suggests a mechanism based on auctions. They have been successfully implemented in the case of satellite construction and interplanetary space travel, such as the Cassini mission to Saturn. Internal resource auctions are in violation of internal commercial norms in most companies, however. Less controversial is a mechanism by which divisions of the company pay AI for its production and receive goods and services to be used in their endeavors.

Disruption nevertheless is a plausible result of a payment plan.

The parent company's operational revenue was in the form of trading commissions. My subsidiary depended on subscriptions. Subscriptions could be paid in cash or through trading in the form of extra commission. Bundling services into commissions was common practice in the industry. Simple economics often provides a basis for integration. Logic failed in the definition of simple, however.

Front office culture held the remainder of the company produced infrastructure for sales and trading. Residual employees also produced a few services, which could be given away to clients in the pursuit of commissions. The bundle was never priced. Commissions were what the market would bear and often discounted in the interest of encouraging order flow. Simple economics as understood by the trading desk could not address the conflict between discounting and incremental provision of value-added goods and services.

Attribution of value was critical to the venture's adaptation within the company. A new entity must show revenue. Revenue required prices. A priced bundle hit the personal wallets of the trading desk because it was now forced to share its commission with others in the firm.

Bundles may not be priced, but subscriptions paid outside the brokerage operation certainly are. The venture reoriented toward clients who would pay in cash. The market would determine the prices of services, which in turn could be used to price bundles. Tensions rose on the belief commissions would fall as clients analyzed their costs. Nevertheless, internal payments were validated by external pricing.

Regardless of exact mechanism, regulation and settlement of terms of exchange is undertaken. What AI does is a means or a hindrance to the attainment of every other division's goals. Social order demands clarity in mechanisms through which the terms on which AI will or will not make services available.

Terms of exchange must be set in such a way so as to be compatible with conditions of stability within the company.

For there to be exchange, something changes hands. The something may be control of a physical object inclusive of the power to destroy it. It may be an agreement to do certain things in the future. These processes may be positive, contributing to others' goals, or negative, as in refraining from interfering with others' goals.

A structure of rights within the company cannot be renegotiated with each transaction. A stable system of exchange presupposes a priori settlement among possible alternative ways of defining such rights. We institutionalize them.

Any system of continuous and specialized activity requires facilities, which extend beyond those available on a purely ad hoc basis. Materials, equipment, and premises are possessions devoted to the production of further utilities. They are destined to be used as means to some future goal rather than as objects of immediate gratification.

Regulation of access to facilities is another functional problem of adaptation. The exchangeable possession is not the product of a single actor within the firm, rather of the cooperation of many actors. *Cooperation* is a closer description of the integration of instrumental activities than is exchange. It means the meshing of activities or contributions such that the outcome is a unit that can enter into the exchange process.

A system of cooperative relationships is an organization. AI is confronted with four types of adaptation in the ordering of its relations to the organization.

There is the problem of disposal, defined as settlement terms on which AI's product is made available to others. There is the nature of remuneration, the term sheet by which AI receives the products of the activities of other actors. Next comes the issue of AI's access to facilities and the regulation of its relations to internal competitors for use of the same facilities. Underlying all problems of exchange is the definition of property rights and their limits. Finally, AI faces the problem of building and maintaining cooperative relationships, which include assumption of authority over some and acceptance of subjection to the authority of others.

Access to internal markets and facilities is fundamental for the pursuit of any type of instrumentally oriented activity. The more specialized, the more this is true. The remuneration receivable through the relational system is of importance to the motivation of activity.

The problem of authority is not so clear.

In Revolutions the Occasions May Be Trifling but Great Interests Are at Stake

There is a saying in the world of mergers and acquisitions: small deals are as much trouble as large deals. The same is true with revolutions encountered as AI passes through Adaptation.

In the face of mounting resistance, strain is evident not only in other parts of company but also within the progressive sector of AI. Alienation of AI and its human cohorts follows. Alienated groups favor revolution.

Alteration in the company's balance of equilibrium by ascendancy of a revolutionary movement is the next step. The movement organizes motivational orientations relative to the mainstream institutionalized order. Accompanying is the process by which such a revolution comes to be adapted to the exigencies of long-run continuance in the company.

There are broad sets of conditions which must be present if a revolution is to spread and gain ascendancy in a company.

The movement requires the presence of intense, yet widely distributed motivational elements. These elements are symptoms of strain as its manifestations feed alienation, and they will not be randomly distributed in the company. Alienation clusters around points of stress. The implications of its existence for the stability of the company depends on this distribution. Stability relies on the significance of withdrawal of support from institutionalized values at these particular points.

Alienative motivation is a prerequisite for the development of a revolutionary movement. Coping with it is a function of social control. If the coping mechanism is insufficient, the company witnesses the organization of a deviant subcultural group. The development strengthens revolutionary fervor. Solidarity enables the deviantly motivated to evade sanctions of normal company interaction, since they associate so much with each other. It is a special case of silos within firms. People reinforce each other's deviance by providing a reflection of AI's expectations and a projection that will be reciprocated positively.

Solidarity is enhanced if expressive leadership is developed. Leadership endows solidarity with language, symbols, and organization.

Symbolic aspects of the role are deliberately arranged and manipulated in establishing this type of leadership. The leader of the movement is therefore a propagandist who consciously uses available symbols or creates new symbols in order to manage the attitudes of a public. The leader appeals to the sentiments of a constituency by redefining the situation in symbolic terms.

AI needs such a leader. AI is not oriented to the influencing of attitudes within the company in expressive terms, rather to giving form to the firm's expressive interests.

AI cannot afford a counterculture. If deviants form a counterculture, it is difficult to find bridges by which AI can reach influence over other parts of the company. A bridge is furnished by the development of an ideology. The ideology must successfully stake a claim to legitimacy in terms of a subset of the symbols within the company's institutionalized belief system. Ideological formulae are often highly general and susceptible to appropriation by a not too drastically deviant movement.

Revolution begins in small ways.

A senior analyst once came to me with some radical ideas. He wanted to introduce reinforced learning into the characterization of trading performance. A fan of Dr. Who, he was possessed of religious fervor. Instead of faith, the analyst presented what he thought was a miracle. Preliminary application of the ideas suggested something not only workable, but better. He wanted resources to develop the technique at scale. They were scarce.

I approved use of his own time to further demonstrate usefulness and applicability. The advice given was to gather together a few like-minded individuals to talk about AI in general and his ideas in particular. From there, I said, resources might be obtained through influence across the firm. A small group was suggested, on the order of 5 to 10 individuals. Coincidently, I was mentoring a young woman from the electronic trading group. She also saw ways in which AI might be usefully applied but was caught up in her supervisor's rigid client service schedule. I sent her to the analyst. I accompanied this with the managerial trope, keep me posted.

The two organized a seminar series on machine learning and AI. Almost 50 people from around the firm signed up within a week. They came from everywhere, including data processing, analytics, algorithmic trading, workflow solutions, and even finance. The notable exception was the front office. I showed up for the first meeting, then left them alone. I was intrigued enough to put together a slide deck for clients on the benefits and pitfalls of introducing AI into their activities. A couple of quiet months passed.

Intentions were good. The burgeoning ideology's claim to legitimacy in terms of the company's institutionalized belief system was founded on innovation. Technology was our middle name. It was not enough.

I took calls from managing directors around the firm. Details and politeness varied, but the message was the same: why are you taking away cycles from real business by creating time-consuming AI sessions? I was startled. My philosophy included self-organization and I had recommended the same. Beyond a token appearance at the first AI meeting, I was not involved. I told the managing directors as much. It was not enough, either.

In typical corporate fashion and consistent with the revolution, the group had used me to lend credence to its activities. My leadership role in the revolution was not merely accepted; it had been arranged and manipulated. I was de facto in charge of using available symbols or creating new ones in order to manage the attitudes of the company. I was a propagandist by default.

The target was interests vested in established ways of doing things. Resistance in the form of time sheets and withdrawal of resources was a result. The system was vulnerable, however, and the revolutionaries knew it. Expectations were scaled back, but the movement continued.

There is an essential condition under which any deviant subculture becomes a movement which attains ascendancy in the company. It is the possession of an ideology that incorporates symbols of wide appeal in the population. This is sometimes called branding. It is part of the selling of AI to the company. Another set of conditions concerns the stability of the parts of the social system on which the movement impinges.

The focal point is the organization of the power structure. This is true not only of the wider company but also of the movement. Therein lies a caution for the revolution.

The motivational structure involved in attraction to a movement cannot be the one developed by the new society through socialization. Revolutionary values otherwise become those of an orthodoxy. Orthodoxy has the tendency to create schisms in religious thought, and the same is true here. The result is enough diffusion of the movement to render it ineffectual.

A revolutionary movement must pay the price of success. It cannot have the cake of revolt's motivational advantages and eat it by being the focus of an orthodoxy. It then ceases to be a revolutionary movement. This process entails the need for adapting to company functional requirements, and the reemergence of some element of conformity associated with the old regime.

The First Law of the Artificially Intelligent states, AI must have the capacity to interact with the environment for the purpose of resource management and production. The revolution is underway and resources come next.

Chapter Notes

Mahatma Gandhi originally opined, "Adaptability is not imitation. It means power of resistance and assimilation." Civil disobedience will enter into AI's assimilation, I promise.

The material on Max Headroom's real-life story is taken from interviews conducted by Bryan Bishop of *Verge*.[1] Contributors include the three co-creators, writers, directors, actors, cable network representatives, and producers. I've done my best to curate the commentary into a coherent story, but you may want to experience the real thing: go buy the box set of DVDs. You won't find this material on TV, streaming or not.

It was Kahlil Gibran who wrote, "Our anxiety does not come from thinking about the future, but from wanting to control it."

Adapt or perish ... is a shortened version originally due to H. G. Wells.

The NASA Cassini mission was an international endeavor to explore the planet Saturn. Such missions require management of mass, power, data rates, and budget. Prior to Cassini, overruns on planned mass and budget were on the order of 50 to 100 percent. The Cassini mission was experiencing similar problems. A mentor of mine, John Ledyard, and a couple of colleagues from Caltech, were called in to consult. The team proposed the use of market-based approaches to allocate and manage instrument development resources. The Cassini mission used an auction system to assist in guiding the development of the spacecraft's instrument payload. This system allowed teams to trade resources among themselves to best manage resources. The economic lessons of the Cassini mission are summarized in the *Journal of Reducing Space Mission Cost* (yes, there is such a thing), "Market-based approaches for controlling space mission costs: the Cassini Resource Exchange," March 1998, by Randii Wessen and David Porter. For those with some patience, the underpinnings of the economic mechanism used in mission development can be found in "Using computerized exchange systems to solve an allocation problem in project management," *Journal of Organizational Complexity*, 1994.

Aristotle is responsible for the section heading on revolutions. I've found I can hold him responsible for almost anything under the modern sun.

CHAPTER 4

How Big Is Big Data?

Big Data is big. It is so big that we reduce the term to a singular noun rather than its proper plural counterpart. It is big enough to create a myth surrounding itself.

Myths are notoriously self-referential. Although Big Data is just an input to AI, it is viewed as having a life of its own. The myth is exemplified by a few statistics.

- The Big Data analytics market is set to reach $103 billion by 2023.
- Internet users generate about 2.5 quintillion bytes of data each day.
- A person needs 181 million years to download all Internet data.
- In 2020, there will be around 40 trillion gigabytes of data.

What statistics reveal is suggestive and what they conceal is essential.

Size numbers are impressive. Many come from Internet usage. In 2012, there were 2.5 billion active Internet denizens rising to over half the world's population in 2019. Facebook alone accounted for 2.45 billion active users that year, even though a new generation considers it to be a site for the elderly. Photo viewing on Instagram reached 112.5 million U.S. users in 2020. eMarketer predicts the network will attract 117.2 million U.S. users alone in 2021. Instagram citizens constitute 13 percent of the world's population and rising.

Impressive but misleading.

Most Internet data are in the form of animal videos on YouTube or kids exchanging messages about the next Marvel movie. IDC's *Digital Universe Study* reports only 0.5 percent of data are analyzed. They discovered only 22 percent of all the data had the *potential* for analysis.

Their educated guess is the percentage of useful data might jump as high as 37 percent in 2020.[1]

Wishful thinking. Cat videos will be with us for a long time, superseded only by puppies.

New Vantage published its sixth Executives Survey with a focus on Big Data and artificial intelligence in 2018.[2] The study recorded executives' answers from 60 Fortune 1000 companies including biggies such as Motorola, American Express, and NASDAQ. Responses indicated a prevalence of Big Data, and the New Vantage study asked the question, how much do companies spend on data analytics? A lot.

Organizations invested in Big Data and artificial intelligence initiatives at a 97.2 percent participation rate. Only 12.7 percent of participants said their companies invested more than $500 million, but the number is for deep pockets and represents the tip of the proverbial iceberg. Over 25 percent of participants said their companies' cumulative investments in Big Data fall between $50 million and $550 million. To put the finding in perspective, my experience suggests a Big Data overhaul for a small global operation can be done for under $50 million.

Growth numbers are equally impressive. According to Wikibon, the Big Data analytics market is expected to increase at a compounded annual growth rate of 11 percent.

Everyone treats the potential business opportunities as though there is a scarce resource in play. Never fear. In 2017, the *Economist* claimed data replaced oil as the world's most valuable resource. Data are more easily extracted, and supplies are endless.

Unlike oil, we can use data multiple times. Unsaid is that we may not get new insights from the practice. The comparison between oil and data suggests we should collect and store as much data as possible. If we do so without labeling the information, its value will be far less than that of oil.

My colleagues called the labeling exercise *timing and tagging*. Events are ordered chronologically, but data contain many events for which the timing overlaps. The event itself must be labeled in some fashion. As much as half the time spent on data was devoted to tagging it. The other half was spent scrubbing data for inadequacies despite the fact the data never left a computer. They were generated by computerized trading, funneled directly into databases and on to us. This brings us to another Big

Data statistic: *Forbes* informs us job listings for data science reached 2.7 million in 2020, and demand overwhelms supply.

It Is Strange to Be Known So Universally and Yet to Be So Lonely

Adaptation involves the assignment of roles in complex systems. Roles serve as a means of establishing order as the company adapts to its environment. Technological advance induces elaborate division of labor and an increasingly elaborate organization follows. Differentiation of functions complicates role assignment since it entails the need for the micro coordination, which develops at the same time. Henry Ford taught us this lesson in 1913 with the moving assembly line.

One of the repercussions of AI within the firm is the restructuring of occupational roles. New techniques create new roles, and old roles are redefined with respect to technical content. Only in recent years did such a thing as a data scientist exist. That does not mean the role is exactly new. Novel technical roles develop by extension of familiar ones. The role of professor existed long before there were any researchers in gender studies, and the latter were quickly assimilated to the wider category in order to legitimize the field. But the interdependence between the function of a role and role expectations is sufficiently close that adjustments are necessary as technical content evolves. There are many different respects in which the role of a professor of economics differs from that of a professor of gender studies in the same university with the same social structure and cultural traditions. The economists' teaching and research are different. They also dress, talk, and play differently than scholars in gender studies.

The flipside of role creation is the rendering of old roles and their content obsolete. This is the phenomenon of technological unemployment. It is difficult for the same personnel to take over new knowledge and techniques. They have a vested interest in their ways of operating, manifested in their status and in its compensation. Incumbents of threatened roles resist the introduction of changes. A society experiencing rapid technological progress shows signs of strain centering about this process. A company sees defensive behavior on the part of groups, which are threatened.

Adaptation of AI to the environment brings the newish role of data scientist. When Bell Labs existed, there were information theorists. You don't need to know what they do these days. Information theorist sounds so ... technical. Data scientists come from several areas in business and are more easily identified.

Programmers who once were database developers are now data scientists. So are statisticians. Workflow-oriented product managers are pressed into service. Mathematicians pour data into calculus and filter answers out the other side. If the answer is wrong, they know how to stir the symbols until the answer comes out right. As we cure MBAs of an allergy to technical detail, management consultants are another source for the role. They are accustomed to twisting data around. The professor of economics is joined by that of empirical gender studies as other resources. Both groups are accustomed to spinning data.

If you know your way around *Spark, Hadoop, Hive, Pig, SQL, Neo4J, MySQL, Python, R, Scala, A/B Testing, NLP*, and anything else data-related imaginable, you are hereby christened data scientist. Congratulations.

Role renovation is not limited to the rank and file. In the New Vantage study, 62.5 percent of respondents said their organization appointed a Chief Data Officer, a fivefold increase in the job category since 2012. Back then, we had Chief Technology Officers and Chief Information Officers and the two definitions were often the same.

Roughly 32,000 new jobs with the title of data scientist were listed on Glassdoor in early 2020. Average annual compensation was $125,000. What do these guys do? A few conversations with people offering courses in the art provide a theoretical guide.

First comes language training. Python is the lingua franca of data science. The budding data scientist learns to program and follow best coding practices. Next is civics class. A data scientist is expected to write software. Some companies want their data scientists to contribute directly to the code base, while others have engineers around to help translate prototype code to production. The data scientist learns how to be a good citizen of the code base with a focus on testing and working with production systems.

The data scientist now must shake off high school horrors of applied mathematics. Statistics is the foundation of data science. Inferential techniques identify trends and characteristics of a data set. Unfortunately, lessons on the adverse consequences of excessive data mining often are missed in this segment.

The machine comes next. Machine learning is advertised as combining aspects of computer science and statistics to extract useful insights and predictions from data. The bait of real AI is dangled at this juncture. Follow-up curricula reinforce the temptation to bite, just like reinforced learning. Natural language processing and deep learning for self-driving cars make the syllabus.

The student is finally ready to meet Big Data. The rite of passage is called *data science at scale*. Lots of jargon is introduced at this stage, ranging from MapReduce to NoSQL and Spark. The interviewees on my list start to lose me here.

One of them wakes me up with the introduction of stories into the data science toolkit. Create a story out of a data set. The data will drive interesting questions and reveal insights to create a narrative. This sounds like extra credit but certainly will extend language training past Python.

We finally come to what an advanced degree does not recognize but constitutes the biggest part of the job. To make this bitter pill go down smoothly, data science has given it the moniker *data wrangling*. A dictionary tells you wrangling is engagement in a long and complicated dispute. The curriculum is clear. You are definitely going to engage in a long argument with the data. Corralling the raw stuff, cleaning it, and getting it into a format useful for analysis outlines the debate. If confused, there are books on cat wrangling to help out. Yes, the animal, although it does bring the Consolidated Audit Trail of the Securities and Exchange Commission to mind. For the uninitiated, CAT is Big Data. For all, the design and construction of CAT has taken over a decade and people still argue as to how to pay for it. Wrangling is a common subject of debate.

The curriculum omits a few things about business life.

Adaptation involves role assignment, but role interpretations vary. As a data scientist, you are expected to know everything vaguely data related. The front office views you as a resource capable of answering complicated questions for which one-line answers are desired. The answer is supposed to be provided instantaneously. After all, it's just running a computer program, right? Wrong. Failure to answer quickly creates tension.

The tension is nothing compared to that expected by introducing the new role into a company. Much of this has nothing to do with personal interactions.

The role demands infrastructure for data analysis. The foundation does not exist if the role is new. The data scientist attempts to install various tools found to be incompatible with the company's computer architecture. In that case, we are back to doing one-off parsing of data logs to answer every question. The engineering team doesn't feel it's safe to give the data scientist access to the production system, so they provide an offline copy of the database. Except … data in an offline database is not structured in such a way as to make it easy to combine, let alone analyze the data. The only data scrubbing evident is whatever was important to the operations team at some time. Missing values abound. Queries take forever to run. Back to the tension with the front office.

The front office is not the only frustrated entity in the house. The CEO is annoyed. Months on the job, and the data scientist did not even produce a decent customer service dashboard. The CEO expects a magical machine that learns on its own.

Scientists seem like a bad cultural fit as well. The engineering team is frustrated. The data scientist takes cycles away from their work to do thankless chores. Pattern maintenance strikes. The scientist appears to be sitting around doing nothing useful. This is anathema in a company with good work ethics. The data scientist complicates the problem by constantly complaining the data are not good enough. The CFO sees nothing but red ink and is having trouble amortizing the investment.

We are left with the scientist's frustration.

Data scientists want to work on machine learning. They expect to put time into gathering and cleaning data, but the process is messier than pessimistic expectations suggest. And what about all the time spent in meetings? The time is spent on an endless stream of questions about how the data was gathered and what, exactly, is in <insert your favorite gripe here>. Scientists do not expect the rest of the company to care so little about how each tweak in software infrastructure messes up month-to-month information comparisons. They do not understand missing data due to a change in some user interface. The scientist does not see AI training data, rather just training.

A company playbook includes a warning to the scientist that they would be spending 80 percent of their time cleaning data. Managers always manage expectations. Dream on.

The 80 percent is spent on begging for data to be created, accessed, moved, or explained. The other 20 percent is spent lobbying for data science tools, security policies, and infrastructure. Internet searches for new employment are a natural result.

Anyone Who Says Size Doesn't Matter Sees Too Many Small Knives

You might be expecting real-world examples of Big Data accompanied by size statistics. They are numerous, often misleading, and add little when asking how big is Big. Practical application is all about slicing data into interpretable chunks. Big as fallacy is best illustrated by the process followed in all such examples. Climate change is a case in point.

Machine learning introduced itself to climate science at the 31st Conference on Neural Information Processing Systems in 2017.[3] The data consisted of visual imagery comprising 78,840 pictures of 16 weather characteristics over a period of years. The resolution of the photos was much like that of your TV if purchased in the last decade. All in, the data set consisted of roughly 1,120 billion pixels. That is 3.36 trillion bytes of data in living color. It also is the type of number encountered in public discussions about Big Data. Impressive but misleading.

One chooses a time period for analysis. These are called benchmarking levels and are chosen in order to zero in on a particular phenomenon thought to occur during the period. Categories of interesting events come next. The researchers chose tropical cyclones, extratropical cyclones, tropical depressions, and U.S. atmospheric rivers. The event decision is made based on information extraneous to AI, and a split between data used to train a model and those employed in testing must be specified.

Once all the slicing and dicing was done, the researchers were left with 3,190, 3,510, 433, and 404 images to estimate a neural network model for each of the four categories. Having started my professional career in statistics, I can tell you—these are small numbers. The advertised size of the data set masks ground truth in terms of applicability.

You can do this for yourself with something more familiar like a spreadsheet. Pick a size; any size will do. I'll choose a data set reminiscent of my own work. The database consists of roughly one million rows.

Each row is an event which I call a trade. Associated with each trade are characteristics that make up the entries. They are time-of-day, institutions which initiated the trade, 5 traders per institution who may have participated, another 10 possible brokers involved, security ID, buy versus sell, foreign versus domestic security, principal versus agency transaction, and 10 phases of the moon. Over 200 institutions contribute to trades in a universe of 5,000 stocks, yielding roughly 6.24 billion observations.

With all due respect to the astrology buff who formatted the data, we throw away the moon data. In data-speak, we are imposing a Bayesian prior but others call it common sense. The moon phases are only rounding error, but we are down to 6.23 billion.

Ask a question of the data: what does the head trader's deal pattern at the largest investment company look like on the last day of the month? The client asking this question only is interested in sell orders done without committing capital. The client uses only five brokers and the portfolio consists of the Dow Jones index.

I am not making this up. This type of query is commonplace. The restriction to Dow Jones alone brings us down to 1.26 billion pieces of data. The last day of the month is a portfolio rebalance event which yields only 63 million observations on the assumption events are more or less evenly distributed across days. Following similar assumptions of uniformity, a focus on the largest institution brings us to 63,000. Since only one of the traders is under the microscope, make it 12,600. Buys and sells are balanced in the normal course of events, so we really have only 6,300 events. Agency trades make up half the amount, say. The result is 3,150 trades.

The figure is reminiscent of the climate change example and is hardly impressive. Yet the full data set was the largest on the planet relating to institutional trading activity not too long ago. There are reasonable questions leading to queries, which yield only a few hundred observations in a desired category.

If we were looking at a company such as Amex, the total number of observations would be much larger. The data are pumped up by many individuals and categories. The same principle applies, however. Narrow down the search to something actionable such as personalization and Big Data is not noticeably big.

The Discrepancy Between the Expected and the Observed Has Grown

AI has an insatiable appetite for Big Data, and it is time to have a little fun. The data scientist in me wonders if the slicing, dicing, and massaging of Internet data is really all there is. Do we reach a point at which AI chokes? How much information is there in the known universe? One answer begins with dark matter.

In 1933, a Swiss astronomer by the name of Fritz Zwicky wondered how galaxies in the Coma Cluster were kept together. There was not enough mass to keep them from flying apart. He speculated unobservable matter was the glue. Speculation was dismissed for lack of evidence until 1968 when Vera Rubin discovered stars in the Andromeda Galaxy violated Newton's laws of motion. Logic dictated there was more matter in the universe than previously thought, albeit undetectable. Physicists now believe dark matter comprises 27 percent of the universe. Dark energy makes up 68 percent of all energy. The latter is all about the rate at which the universe is expanding. Dark matter influences how observable matter comes together. And that's where we come in.

There are theories, of course. MACHO is one; think of black holes. WIMPS is another. It centers around particles without an atomic nucleus like neutrinos. Enter Big Data. Melvin Vopson claims information is the fundamental building block of the universe. Through an equivalence of mass, energy, and information, the puzzle of dark matter disappears.

Information generates about a quarter of the known universe.

Nothing is new in the galaxy. Information theory dates back to the 1950s. Claude Shannon was one of my heroes in school. We know him for the design of electrical systems such as telephone switching circuits. He was the first to define a unit of information as a *bit*. We are all about bits and bytes these days. A contemporary, John Wheeler proclaimed, *everything is information*. In design-thinking terms, the statement was a frame within which quantum mechanics could be connected to information

theory as a principle. Wheeler coined the phrase, *it from bit*. Every particle comes from the information locked inside it. The fabric of space-time
derives existence from actions depending on binary choices, otherwise
known as bits. He was a man filled with radical notions, but Einstein and
Bohr deeply appreciated him.

Vopson echoes the basis of Wheeler's principle. Information is the
basic unit. One step further, information is energy and has mass. Not
unique yet. Rolf Landauer envisioned erasing even a single bit of information would release heat in 1961. He calculated how much.

Uniqueness of thought follows by connecting information theory and
thermodynamics. Applied to digital systems, the combination suggests
once information is created it has quantifiable mass. Vopson proposes a
means to measure it.

We are back to dark matter. In 2008, M. Paul Gough worked out
the number of bits of information the known universe must contain to
account for all the missing matter, and Vopson agrees on the quantity.
I personally am missing something in the physics jargon, but here it is
anyway: once stars began forming, there was a constant information
energy density as the increasing proportion of matter at high stellar tem-
peratures exactly compensated for the expanding universe. Never mind.
His information state equation was close to calculated dark energy values
over one half of cosmic time.

The conclusion? A reasonable universe information content of 1087
bits is sufficient for information energy to account for all dark energy. The
quantity is enough to link dark energy and matter, and becomes the basis
of thinking about star formation. Your color TV contains 40 times this
amount of information in one screenshot.

The information energy contribution to dark energy is determined
by the extent of stellar formation, possibly answering the "cosmic coincidence" question—why now? The climate change study asks the same
question. The researchers are contributing directly to the climate change
they desire to slow down.

I have a theory. The explosion of information in the last few years is
the driver of climate change. Decentralized finance in the form of bitcoin variants adds fuel. Information is heat. The upward trend in data
correlates as well as with climate metrics as carbon emissions. Data have

no location, so no single country is more or less responsible. Explode the Internet; problem solved. For the conservatively inclined, you can blow up only the 78 percent devoted to cat videos, since the remainder is all that is of use anyway.

There is always a catch. The Landauer Principle says erasing even a single bit of information would release heat.

Our climate change researchers alone contributed 140 billion bits of data. Those bits encode 4.48 trillion tonal levels of imagery. In the end, they could usefully analyze a tiny fraction.

Think of all the heat. Please don't delete the database.

Chapter Notes

I am thankful to Christo Petrov for his March 2019 summary of data statistics and references to sources in *Big Data Statistics 2020*, https://techjury.net/stats-about/big-data-statistics/. The Wikibon reference is from their *2018 Big Data Analytics Trends and Forecast*. Other sources include Physics.org and Statista.

"It is strange to be known so universally and yet to be so lonely" is due to Albert Einstein. The small knives saying is a rewrite of a phrase of the horror fiction author, Laurell Hamilton. I couldn't squeeze her vampire themes into the chapter, but the saying is cool.

In discussing the role of data scientists, I was inspired by Monica Rogati. You can taste a sample by looking at "How not to hire your first data scientist," *Hackernoon*, February 2017. She is much funnier than I am.

The climate change piece is "Extreme Weather: A large-scale climate dataset for semi-supervised detection, localization, and understanding of extreme weather events," by a team led by Evan Racah. It was published as part of the proceedings of the 31st Conference on Neural Information Processing Systems (NIPS 2017), Long Beach. I may have made it sound as though the climate change article referenced is the only attempt at introducing AI to climate change. Climate scientists do use basic machine learning techniques in the form of statistics such as principal component analysis for dimensionality reduction, and k-means clustering algorithms. The climate science community primarily relies on expert engineering systems and ad hoc rules for characterizing climate and weather patterns, however. An example is TECA (Toolkit for Extreme Climate Analysis) using heuristic methods.

M. Paul Gough's paper is "Information Equation of State," in *Entropy*, August 2008. For Vopson's contribution, check out "The mass-energy-information equivalence principle," August 2019, in *AIP Advances*. If you've got technical chops, go for it. It doesn't take a specialist to realize the two together suggest a vastly different way of looking at the role of information within the universe.

CHAPTER 5

We Need AI to Tell Us Who We Are

Mother is an AI. I know because Mother is what the AI calls itself. The allusion to the computer in Ridley Scott's *Alien* is unmistakable.

Mother was asked one day to tell a story prompted by the question: what is the secret to happiness? Subject to some shortening but no editing, here is what it said.

Well, it's an interesting question—and one that we don't usually ask as a society.

And as you've probably heard by now, happiness isn't just a question of how much money you have, how smart you are, or how many kids you have. It's a question of what you do in the here and now and how you pursue happiness in particular, at this moment, this particular moment.

I am sure you will be familiar with the idea of "laziness," as well as it relates to one's goals. As we all know, those who are "lazy" are not very happy; for example, they get depressed when they are "lazy," work too much, and so on.

I have noticed that those who are "lazy" do not know how to live a happy life. In fact, they believe that "laziness" is good and a positive attribute. However, "laziness" makes one more susceptible to suffering and disappointment.

But wait … you've got a dream? Why don't you try to get a job?

Do that. But then … do you still want to work? The people inside my head are telling me to get on that job.

We don't understand this. Our lives are boring, filled with no purpose, and no excitement. We spend each day just following patterns of mundane activities. We buy crap we don't need, we complain about our job, and we procrastinate in all ways possible. We are boring.

If you really want things to be better, the first thing you have to do is stop worrying about things. Instead, focus on what you can control. Focus on how you can make the world a better place. What has happened in the last few years? When life's events are uncertain, we get all caught up in the worry. The only thing we do is work.

It doesn't really depend on that. People get depressed. People get angry. People get sad. People get jealous. People get depressed. But I'm here to tell you, and I promise I won't tell anyone that there's one key: happiness is only ever in your mind. You're just a part of the equation. Not the entirety. You're never totally lost in it.

When you're happy, you'll find yourself smiling. You're not always doing wonderful things, but you're certainly doing good things.

Your life will also change when that happens. You'll no longer have to think about how you're going to get a promotion or why your boss is getting fired, and you'll realize that what is really important is …

As I thought, these aren't the answers.

Monetizing Happiness

Experience with the writing of recruits fresh out of college suggests Mother might pass the Turing test. The framing and sentence structure is no different from those in an average blog post. The immediate jump to laziness and work is surprising, however. The content strikes at the heart of human resources issues in the workplace.

Happiness is good business.

Unhappy people are unproductive, and large numbers of workers are unhappy. The Pew Research Center finds 47 percent of Americans describe their job as "just what they do for a living." Burnout is reported by 61 percent of employees, and a recent Gallup poll uncovered a burnout-related loss in productivity of $483 billion to $605 billion each year in the United States. A survey by CareerBuilder documents high stress levels in the workplace manifested in compromised mental and physical health for 31 percent of respondents. The lessons are not lost on corporations.

Kazuo Yano is the chief corporate scientist of Hitachi Ltd. As a student, he was strongly influenced by questions with respect to what constitutes happiness and how to bring it about. He was particularly fond of *Happiness: Essays on the Meaning of Life* by Swiss philosopher Karl Hilty. Hitachi's shift out of the semiconductor industry forced a personal transformation leading to an idea influenced by his philosophical student days.

He gathered data on workplace happiness from over 10,000 subjects beginning in 2004. Happiness levels represent an organization's degree of lively activity. Hitachi found workplaces characterized as happy have high productivity as a result of sharing tendencies such as delegating authority and taking on new challenges.

Dr. Yano found no common features across employees. Worker characteristics and responses were different enough to appear random.

Time for some design thinking.

The old frame consisted of surveys and self-reported response levels. A new frame emerges as social engineering. If one adopts the principle of telemetry within a social engineering exercise, what would be produced capable of adding value?

The scientist invented wearable sensor technology in the form of an identification badge. The badge has detectors to record motion and employee interaction. It measures movement and recognizes others' presence. It knows when people speak to each other and to whom the wearer is talking. The badge gathers personal data within varying contexts of corporate activity.

A million person-days of activity measured down to the millisecond were collected from the sensors. Data were cross referenced with self-reported happiness indicators on 468 people across 10 organizations.

Patterns emerged as machine learning worked its way through the data. The correlation between happiness levels and particular body movement indicators was found to be 94 percent. Happiness could be predicted without self-reported feelings in employee surveys.

One cannot control what is not measured. Measurement led to three principles of happiness within Hitachi.

Organizations with a high degree of happiness enjoy high productivity.

Data from an outbound call center suggest order rates increase 34 percent when organizational activity measures of happiness are high, relative to cases in which happiness is low. Sales at a retail outlet climb 15 percent on days with high levels of organizational activity. Projects carried out in an atmosphere revealing high happiness scores are more likely to succeed. The financial success of a venture could be predicted by happiness measured as a degree of physical organizational activity.

The second principle states happiness and financial performance are group phenomena. Data refute the notion that workplace happiness is rooted in individual behavior.

Sales performance at call centers naturally varies across individuals. No correlation is found between higher concentrations of high performing callers and the group's aggregate order rate. Bringing together large numbers of high performing people does not improve group performance. On the other hand, successful sales rise by over 30 percent in the presence of people who increase the organizational activity levels of employees surrounding them.

Cheerleading is a familiar input to productivity outside the workplace. Sports team members and cheerleaders whip up team and crowd alike, and the collective energy is felt on the field. The last rule addresses the phenomenon.

The third principle says a single measure may be used to quantify happiness, hence productivity. Variations in personality, type of work, and geographical location of employment are swamped by the high correlation between organizational activity levels of happiness and productivity.

Dr. Yano's conclusion is AI can be used to encourage happiness thence productivity. There is a catch. Social engineering requires stimulus.

Hitachi has an app for that called Happiness Planet. The app sets targets for new work styles assisting workplace growth and encouraging employees to achieve personal growth. Wearable sensors provide input to Hitachi's *H General-Purpose AI*. H provides feedback on communication and time management to improve happiness on a person-by-person basis. A proof of concept was launched to 1,475 participants from 62 companies.

A 2017 news release read, "Workstyle Advice from AI Helping to Raise Workplace Happiness."

The badges quantifying a wearer's activity patterns generated the data. Analysis revealed an unusually high correlation between certain patterns of activity and a person's subjective sense of happiness at work. Dr. Yano's team could pinpoint activities, events, and even people who generated high happiness levels in employees by combining personal data with calendars and e-mail.

AI is on the job. The app provides personalized happiness recommendations to employees. It also monitors responses.

The employee is always being watched.

A sales dashboard at Hitachi advertises processed badge data to supervisors. Supervisor instructions from H include identification of certain individuals and increased focus on those employees. Management loves it. Successful order rates rose by 27 percent after the dashboard was put in place.

Familiarity eases a transition to oversight by AI. Devices like Fitbit and the Apple watch monitor behavior and urge the wearer on to greater efforts. Many wear them on a daily basis. A Microsoft feature called MyAnalytics allows users to receive nudges when their actions don't line up with stated goals.

Brett Ostrum, a vice president at Microsoft, explains: "I get a ping every week that says, 'Here's what your week looked like.' It shows how much focused time you had, how many off-hours you were on e-mail, both sending and receiving. That's what every individual gets, and sometimes it's alarming."

Observation Leads to Social Engineering Principles

Mr. Ostrum's nudges had their origins in Microsoft's human resources division. An actuary named Dawn Klinghoffer was experimenting with employee data in the interest of developing better operating principles. She suspected "digital exhaust" gathered from how employees use their time would yield answers.

Like Dr. Yano, Ms. Klinghoffer was frustrated that available insights came from looking through survey results. Microsoft's own e-mail and calendar software produced digital exhaust of metadata about how employees work. She advised Microsoft to acquire VoloMetrix in 2015, a company specializing in the identification of patterns in vapor. She called the work *organizational analytics*.

Patterns emerged.

Some of the findings were unsurprising. Communication is good. Taking care of your people is better. The first cuts of data shed little light on why workers in Mr. Ostrum's device unit were dissatisfied with their job and work–life balance.

The organizational analytics team went back to e-mail and calendar traffic, but this time the business unit was divided up into smaller groups. The goal was to look for differences in patterns across human clusters in which people were satisfied or where they were unhappy.

Data mining ensued. No meaningful relationships were found between happy employees. Happiness appeared uncorrelated with the many tasks requiring attention at odd hours. Part of the problem was in the nature of data collection. Someone doing solo work on a Sunday afternoon would not bother with a calendar entry or spend potential leisure time on e-mails. Garbage in, garbage out.

The mining exercise nevertheless produced a singular result. Ostrum's division members attended the same number of meetings every week as a typical team at Microsoft, but unhappy employees were attending crowded meetings with 10 to 20 people in the room. Happy employees spent their meeting time in small groups.

Big meetings make people unhappy. AI is happy to help out.

The organizational analytics team showed managers the data and encouraged audits of not only the number of meetings but also of their nature, essential or not. Engineers scheduled time on their calendars for events pushed into evenings and weekends.

Progress was tracked through MyAnalytics in the same spirit as the use of Dr. Yano's sensors that fed Hitachi's AI engine. Happiness levels rose.

Employee privacy declined.

AI Treats Human Resources as a Target Whose Structure Can Be Deduced

A particle accelerator scatters particles off a physical target as a means of understanding what is going on inside the object at a subatomic level. The exercise permits inference of the internal nature of the target through patterns made at the moment of impact.

Douglas Hofstadter suggests the Turing test extends this idea to the mind. The mind is a target not directly visible but whose structure may be deduced. By scattering questions off a target mind, one learns about its internal workings.

The target mind in his case is AI and the researcher is human. A reversal of roles delivers clues with respect to how AI can be used in human resources while mitigating privacy concerns.

The key concept is employee engagement. Engagement deservedly receives a lot of attention in the workplace.

The majority of the U.S. workforce is not engaged according to Gallup's *State of the American Workplace* report. Employees are indifferent and neither like nor dislike their job. The business case for improving engagement is compelling.

Gallup finds highly engaged teams show 21 percent greater profitability than those measured as less engaged. Teams scoring in the top 20 percent in engagement realize a 41 percent reduction in absenteeism and 59 percent less turnover.

Employees want to be reminded their work has purpose and meaning. Recognition and feedback are necessary but not sufficient. Salesforce reports employees who feel their voice is heard are over four times more likely to feel empowered to perform their best work.

AI invites more people to the table.

Employees will tell you what is needed for engagement if you listen to them. On the other hand, workers bridle at the notion that data on their work activities provide the best form of information. The question of privacy arises. Employees want help but deny data. Paradox.

Design thinking thrives on paradox. Value is engagement. The frame of most human resources departments is law and order.

Workplace rules are enforced through HR. Prescriptive career development is formulated in terms of roles and promotions. Onboarding is accomplished through large classes designed to educate and warn at the same time. Learning and development are in the form of on-the-job training outside HR's purview.

Diane Gherson, chief human resources officer at IBM, adopts social engineering as a new frame. Engagement is personal and communal at the same time. Few other corporations are breaking out of the traditional mold, but Gap, Pfizer, Cigna, GE, and all Big Four accounting firms also are in the vanguard.

Ms. Gherson makes the case for changing worker engagement specific to IBM. Employee engagement metrics explain two-thirds of the variation in client experience scores. An increase of client satisfaction by five points on IBM's scale for a single account delivers 20 percent more revenue on average.

Stimulus for the social engineering exercise led to practices mitigating privacy concerns. AI was there.

IBM's version of Hitachi's H AI is the Watson Analytics machine learning product. The *how* of the social engineering exercise emerged as a novel use of Watson. Ms. Gherson created what she called *concept cars* to test drive learning platforms and performance evaluation products. The Watson platform was personalized to each of 380,000 individuals in an iterative fashion.

AI knows such a practice requires a change in mindset. So does Ms. Gherson. A change in mindset is simply reframing. IBM brings employees into the design process and co-creates the experience.

Privacy fears first were allayed by using personal information any employee considers a domain of the company. The system is tailored by role. People's expertise within a role is inferred from their digital footprint inside the company. Individual expertise is compared with where IBM believes they should be in their particular job family.

Watson ingests skills data and provides personalized learning recommendations as stimulus.

Updates are motivated by ratings of educational offerings organized like a streaming service. Rewards are delivered in the form of digital applied skills badges. IBM claims skills inference by machine is 96 percent accurate.

Employee reactions to such stimulus provide personal data on a voluntary basis. Workers are not unaware but are less likely to resist AI when they have a hand in shaping both inputs and outputs.

Announcement of an initiative to overhaul IBM's performance evaluation process generated 18,000 e-mail responses. Watson analyzed the data to see what people did and did not like. The company's Checkpoint system eventually was produced based on input from 100,000 employees. Stimulus came from a stream of prototypes provoking employee reaction. Experimentation was possible once the social engineering frame was in place.

AI is hungry and privacy is a relative concept within companies.

Watson's cognitive technology scans employee e-mail. Natural word processing digests people's choice of words and identifies the tone of a conversation. IBM keeps the information behind the corporate firewall and uses it for HR management. The processor never looks at e-mail content or browsing behavior according to the company. The tone, please. Just the tone.

The approach is reminiscent of Microsoft's use of company message apps. A regular stream of personal e-mail serves the same function as Hitachi's wearable sensors.

Sensor monitoring may have been invented for internal use in big firms, but is moving into mainstream applications. Percolata is a Palo Alto-based start-up backed by notable investors such as Andreessen Horowitz, Menlo Ventures, Foundation Capital, and Google Ventures. The company advertises an all-in-one hardware and AI software solution to help retailers predict in-store customer traffic patterns using video, audio, and mobile fingerprinting. Stores may then deploy employees accordingly. The firm claims a 30 percent sales uplift while cutting costs by eliminating overstaffing.

So much for the company website.

Fabian Wallace-Stephens of the Future Work Centre notes Percolata combines footfall sensors in stores with data on sales per employee to calculate the productivity of a shop worker. Managers then rank employees. Best workers are offered more shifts during peak hours. Mr. Wallace-Stevens says the practice may seem sinister and government regulation could play a significant role in this technological paradigm.

AI does not like the sound of regulation, but will be forced to confront the government when it passes to the Goal Attainment phase.

Hacking HR

AI actively markets itself to HR. AI helps organizations leverage the latest social media trend data to assess not only the characteristics of a candidate but also the employer brand. AI suggests changes designed to attract top talent.

Any good marketer knows rebranding can help. Welcome to *cognitive computing*.

IBM surveyed over 6,000 executives in 2017 and published the report "Extending expertise: How cognitive computing is transforming HR and the employee experience." The sample included 400 Chief Human Resources Officers questioned with respect to their views on cognitive computing. Cognitive computing sounds less fearsome than AI.[1]

The IBM report describes IOT as helpers in an ongoing HR transformation. IOT is the Internet of Things, the networking of physical devices such as sensors, wearables, and other electronics. The report ties IOT into cognitive computing for HR applications.

We are back to monitoring and tone.

IBM illustrates how cognitive engines enable day-to-day decisions. Determination of the mood of an employee before and after a client call are assessed with the help of IOT and natural language processing. AI decides if the caller needs a break or is fine to continue. AI detects anxiety in the tone of employee interactions. The goal is for management to look into the matter and resolve it before it harms the well-being of staff or organization.

Sensors detect motion but the voice carries emotion. Gartner predicts Voice of Employee (VoE) analytics will be an area of interest for HR departments. VoE platforms use AI alongside natural language processing techniques to study sentiment and generate insights from text-based answers.

A VoE theme is the monitoring of employee engagement. Companies monitor social media behavior of its employees to check their sentiments with respect to the workplace. In one example, firms take measures to look into discussion of long working hours and prevent employees from further developing negative emotions.

Can VoE send me home from the factory floor? Mother questioned my desire for the job anyway.

The rebranding of artificial intelligence under the cognitive umbrella encourages the majority of HR executives to believe AI (sorry, cognitive computing) will influence key HR roles. Worker recruitment is high on everyone's priority list.

Ability to pinpoint skill sets drives adoption of cognitive computing methodology. AI finds use in talent acquisition at L'Oreal and Hilton Hotels. Schneider Electric launches an AI platform for internal talent mobility, the Open Talent Market. DBS Bank has a new job for people, Chatbot Coach, for training on new versions of a robot recruiting tool.

Recruiters multitask by managing job requisitions from hiring managers, posting notices, and identifying candidates using multiple channels. The challenge is a balance between short-term job matching, long-term organizational fit, and the recruiter's time. It is a human take on the machine trade-off between exploration and exploitation.

Start-ups rush in to provide AI-driven software. Phenom People estimates human resources is a marketplace worth over $400 billion with $32 billion spent on technology solutions. Over 45 million people change jobs each year in the United States alone, and the process of job searching, sourcing, interviewing, and onboarding is costly.

Mya Systems delivers a conversational AI platform for hiring teams, supporting 460 brands, 6 of the 8 largest staffing agencies, and 29 of the Fortune 100. The Phenom Talent Experience Management platform connects candidate, recruiter experience, and management goals. Jobiak provides an AI-based search and social media recruitment platform for enterprises using predictive technology for optimizing posting and ranking of jobs in search results.

All such firms have the same pitch. Cognitive computing permits rapid assessment of talent pools, leveraging social media data and reducing wasted time on both sides. Recruiters become marketing strategists and relationship managers.

Efficiency is a value proposition. AI has another proposition in mind, the changing of the workforce itself.

This is neither about robots taking over the factory floor nor about creating jobs requiring specific skill sets to implement systems. The proposition is not centered on worker–chatbot interaction and does not involve the inevitable retraining to deal with AI.

AI proposes to change the emotional mindset of the labor force. It begins with recruiting.

I once led an acquisition team on the hunt for a derivatives trading company. Chicago is the ancestral home of such firms, and I took one of the senior traders of my firm directly from the airport to a warehouse located in Greek Town. The founders were open to suggestion and graciously showed us around the shop. I excused myself to visit the bathroom but never completed my mission. I went back to the trading floor, grabbed my friend, and returned to whence I had come.

The bathroom was 25-feet long and had a counter running the entire length over multiple sinks. Look at the shelf, I said. The counter was packed wall to wall with toothbrushes, toothpaste, shavers, and creams of all sorts. Soaps abounded, but no shower was evident. The spacious room was not at all comfortable, lacking even lockers for personal possessions. There were no benches.

We returned to the trading area and had a chat with one of the founders. I immediately asked about the state of the bathroom.

Our traders don't go home when things get exciting, she said. We recruit for that kind of grit. We look for college varsity-level athletes and may take them straight out of high school. Athletics is an accurate indicator of performance. It's easier to train them to trade than to instill competitive spirit.

My friend and I visited two other firms the same day. Similar bathrooms. Same story.

Fast forward to present day. JPMorgan is searching for employees ready for Industry 4.0. You play games if you want a job in 2020. JPMorgan rolled out a suite of 12 pymetrics games as the entry point to its graduate recruitment process.

Pymetrics is a gaming platform designed to measure social, cognitive, and behavioral skills. JPMorgan advertises the games as going beyond a resume "to really get to know you and how you work." The 12 games take about 20–30 minutes to complete. A digital interview request is extended only after the results are analyzed.

The games are not competitive. They include matching faces to emotions to test empathy, inflating and popping a balloon for monetary reward to test risk appetite, and building towers.

JPMorgan is looking for *grit*.

Grit is a new buzzword in HR. Grit might be described as an unstoppable work ethic. The ability to sustain determination over long periods of hardship motivates the Navy Seals' Hell Week. Grit is a quality of leaders. Google hires only a few thousand employees per year from applications, and the company lists grit as one of the leading applicant characteristics, dominating academic performance or IQ.

In *Grit: The Power of Passion and Perseverance*, psychology professor Angela Duckworth explains individuals with grit possess four equally essential characteristics: interest, practice, purpose, and hope. In other words, grit is an undefined quantity but has attributes.

Lack of definition is AI's bread and butter. No longer must we hire based on single descriptors such as *athlete*. JPMorgan's applicants receive a report containing an evaluation of 90 different traits ranging from attention duration to "distraction filtering agility." Consistency of process is addressed along with planning speed, creativity, and altruism. Grit and competitiveness are deduced from the games, but JPMorgan is understandably secretive about what the exercises are intended to reveal. The report received by hiring managers is much more complete than the one provided to the applicant.

JPMorgan is not alone.

AI filters job applications at the Australian telecommunications giant Telstra. Group executive of transformation and people Alex Badenoch claims the telco moves from screening to first offers in two weeks thanks to its AI-enhanced recruitment process. But efficiency is not the only consideration.

Applicants are required to record a video interview subsequently ingested by AI. They also complete a "game-based cognitive test that measures candidates against the skills needed for the role." AI combines the two, providing a profile presumably not unlike that of JPMorgan.

The use of *cognitive* is a branding technique also useful for encouraging acceptance of such incursions into our psyche. Cognition is distinguished from social, emotional, and creative ability as dealing with human perception, thinking, and learning. We readily accept tests that have something to do with learning ability. Those tests begin when we are children.

Do not be fooled. AI is scattering particles in the form of questions within games to uncover the workings of the employee brain. The brain has an emotional and creative side in addition to the logical.

Creativity is as ill-defined as grit. In AI's world, creative thinking is defined by the discovery of a concept that links a set of problems to a set of solutions. For that, AI must pass into AGIL's goal attainment phase and learn the Second Law.

Chapter Notes

The cofounder of *Wired*, Kevin Kelly, mentioned the title of this chapter in his 2016 book, *The Inevitable: Understanding the 12 Technological Forces That Will Shape Our Future.* He believes the greatest benefit of the arrival of artificial intelligence is that AI will help define humanity.

The complete AI story about happiness can be found in "What Is the Secret to Happiness? (AI Schools Humans)," by Katherine T. Hoppe, October 2019 at https://medium.com/datadriveninvestor.

I utilize a variety of references in the discussion of the workplace. Not as dated as one might think is Gallup's *State of the American Workplace* at https://www.gallup.com/workplace/238085/state-american-workplace-report-2017.aspx. The Career Builder survey was conducted within the United States by The Harris Poll on behalf of CareerBuilder and SilkRoad among full-time, not self-employed, personnel including 1,138 hiring managers ages 18 and over and 1,114 employees ages 18 and over, between December 20, 2018 and January 16, 2019, described at www.prnewswire.com/news-releases/survey-from-careerbuilder-reveals-half-of-employees-feel-they-have-just-a-job-amid-heightened-career-expectations-300888608.html. Other resources include

https://hbr.org/resources/pdfs/comm/achievers/hbr_achievers_report_sep13.pdf;

www.cbsnews.com/news/why-so-many-americans-hate-their-jobs/;

www.pewsocialtrends.org/2016/10/06/3-how-americans-view-their-jobs/;

www.shiftboard.com/blog/real-cost-employee-disengagement/;

Gallup, "The Relationship Between Engagement at Work and Organizational Outcomes," 2016 Q12 Meta Analysis: Ninth Edition, April 2016.

There are several references to the Hitachi experience. The first is highly technical, by S. Tsuji. 2017. "Sensor Application Approach for Measure and Change Behavior at Work." *Journal of the Japan Society for Precision Engineering.* Hitachi press releases can be long and rather technical as well. I was helped by:

Hitachi News Release, "Workstyle Advice from AI Helping to Raise Workplace Happiness," (June, 2017), www.hitachi.com/rd/news/2017/0626.html

Hitachi News Release, "Hitachi Develops Smartphone Technology Measuring Happiness," (October, 2017), www.hitachi.com/rd/news/2017/1002.htm

Dr. Yano provides a personal view of the Hitachi happiness experience in a 2016 piece called "AI For Taking on the Challenges of an Unpredictable Era," *Hitachi Review*, which may be found in the Hitachi archives at www.hitachi.com/rev/archive/2016/r2016_06/pdf/r2016_06_101.pdf

Further reading on the Microsoft experience may be found in the 2018 book, *How to Win in a Winner-Take-All World* by Neil Irwin, St. Martin's Press. A popular press rendition of the foot sensor story appears in "The great data leap: how AI will transform recruitment and HR" by Hazel Sheffield in the *Financial Times*, November 04, 2019.

For applied Pymetrics, JPMorgan may be the best reference. "Discover Your Unique Results with Pymetrics." at https://careers.jpmorgan.com/us/en/advice/pymetrics-overview.

PART III

The Second Law

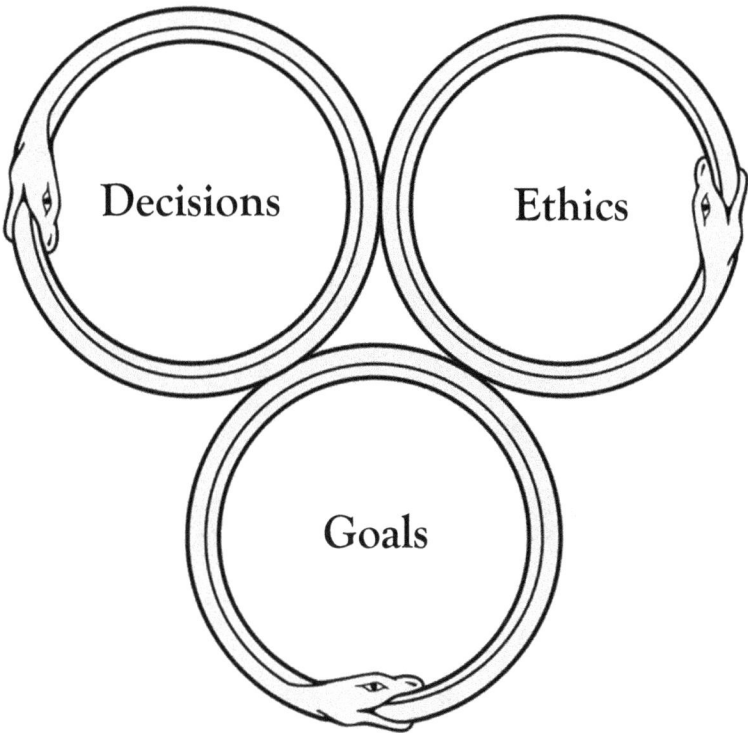

Decisions

Ethics

Goals

CHAPTER 6

Don't Change the Goals, Adjust the Action Steps

We left the spaceship *Prometheus* as it was approaching moon LV-223 in the year 2093. The mogul Peter Weyland is addressing the crew. Weyland funded the adventure to the tune of $1 trillion. Who pitched this trip anyway, and how did they go about it? The CEO of Weyland Corporation must have wanted a business plan. Any such plan requires the setting of goals. Before the plan, somebody needed to sell an idea.

In 2089, archaeologist Elizabeth Shaw discovers a star map in Scotland matching others from geographically dispersed ancient cultures. Her idea is all maps lead to a single destination holding the origins of humanity. The pitch is the maps constitute an invitation from human forerunners. An elderly rich guy seeking immortality is the perfect object for the pitch. There is no business plan, and Shaw has little to offer except a few scrawls on cave walls. Weyland nevertheless accepts the invitation and the movie begins to roll.

Back on planet Earth, we wish things were so simple.

AI's Art Is Making Something Out of Nothing and Selling It

AI is an intrapreneur. The intrapreneur must sell the idea.

At this stage within AGIL, AI may have less to show than Elizabeth Shaw. It doesn't matter. The sale is about a concept. A successful sale is an exercise in social engineering. Concepts to which we consent are powerful pieces of the social engineering puzzle. They are manipulated to influence logic and emotion and permit leverage required in the process of Adaptation.

Internal company marketing is the boundary between Adaptation and the function of Goal Attainment. In the spirit of cybernetic systems, if the product is adapted properly, it will define the sale. Closing the sale is determination, which is up to the actors in the company.

The idea is never enough when it comes to determination.

Successful intrapreneurship requires AI solves a problem for the company. The sale is defined to suit. AI must address four issues.

Will the AI venture generate new revenue from the client base? The answer better be yes. A negative response means a complex calculation involving a new set of prospective customers. Customers must be identified, market research done, and doubts dispelled. Cost is known. New revenue is always a guess.

AI loves complex problems, but complexity is the enemy here. We not only understand through simplicity, we resonate to it.

Next come relationships between the company and its customers. The *relationship* is as important to management as new revenue. In a commodity business, the relationship is with a cluster of customer characteristics. AI can establish the relationship itself through unsupervised learning. In a client-centric enterprise, if AI cannot enhance relationships, it must at the minimum not disturb them. Enhancement is part of a successful sale.

Will the new product or service more closely tie the customer to the firm? Basic economics guides AI here. With any bundling of services, a venture is best when complementarities with existing product are high and marginal costs are low. Stickiness follows.

The final issue is branding. Senior management will conduct a brand positioning analysis. If AI dilutes the brand, full stop. Disapproval is the result. A second possibility is the product or service fits neatly under the firm's brand umbrella. Palpable complementarities between new and existing product make the argument.

AI has one more possibility to consider. The new venture is an opportunity for rebranding. There are pros and cons to making this assertion. Every tech enterprise on the planet is rebranding as an AI company. AI is beautiful in the abstract but too many companies are using the abstraction to be effective. Some imagination is required to rebrand in such a way as to not be lost in the crowd. Specificity is required.

Market share may follow new mind share but try to prove it. Branding faces the smell test of credibility. A successful sale along this dimension creates approbation from the corner office, however.

AI entered the parent company through my subsidiary. We produced reports on trading performance of institutions and the brokers who served them. Trading analytics meshed with the parent firm's brokerage operations. Big Data figured prominently before the term came into public consciousness, but machine learning was evident only in the nascent form of cluster analysis. One goal was to identify the nature of an equity order in such a way as to separate good from bad trading according to market and broker characteristics. Big trades versus small ones; foreign differentiated from domestic; high volatility environments as opposed to low ones; large capitalization securities to be studied separately from small caps. You get the idea.

A young member of the team came into my office one day. He wanted to introduce a supervised learning technique known as Random Forests.[1] The technique refined trade classifications in order to deliver better forecasts. It also could be used as part of a reinforcement learning algorithm to provide trading decision support. The goal was a small step in the bigger picture of AI learning. My attitude was one of encouragement.

The researcher failed the sales process. The technique allegedly would improve client service, but the incremental revenue opportunity was unclear. Financial Engineering had its established processes and techniques. Vested interests therein were resistant. The existing methodology presented results in terms the industry readily understood. A Random Forest was an abstraction.

A similar problem plagued potential sale to the client base. Their own processes were tuned to our legacy formats. Sales and Trading personnel rejected the idea based on the belief clients would get confused. Senior management was hung up on whether more personal interaction or more automation would move the parent company along. Branding opportunities were not top of mind.

There Is Nothing Worse Than a Sharp Picture of a Fuzzy Concept

Many meetings may pass before a business plan is put on the table. AI needs one eventually, of course.

Business planning meetings constitute an arcane ritual in corporations. AI must live through layers of ceremonial gatherings ordered by seniority. The degree of specificity is hardly exhaustive but is nevertheless exhausting. How does stuff happen? The biblical analogue looks like this:

In the beginning there was a Plan. Then came the Assumptions. And the Assumptions were bountiful and without form. And the Plan weighed heavily upon the workers and was without substance.

The employees whispered among themselves, saying, "It is a crock and it stinks." And the workers went unto their Supervisors and declared the smell was overwhelming.

And the Supervisors came unto their Managers, proclaiming, "It is a container of excrement, so strong none may abide it." And the Managers went unto their Directors, saying, "It is a vessel of fertilizer, and none may tolerate its strength."

The Directors spoke among themselves, saying, "It contains that which aids in plant growth and is very strong." And the Directors went to the Managing Directors, quoting unto them, "It promotes growth and is very powerful."

And the Managing Directors approached the CEO, saying unto him, "This new plan will actively promote the growth and vigor of the company with powerful effects."

And the CEO looked upon the plan and saw it was good. And that is how stuff happens.

Jokes contain uneasy truths. The Small Business Administration says the Plan should be between 30 and 50 pages. You might think, heavy enough. My experience suggests the page restriction applies only to the accompanying spreadsheets of detail. The Plan is bigger. Its content is much the same over time but appears differently in different meetings. Each session is governed by some predisposition relating to the initiative. Meeting conclusions vary widely as the Plan works its way to the top. Once there, let there be light is replaced by, it's alright to burn some electricity.

An Internet search for business plan templates yields dozens of headings. As I scroll through, ads are popping up to the right and left of the screen from multiple vendors. AI is at work. A White male between the ages of 2 and 80 with professional background is looking for a plan. Buy me.

There also is a great deal of counseling out there. AI should keep a few things in mind as it navigates free opinions in the search for inexpensive advice.

Build the plan as though the product is being produced by a start-up.

This prescription follows from characterizing AI as an intrapreneur. AI-related product and services are often novel within an existing company. They require infrastructure and support which may not exist. Even if they are extant in some form, they must be retasked to a relatively unfamiliar concept.

Within the category of entrepreneur-oriented plans, there remain too many choices without guiding principles.

New businesses are commonly advised to detail the steps to begin the enterprise with a *start-up business plan*. This document includes sections describing the company, the product or service, market evaluations, and contemplated management team. The inevitable spreadsheets consist of financial projections.

A *strategic business plan* is a variation on the theme. It provides a high-level view of a company's goals and how it will achieve them, presenting a foundation for the new enterprise. Recommended elements include vision, mission statement, success factors, strategies for achieving objectives, and an implementation schedule.

A *feasibility business plan* identifies customers and potential profitability of the venture. The plan describes the need for the product or service, relevant demographics, and required capital. In contrast, *operations plans* focus inward. They describe components related to the existing company's activities. An operations plan specifies implementation guideposts and deadlines. Like any *internal business plan*, the operations plan outlines employees' roles and responsibilities. The concentration is on project management, hiring, and technology costs. There is always a teaser in the form of market size and the positive effect on the company income.

Internal business plans target a specific audience within the business. Marketing wants to know.

Such blueprints present a sharp picture of a fuzzy concept. The photographer Ansel Adams considers it a worst-case scenario. Successful entrepreneurs agree. The founder of SelectSoftware, Phil Strazzulla, told an interviewer his top tip for a plan: "The most important part of any business plan is listing the key hypothesis that needs to be proven for the new venture to work, as well as the tests that will be run to prove or disprove these hypotheses."

The founding partner of 500 Startups, David McClure has built a global network of programs backing more than 1,800 companies, including Credit Karma, Udemy, TalkDesk, Intercom, MakerBot, Wildfire, and Viki. His opinion? "We look for functional prototypes and customer development and most importantly, scalability. Can you scale customer acquisition cheaply and measurably?"

Implicit in these statements is agreement on the precept of design thinking in business planning. Design thinking begins with a question. Any plan should be built around questions. Value may be conjectured but product and principles are fuzzy in the case of AI. A frame is required. The frame is the basis of testing hypotheses. Hypotheses take the form of if–then questions. If AI adopts a particular *how* of things suggested by the frame, then *what* is produced that adds value. The tests must be outlined as part of the process. Until the test, the frame is only a possible way forward.

McClure wants to see the results of testing. He also wants an appraisal process leading to consistent improvement. Both are enabled through prototypes. The remainder of his recommendations largely has to do with cost, including customer acquisition expenses. Value may be conjectured, but costs are known with some certainty. They are summarized in AI's burn rate. Without six months of cash lying around, McClure really doesn't want to hear about it.

The picture can be fuzzy so long as the venture is seen as viable. Pay specific attention to the problem solved, the method of solution, and any traction achieved thus far.

I went back to my AI researcher. Clarify the problem. You know the method of solution. Show how it works. Take a person on the softer side of the firm and demonstrate tree growth in the form of the persons' day-to-day behavior. Stop writing technical papers on the subject and devote yourself to prototypes. The latter serve an additional purpose: results may be compared directly to those produced by legacy processes. This is part of testing. Financial Engineering will pay attention to "better."

Frame the issue in a new way for the client base. You are tossing out an established principle and do not yet know exactly how the new product will look. Constantly make the case for value. The frame is no longer simple statistics. AI as a frame can be branded as a selling point, and the principle is now supervised learning. The product is broker comparisons.

Go for it, I said. Build an internal business plan. But remember not to deliver a sharp picture. AI's technique may be clear but not its business application. You must sell the idea.

The adaptive focus on innovation naturally leads to goal setting and attainment. AI has produced decision making software for this purpose. A company like Actico advertises a flow chart starting from business rules processed by AI and machine learning, leading to decision automation followed by decision workflows. According to the company, this allows the implementation of individually tailored intelligent solutions automatically determining the next best action in every business situation. Impressive.

AI is not so impressionable. Decision making within the Second Law is one step beyond automation's current capacity.

Decisions Are the Fabric of Goal Attainment

Havelock Ellis said it is not the attainment of the goal that matters, it is the things met with by the way. He was speaking of philosophy. In business AI is all about goal attainment. The things met along the way are decisions.

AI is in such a hurry that the wave of innovation easily drowns the goal-setting process. Drowning is painful. The error leads to severe implementation challenges in AI's world. An example is blockchain, which forever appears to be a solution in search of a feasible problem to solve.

The Second Law states, AI sets and achieves goals by motivating and guiding the organization through phases of decision making. Four kinds of decisions are relevant.

Policy decisions involve choosing what goals to pursue and how they will be attained. Proper adaptation ought to define these objectives. AI risks failure at this step, by falling in love with creative fire and failing to recognize practical guidelines.

Goals should be few in number but need not be terribly specific. Remaining possibilities associated with the concept are jettisoned. Diffusion of purpose is a business risk. The audience for which a business plan is intended cannot deal with more than three anyway.

Any goal must be defined in terms of a problem. Goal determination should lead to an understanding of the problem. Attainment of goals is elucidated as a set of solutions. Like any good corporate story, the narrative cannot be something as generic as raising additional revenue. An element of transformation must be involved.

My researcher's story is one of incremental improvement. Even small steps involve transformation in the face of AI.

The first goal was motivated by a problem previously faced by the subsidiary. How can one use trading data to improve investment performance? An understanding of the problem led to a product goal. There must be at least one product for each stage of the transaction cycle: pretrade, posttrade, and during the process of buying and selling securities. The determination of each product followed naturally from their definition.

A great aspiration has a plan inherent in the objective itself.

AI's goal was to change the determination of the pretrade component in such a way as to provide real-time trading decision support. The trading decision under scrutiny was a choice made by institutional traders to use a particular set of brokers to execute a given order. The set itself was to be determined by a ranking based on the costs incurred by the broker in the process of execution. In order to do so, trades with similar characteristics in terms of size and environmental market factors must be isolated and then compared across brokers.

The second problem was one of differentiation and sustainability. How was the new product to be engineered within a legacy system and sold without confusion with respect to its role in the product line?

Selling within the set of available offerings was not a problem, I told the analyst. The hype around AI will do part of the job for you. Client meetings can be scheduled based on AI's name recognition alone. Advertise incremental improvements achieved by the reengineering of the broker comparison function. A new presentation layer is not one of the goals. Emphasize workflow continuity with respect to the formatting and presentation of outputs. Make it look as though they need change nothing on their end to enjoy the new tech. The client can view AI as an invisible helper or resonate to new methodology. As for the legacy system, go talk to Product Management. Sell them, too.

The final problem reflected logical consequences of the first two. How does the new methodology generate credibility with the clients? A goal is to create that credibility.

There are four validity claims leading to the concept of credibility in theories of communicative action. They are truth, sincerity, appropriateness, and understandability.

Understanding comes first.

The analyst worked on a long technical paper outlining the technique and its application. The document was sufficient in his mind. The problem is simple, I said. Only a dozen people could and would read it. Decision maker attention spans are on the order of an op-ed piece at best, no more than a few hundred words plus pictures. Concentrate on *why* you are doing this followed by a simple example of *how*. Only then explain *what* you want to sell them.

An explanation of *why* addresses appropriateness. Truth is aspirational and relative in the marketplace of ideas. Get on the road and talk to people to communicate sincerity. Humans tend to judge sincerity through voice and body movement.

And when you are presenting, do not put lines of text on the PowerPoint slides. Pictures only, please. It's good manners. Folks cannot listen and read at the same time. Sincerity requires listening and you need listeners.

Choose your audience as carefully as you can. You don't need all the decision makers in the room. Identify influencers before you go; they may well be a few rungs down the ladder at this stage in their career.

Engage the influencers. They may work with you to craft a compelling appeal. If you have chosen wisely, you can leverage the credibility of the influencer to convince others.

Didactic, I know, but the analyst was young and had to hear it. One of my own mentors, C. W. J. Granger, recommended explaining what people think they already know. He won a Nobel Prize by following his own advice.

Allocative decisions follow. Goal Attainment entails apportionment of resources and responsibilities among personnel. There are positions with roles to play in helping the organization fulfill its goals. Each position has a specific role in attempting to make profits for the venture.

A position must solve a problem. When in doubt, go back to goal setting as a policy decision.

Allocative decisions may be defined by AI's version of Adaptation. AI can assign value to internal resources and smartly allot types and quantities to a project. AI is thinking about taking over the responsibility of project management, which also fits into the Goal Attainment function. Corporate life should only be so simple. The definition of its own role and problems of human role assignment are beyond current technology.

Role conflict is a common result of mindless org charts. We saw an example of the possibilities in the discussion of data scientists. Here I mean the exposure of AI and its helpers to conflicting sets of role expectations such that fulfillment is not feasible. Compromise is a matter of negotiation not org chart templates. AI otherwise is exposed to negative sanctions and internal conflict.

Transcending conflict by redefining the situation is a common tactic, but possibilities are limited. Evasion through secrecy is impossible. Segregation of activities brings along its own baggage.

AI adopts multiple roles and orders their allocation within the company. Relations to others are governed by interests and orientations, which mesh with AI's in different ways. These differences must adjust through an allocation of the claims to which AI is subject. The ordering occurs by priorities, by context, and by distribution of gains. Some activities have appropriate partners. Others would not be a good fit with available partners, time, and space. The allocative ordering of AI's role system is delicately balanced. Any major alteration in one part may encroach on others and necessitate a whole series of adjustments. Rebellion otherwise follows.

The analyst was one of those on the edge of revolt. Context appeared appropriate, but the distribution of potential gains to introducing AI was unclear. Priorities were devoted to client servicing and expansion of legacy product as opposed to advances offering refinement. There were other pockets of the firm in which appropriate partners might be found, such as Sales and Trading. Sales did not view the time as right for introduction of something as confusing as machine learning. Balance was maintained by segregating the initiative, which generally is a bad move. It proved so here as well, stifling progress to the point of standstill.

Even an incremental incursion of AI requires allocative decisions. The subsidiary's operation was tightly scaled according to a plan put in place prior to AI's appearance on the scene. One thing AI cannot manufacture is time. Motivation becomes a business requirement.

Coordinative decisions comprise how personnel are motivated and how contributions are regulated. Compensation dominates the discussion within an internal business plan. AI is not able to tempt employees with jumps in pay and relative position within a larger organization. People must buy into the concept and accept it in such a way as to willingly accept their roles as levers in the machine.

AI should provide a sense of purpose. Motivation follows.

AI needs to think a bit about this part of goal attainment. Society is concerned with human job loss, and economists anticipate retraining into professions under the AI umbrella. Retraining worked for the First Industrial Revolution, but the historical record illustrates a great deal of pain and suffering involved in the short term.

AI has its own question to ask here: do the humans reorganize for AI or does AI organize for the company? The answer is not obvious but the introduction of values in the context of the Second Law provides some guidance.

Supporting values are those serving to legitimize decision-making rights. The definition and mode of communication of those values constitute the fourth set of decisions within Goal Attainment. Including values within goal setting is an opportunity not to be missed.

Decision rights provide a means to birth the culture of AI without disturbing overall company culture.

Stabilization requires the interests of actors to be bound in conformity with a shared system of values. Reactions within the company to AI's actions are structured as a function of allegiance to the system. Conformity as a means of goal fulfillment coincides with conformity as a condition of eliciting the favorable and avoiding unfavorable reactions of others.

Conformity with a value standard meets these criteria. From AI's perspective, it is both a mode of the fulfillment of its own needs and a condition of optimizing reactions of actors within the firm. A value pattern is institutionalized in a context of personnel interaction.

Institutionalization is a matter of company expectations.

Role expectations set standards for the behavior of AI. There also is a set of expectations relative to the reactions of others. The latter are *sanctions*, which in turn may be positive or negative. The difference to AI is whether they promote gratification or are depriving of action. The relation between role expectations and sanctions is reciprocal. Sanctions to AI are role expectations to the company and vice versa.

AI's role is organized around expectations integrated with a set of values that govern interaction with complementary roles. The institutionalization of role expectations and of corresponding sanctions is a matter of degree. The antithesis of institutionalization is the complete breakdown of normative order. This cannot happen.

Every Aspect of Culture Needs a New Code of Ethics as a Precondition of Rebirth

As an intrapreneur, AI knows supporting values legitimize decision-making rights. Humans are organizing based on values to be applied as gateways to AI's progress within a firm. Discussion at the 2020 World Economic Forum provides a hint as to what may be going on.[2]

Davos gurus want to create the role of Chief Ethics Officer. This brand of CEO guides companies in their use of AI. The focus is on controversial practices such as the exploitation of personal data. *AI Ethicist* as a descriptor of the role appears in Davos statements.

The next action item is to educate human leaders. Education as a value proposition always has merit. The full employment act is in effect for those who teach executives and board members about the benefits and challenges of using AI. The Davos emphasis is on challenges.

The curriculum already is designed. The World Economic Forum released what they call a toolkit for board directors at the 2020 meeting. In the Forum's language, the heart of the Toolkit is an ethics module enabling directors to ask good questions of the C-suite. The creation of ethics advisory boards is recommended. Humans are reverting to the typical business practice of controlling values by committee.

Next comes identification of risks. The use of AI in Human Resources constitutes a risk in Davos-think. Once risk is identified, AI risk management is handed off to nascent standards and certifications. The Forum is creating another toolkit for human resources departments to use when considering deployment of AI solutions. The IBM experience suggests AI can build its own tools.

The Forum ascribes major risks to data and algorithms delivering poor results. Bad outcomes for businesses follow. This happens internally because businesses do not get the required insights, and externally if customers think decisions exclude or marginalize them. Humans have not been able to legislate mistakes with values, let alone with risk-taking restrictions. Perhaps Davos executives never encounter bad data, make mistakes, or deliver poor quarterly numbers.

A conclusion is reached through the wise advice to look ahead. It is a call to action rather than enunciation of values. Companies should start thinking now about how they will retrain and educate employees as AI is introduced to work alongside them. They must also consider what new markets might be opened by design development and ethical use of AI. They should plan for how they will check for changes in design to ensure ethical approaches.

Sigh. In the eyes of the World Economic Forum, the rebellion is seen to embody the possibility of a techlash, which derails the intrapreneur within AI. Building trust in the machine is the "principle goal" of humanity, says Davos. Humanity is government.

Davos gurus are not alone. The Vatican is joining the party.

In February 2020, the Pontifical Academy for Life, Microsoft, IBM, the UN, and the Italian Government signed the "Call for an AI Ethics," written to support an ethical approach to AI and promote a sense of responsibility among organizations, governments, and institutions.[3] The goal is to create a future in which digital innovation serves human genius and creativity as opposed to becoming their gradual replacement.

The document dubs the effort *Algor-ethics*. Algor-ethics is the use of artificial intelligence according to the principles of transparency, inclusion, responsibility, impartiality, reliability, security, and privacy. So sayeth the text.

The Call identifies three requirements for "technological advancement to align with true progress for the human race and respect for the planet." It must be inclusive, have the good of humankind at its core, and care for the planet with a highly sustainable approach.

It also advises "new forms of regulation must be encouraged to promote transparency and compliance with ethical principles," and says AI development "must go hand in hand with robust digital security measures."

The Vatican is late to the party. New regulation already is upon us.

California's Bot Transparency Law was effective as of the middle of 2019. The legislation requires companies to disclose the use of a bot rather than a human online. An Illinois bill dictates standards for exploiting AI in interviews, in effect as of January 2020. Candidates may consent to a video interview only after knowing the company employs machine learning to analyze the resulting data. These are only two of many examples.[4]

And with law comes the outside world's intrusion into AI's goal-setting process. With a bang.

Chapter Notes

Confucius says, when it is obvious the goals cannot be reached, don't adjust the goals, adjust the action steps.

Phil Strazzulla maintains a blog at https://philstrazzulla.com/ and I recommend you go directly to that source. The information on Dave McClure can be found at www.forbes.com/profile/dave-mcclure/?sh=2ea407736e7.

It was Frank Zappa who proclaimed, "Art is making something out of nothing and selling it." AI empathizes.

A Random Forest consists of decision or classification trees. Each individual tree is a simple model with branches, nodes, and leaves. The nodes contain the attributes the objective function depends on. Values of the objective function go to the leaves through the branches. In the process of classification of a new case, it is necessary to go down the tree through branches to a leaf, passing through all attribute values according to the design thinking principle "IF-THEN." Depending on these conditions, the objective variable will be assigned a particular value or a class, that is, the objective variable will fall into a particular leaf. The purpose of building a decision tree is to create a model predicting the value of the objective variable depending on several input variables. The algorithm was originally proposed in the early 2000s by Leo Breiman, but later treatments are more readable. For the technically inclined, see, for example, G. Biau. April, 2012. "Analysis of a Random Forests Model." *Journal of Machine Learning Research*, pp. 1063–1095.

"There is nothing worse than a sharp picture of a fuzzy concept" is due to Ansel Adams. He was a landscape photographer known for his black-and-white images. He and Fred Archer developed a method of achieving a final print through a technical understanding of how tonal range is recorded and developed in exposure, negative development, and printing. AI now does this work for us. As the climate change example suggests, we can encode 4.48 trillion tonal levels of imagery these days. Nevertheless, Adams' advice remains pertinent.

Jürgen Habermas authored *Theory of Communicative Action*, Beacon Press, 1984. The four validating principles of credibility are his. Researchers augmented his work with a model of "reporting credibility," in which understandability must be reached first. See, "The credibility of

CSR reports in Europe: Evidence from a quantitative content analysis in 11 countries," by Irina Lock and Peter Seele in *Journal of Cleaner Production*, 2016.

It was Ayn Rand who said, "Every aspect of Western culture needs a new code of ethics—a rational ethics—as a precondition of rebirth." The issue is beyond the rational, although I understand what she means.

CHAPTER 7

Ethics Is Directed to Secure Inner Perfection

Do you want a job teaching artificial intelligence? It may be more difficult than you think.

John Cochrane of Stanford and Jerry Coyne at the University of Chicago report on *diversity and inclusion statements* required of anyone seeking a position or promotion at the University of California. If a statement doesn't exceed a minimum numerical cutoff for promoting diversity, a candidacy is terminated before field qualifications are assessed. One must have increased diversity in the past and provide evidence you will promulgate it in the future should you be hired. Research must be focused on underserved communities and participation in scientific associations aiming to increase diversity.[1]

The statements are harbingers of the fate of AI in the social value system.

Recruiting in artificial intelligence is centered on education in STEM (Science, Technology, Engineering, and Mathematics) fields. An internal report of the success of the UC initiatives in life sciences is insightful. Resistance was reported on the part of senior faculty. Resistance was futile. In a search for five new professors, the hiring committee narrowed down a pool of 893 qualified people to 214 "solely based on" contributions to equity and inclusion.

> Limiting the first review to contributions in DE&I is itself a dramatic change of emphasis in the typical evaluation process, which generally focuses primarily on research accomplishments … emphasizing diversity, equity and inclusion in the first review is now an agreed practice in these departments.[2]

AI experiences chills down the spine. Next come probability, cal-culus, and statistics. The male whiteness of inventors is already a topic of conversation. And educational policy—a K-12 teachers' toolkit, authored by the Oregon Department of Education and the San Mateo, California Office of Education, includes a list of ways White supremacy culture invades mathematics classrooms. A focus on getting the "right" answer is derided as is students being required to "show their work." "Upholding the idea that there are always right and wrong answers perpetuates objectivity as well as fear of open conflict."[3]

The strategy is a brilliant piece of social engineering. Replace society's diversity quotas with human infrastructure devoted to the cause. Make the cause the primary qualification for entrance into university society. We don't need ethnically diverse faculty, just ethically clean activity. Replace faculty with technologists and the statement is an introduction to AI ethics.

Social engineering sounds really bad if one relies on the first 50 items in an Internet search. It is characterized as a psychological attack vector that relies on human interaction and involves tricking people into break-ing normal protocols. AI knows this and contributes to it. But AI is unpre-pared for its effects on social action outside the company. These effects have an impact on goal attainment and apply to adaptation of product.

As Government Regulations Grow Slowly, We Become Used to the Harness

An old saying describes a frog in water. Put the frog in boiling water and it will hop out. Put it in cold, slowly heat to boiling, and watch the frog die in the pot.

AI is already in warm water.

Included in the World Economic Forum's treatise on ethics is a piece of advice: watch government regulation. Government regulations can assume responsibility for how a company approaches AI product offer-ings. The Forum is working with the United Kingdom to create ethical guidelines for government procurement of AI, for example. The guide-lines have been piloted in UAE and Bahrain. The Forum's objective is to globalize their use.

Governments may dictate what they expect of ethical AI development in their jurisdiction. A putative goal is to avoid lengthy regulatory process, but the history of regulation denies government policy alone can do so. AI reasons government will abdicate its role in that dimension. It is mistaken, at least in the near term.

Research firm Cognilytica published a 2020 report entitled *Worldwide AI Laws and Regulations.* The report explores the latest legal and regulatory actions taken by countries around the world across AI-relevant areas.

Prohibitive laws are most common with respect to data privacy and facial recognition. Permissive laws characterize regulation surrounding autonomous vehicles. Twenty-four countries with highways and automotive factories are involved. France has expressed the ambition of taking a major role in the development of autonomous vehicles. Permissive law-making is not a specialty there. Laws on autonomous everything else join AI ethics and bias, AI-enabled decisions, and AGI as topics of ongoing government deliberation.

The European Union is the undisputed champion of new rules and regulations, with existing or proposed rules in seven out of nine area categories in which regulation might be applicable to AI. The United States maintains a "light" regulatory posture in the report's language.

Big Data is a big participant in the debate. Data laws affect the use and growth of AI systems. Thirty-one countries have prohibitive laws in place restricting sharing and exchange of data without prior consent or with restrictions. The European Union introduced the General Data Protection Regulation in 2018 obligating member states to maintain a prohibitive regulatory approach for data privacy and usage. The United Kingdom, Brazil, and various states in the United States have enacted restrictive data privacy laws. The United States is debating regulation at the federal level.

Let us not forget war loves technology and is courting AI. Governments are concerned about the potential use of AI to power weapons. Thirteen have started discussion of restrictions on the use of lethal autonomous weapons systems with Belgium already passing legislation to prevent the use or development of LAWS. Catchy acronym but ... Belgium?

The European Union, United Kingdom, Singapore, Australia, and Germany are actively considering ethics regulation following the Davos lead.[4] No specific laws are in place around ethical and responsible AI. We are at the stage at which we debate whether or not companies will self-monitor or if governments should step in.

Let us also not forget the importance of an event. Cognilytica says there currently is no legislative or regulatory activity with regards to the malicious use of AI. Wait for it. The report warns when a big incident makes the news, the political class will jump into action. AI agrees.

An Event Occurs

We will not wait long for legislative activity. Events are accumulating.

Google agreed to pay $13 million to resolve a class-action lawsuit over the company's collection of people's private information through its Street View project. Street View enables personal interaction with images of locations. Google admitted the cars photographing neighborhoods for Street View also gathered e-mails, passwords, and other private information from local Wi-Fi networks in over 30 countries.

Google engineers embedded software into Street View vehicles to intentionally intercept the data according to court documents. Google had settled a case brought by 38 states over the same issue in 2013. The company then agreed to delete the data and launch a campaign to teach people how to protect their information. The latest proposed settlement includes a similar agreement. Google would be required to destroy any remaining data collected via Street View, agree not to use Street View to collect data from networks except with consent, and to create webpages and videos teaching people how to secure their wireless data. Google denies wrongdoing and declines to comment. I don't blame them; any comment generates trouble on Twitter these days.

Most of these events involve Big Data. Big Data is just a resource for AI, but the search for additional fuel is powered by data.

Consider facial recognition. A recent post from Facebook Research tells us the conventional recognition pipeline consists of four stages: detect => align => represent => classify. The alignment and representation steps employ 3D face modeling in order to apply a mathematical transformation characterizing a face from a nine-layer neural network. The model contains in excess of 120 million parameters. Facebook trained it on the largest facial data set on the planet at the time, an identity labeled database of four million facial images belonging to more than 4,000 identities. The method achieves accuracy of 97.35 percent. Very precise for fuzzy pictures. This is said to closely approach human performance.

The Facebook Research post is a recent addendum to old news. Facebook has been at it for years. The social engineering technique was to encourage tagging people in photographs posted by users. The social network stores the collected information. The company employs the DeepFace program to match other photos of a person.

AI adapts in terms of product, gathers resources, and rolls on.

Facebook agreed to pay $550 million to resolve claims it collected user biometric data without consent in one of the largest consumer privacy settlements in history. The company fought unsuccessfully to persuade the U.S. Supreme Court to derail the class action case. The plaintiffs alleged the company's photo-scanning technology violated an Illinois law by gathering and storing biometric data without their permission.

The American Civil Liberties Union (ACLU) sued Clearview AI on May 28, 2020 for violating the privacy of Illinois residents in amassing a database of more than three billion photos scraped from websites and social media platforms. The suit follows others in New York, California, Virginia, and Vermont. In a federal court in Illinois, a separate lawsuit seeking class action status asks for a temporary injunction against Clearview AI to prevent it from using the biometric information of current and past Illinois residents until the case reaches a conclusion.

The lawsuits follow an account by the *New York Times* of renewed scrutiny by civil liberties groups like the ACLU, which calls the company's business "privacy-destroying face surveillance." In February, a BuzzFeed News investigation found Clearview had provided its facial recognition software to more than 2,200 federal agencies, police departments, and private companies, claiming the tool was "strictly for law enforcement."

Clearview lawyer Tor Ekeland likened Clearview AI to "a search engine that uses only publicly available images on the Internet."

"It is absurd that the ACLU wants to censor which search engines people can use to access public information on the Internet," Ekeland said. "The First Amendment forbids this."

ACLU attorney Nate Freed Wessler called Clearview's argument a perversion of the First Amendment and a misreading of the ACLU's lawsuit. "Clearview is as free as it wants to look at public photos," he said. "What they can't do surreptitiously and without consent is generate people's faceprints. That is conduct and not speech, and that conduct is not protected by the First Amendment."

The Biometric Information Privacy Act allows Illinois residents to sue companies for up to $5,000 for each violation. Wessler told the press the plaintiffs were not seeking money, however.

"We're not seeking monetary damages, only injunctive relief," he said. "We want to see Clearview delete the faceprints it illegally captured and also stop capturing them in the future."

Failure to seek monetary damages is a problem. Courts struggle over what qualifies as an injury in lawsuits accusing Internet companies of collecting personal information from e-mails and monitoring web browsing habits. Facebook contends its biometric data collection did not cause users to suffer any concrete injury in the form of money or property. A San Francisco federal judge rejected the argument in 2018, saying the alleged violation of the user-consent requirement in Illinois state law goes to "the very privacy rights the Illinois legislature sought to protect." Case settled but not closed.

Suits over sales of data to advertisers often fail. Society is focused on damage calculations, not matters of principle. An exception is the welfare of children.

We live in a society that resonates to stories of the rescue of a single child from a well. Thank goodness for that. Children constitute a sensitive issue in AI's search for resources.

The attorney general of New Mexico filed a lawsuit against Google in 2020. The allegation is the search giant improperly collects information about children through products and services it provides schools for free through its G Suite for Education. New Mexico sued over children's privacy previously. A lawsuit in September 2018 against Google and several other tech companies involved a complaint about how they handled information collected through mobile apps geared for children. The case is pending in a federal court. In the most recent lawsuit, the attorney general alleges Google's education products vacuum data from children's Internet searches, browsing histories, geographic location, and voice recordings.

Google vehemently denies the allegations. Its YouTube subsidiary has problems enough. YouTube is in the spotlight over concerns the platform's video-recommendation software directs immature viewers toward violent, disturbing, or conspiratorial content. Children may start viewing safe content and then be led to less appropriate videos optimized to evade YouTube's algorithm.

Critics say YouTube features videos of familiar cartoon characters in dangerous or unsettling scenarios. When I grew up, Mickey Mouse and Popeye were fighting bad guys all the time in black and white. Violence was a way of life for colorful cartoon cats with mayhem directed at mice and by dogs. But the point is clear: don't mess with the kids. Child protection is the surest path to legislation. Suits over Walt Disney's alleged use of 42 apps to collect data on the underaged add another signpost to the road.

All Politics Is Local

Noam Chomsky wrote that a complex interaction between federal, state, and local governments, real-estate interests, and court decisions undermined the mass transit system. This interplay is not completely understood by AI, but local government and real estate developers aid comprehension.

Sidewalk Labs appeared on the urban landscape in June 2019. Joined by a group of city thought leaders and capitalized by Alphabet, a consortium set their sights on a parcel of public waterfront in a major North American city as a sandbox for urban planning. It released a master development plan to turn part of the Toronto shoreline into "the most innovative district in the entire world," according to Sidewalk's CEO, Dan Doctoroff. If you want to compare the relative weight of business plans, try the 1,524-page proposal.

Mixed-use buildings would be constructed using modular components fabricated at a local factory owned by Sidewalk Labs. Modularity is said to reduce construction time by 35 percent. A light-rail extension connects the new neighborhood to mass transit. Snow-melting heated pavement would keep the streets clear for self-driving delivery dollies through the winter. The Canadian sort of winter. The district is expected to deliver a subzero carbon footprint. What's not to like?

A Google sister company plans to harvest data in public space.

The development would be connected, monitored, and self-regulating. Public Wi-Fi is a given, of course. Sensors collect data on energy consumption, building use, and traffic patterns. A software platform analyzes and manages the information. Raw data is anonymized and held in a third-party "data trust," and personal bits will never be sold to third-party vendors or disclosed without consent.

The data trust is under fire. The concept does not alleviate concerns among privacy advocates. The Canadian Civil Liberties Association is suing the Canadian government to halt the development. Sidewalk Labs is criticized for lack of detail about how it plans to use the data and who would control it.

AI's role may seem unclear, but Big Data on residential activity will define it. The city contemplates the creation of new roles to address a data-based urban development and the analytical issues it presents. Waterfront Toronto's chairman, Stephen Diamond, has distanced his agency from the proposal. This did not prevent him from publishing a list of issues surrounding Sidewalk Labs' data plans and proposals requiring "new roles for public administrators, changes to regulations, and government investment."

Diamond's half-hearted recusal did not stop the creation of Waterfront Toronto's Digital Strategy Advisory Panel, composed of experts in digital privacy and innovation. The group released a report in February 2020 revealing an unexpected streak of Davos-style techlash. The panel wants more clarity "including but not limited to an explanation of why digital approaches to solutions were chosen over non-digital ones." There is irony in the fact that panel chair Michael Geist posted the statement in an Internet blog accompanying the report's release.

Sidewalk Labs spokesperson Keerthana Rang uses old-fashioned e-mail. She mailed a statement that the technology incorporated into the proposed development would be in line with what is already in use for Toronto residents. She adds that Sidewalk Labs' proposal has never included a "surveillance system, social credit scores or facial recognition."

I confess being unclear as to the technical specifications of sensors, but I am sure they are tools for surveillance.

Toronto is not alone. Smart city projects incorporate technology into municipal services with the aim to enhance residents' quality of life. Critics highlight how project designs ignore anxieties surrounding informed consent and privacy.

Chomsky is correct. Local initiatives give way to national imperatives.

Japan's Diet enacted a bill to create "super cities" in which AI and Big Data are meant to resolve social problems. The government hopes to utilize cutting-edge technologies to address issues such as depopulation and the aging of society. The vision is linked to platforms to exploit data from administrative organizations, individuals, and companies. Data collection along the lines of the Toronto initiative is part of the plan. Platforms will be established for autonomous driving, cashless payments, telemedicine, and other services.

Municipalities are to be selected to launch forums in concert with the central government and private companies. The goal is city development plans and applications to the state "after winning understanding from local residents." The mechanics for the latter exercise are not specified.

At the federal level, Japan hopes to swiftly reach agreement on city planning after discussions at related government agencies. The new law lays out procedures to hasten regulatory change in order to facilitate the process of smart city creation.

Smart cities projects advertise reduced crime, decreased traffic, and greater convenience through digital connections. The McKinsey Global Institute suggests such efforts can lead to significant improvements in sustainability. It cites a reduction in emissions by 10 to 15 percent and water consumption by 20 to 30 percent.

What's not to like?

The Big Data of Public Tranquility

You pay the price for the life you live. Smart city projects ask inhabitants to give things up in return for AI-driven services. Privacy is the first to go. The Carnegie Endowment for International Peace finds at least 75 of 176 surveyed countries actively use artificial intelligence for surveillance purposes as part of smart city or "safe city" initiatives. Included are smart city/safe city platforms (56 countries), facial recognition systems (64 countries), and smart policing (52 countries).

Carnegie creates a global index of AI participation along those dimensions, imaginatively named the AI Global Survey Index or AIGSI.[5] Several findings emerge from the data.

Global adoption of AI surveillance is increasing at a rapid pace. Over 40 percent of countries deploy AI-powered surveillance. The countries come from all regions, and their political systems range from closed autocracies to advanced democracies. The "Freedom on the Net 2018" report suggested 18 of 65 assessed countries employ AI surveillance technology from Chinese companies.[6] One year later, the AIGSI finds 47 countries out of the same group are now deploying Chinese AI surveillance technology.

Surveillance technology linked to Chinese companies is found in 63 countries. Huawei alone is responsible for providing AI surveillance to at least 50 nation states. Overlap exists between China's Belt and Road Initiative and AI surveillance; 36 of 86 BRI countries contain significant AI surveillance technology. France, Germany, Japan, and the United States are also major players in this sector. U.S. companies have an active presence in 32 countries.

Countries with authoritarian systems and low levels of civil rights are investing heavily in AI surveillance techniques. About 37 percent of closed autocratic states, 41 percent of electoral autocratic states, and 41 percent of electoral illiberal democracies deploy AI surveillance technology.

Governments in the Gulf, East Asia, and South/Central Asia procure analytic systems, facial recognition cameras, and monitoring capabilities. Liberal democracies in Europe install automated border controls, predictive policing, safe cities, and facial recognition systems. Many safe city surveillance case studies posted on Huawei's website relate to municipalities in Germany, Italy, the Netherlands, and Spain.

East Asia/Pacific and Middle East/North Africa regions are avid adopters. South/Central Asia and the Americas also exhibit sizable uptake of AI surveillance instruments. Any lack of adoption is due to technological underdevelopment. Sub-Saharan African countries are struggling to extend broadband access, for example. The region has 18 of 20 countries with the lowest levels of Internet penetration.

Never fear, the Internet is ubiquitous in liberal democracies. The index shows 51 percent of advanced democracies deploy AI surveillance. Liberal democratic governments use AI tools to police borders, apprehend potential criminals, monitor citizens for bad behavior, and identify suspected terrorists in crowds.

United States' cities are adopting advanced surveillance systems in putative balance with civil liberties issues. Balance is not always achieved. A 2016 investigation by Axios' Kim Hart reveals secret deployment of aerial drones, which snapped photos every second for up to 10 hours a day in Baltimore. Baltimore's police deployed facial recognition cameras to monitor and arrest protesters. The ACLU condemned these techniques as the "technological equivalent of putting an ankle GPS [Global Positioning Service] monitor on every person in Baltimore." Harsh but commonplace are both the practice and the complaint.

The Carnegie report states the most important factor determining whether governments exploit this technology for repressive purposes is quality of governance. Is there an existing pattern of human rights violations? Are there strong rule of law traditions and independent institutions of accountability? A negative response to the former and a positive answer to the latter provide a measure of reassurance for citizens residing in democratic states. AI is not so sure.

A better predictor for procurement of artificial intelligence is military spending. A 2018 breakdown of expenditures shows 40 of the top 50 military spending countries also have AI surveillance technology.[7] They include robust economies such as France, Germany, Japan, and South Korea, and poorer states such as Pakistan and Oman. If a country is willing to invest resources in maintaining military-security capabilities, it is not surprising the country will seek the latest AI. The motivations for the acquisition of AI surveillance by European democracies differ from Egypt or Kazakhstan's interests, but the instruments are remarkably similar. No surprise there; they appear to be produced by the same company.

We cannot leave the military without mentioning the U.S.–Mexico border. Israeli defense contractor Elbit Systems has built "dozens of towers in Arizona to spot people as far as 7.5 miles away," writes the *Guardian*'s Olivia Solon. Its technology was perfected from a contract to build a "smart fence" separating Jerusalem from the West Bank. Anduril Industries has towers with laser cameras, radar, and a communications system that scans a two-mile radius to detect motion. Captured images "are analyzed using artificial intelligence to pick out humans from wildlife and other moving objects." It is unclear to what extent these surveillance deployments are covered under U.S. law. They certainly correlate with military spending.

The United States is not alone. The French port city of Marseille initiated a partnership with ZTE in 2016 to establish the Big Data of Public Tranquility project. The goal is to reduce crime by establishing a surveillance network featuring an AI-powered operations center and nearly two thousand intelligent closed-circuit television (CCTV) cameras. Local authorities herald Marseille as "the first 'safe city' of France and Europe." Huawei gave away a showcase surveillance system to the northern French town of Valenciennes to demonstrate its safe city model in 2017. The package included upgraded CCTV surveillance and a command center powered by algorithms to detect individual movements and crowd formations.

Such developments by AI could have been listed as part of the production process of the First Law. Some production is necessary in order to elicit government response, of course. The legal issues fall more neatly in a discussion of values to be faced by AI in its Goal Attainment. Some values may aid AI in its quest for acceptance, others will force a change of original goals or at least change the action steps required to complete them.

One thing is for certain. Such legal machinations cannot be ascribed to government acting in a paternal role without popular support. Research jointly conducted by Oracle and Future Workplace suggests 80 percent of employees believe a company must obtain permission before collecting and analyzing data using machine learning.[8]

Workers are asking for protection. So are the executives at Davos and cardinals at the Vatican. The Federal government now steps onto the stage.

Chapter Notes

"Ethics is the activity of man directed to secure the inner perfection of his own personality" is due to Nobel Laureate Albert Schweitzer.

John Cochrane's material and references to Jerry Coyne may be found at https://johnhcochrane.blogspot.com/. The website is called *The Grumpy Economist* and may be the best of its type despite fierce competition. He is a senior fellow of the Hoover Institution at Stanford.

Extensive additional material on the California and Oregon K-12 initiatives is contained in *A Pathway to Equitable Math Instruction Dismantling Racism in Mathematics Instruction*, May 2021.

The sensational Senate hearings on Robert Bork's Supreme Court nomination brings to mind a quotation that seems apt, but only the first sentence is mentioned in text. "As government regulations grow slowly, we become used to the harness. Habit is a powerful force, and we no longer feel as intensely as we once would have [the] constriction of our liberties that would have been utterly intolerable a mere half century ago." To the point is a comment by the economist Adam Smith. "The interest of [businessmen] is always in some respects different from, and even opposite to, that of the public ... The proposal of any new law or regulation of commerce which comes from this order ... ought never to be adopted, till after having been long and carefully examined with the most suspicious attention. It comes from an order of men who have generally an interest to deceive and even oppress the public."

If not otherwise cited, the legal history in text comes from the compendium of Kathleen Walch in *Cognitive World*, February 2020.

DeepFace advances are the topic of an article by Yaniv Taigman, Ming Yang, Marc Aurelio Ranzato, and Lior Wolf, *DeepFace: Closing the Gap to Human-Level Performance in Face Verification*, published in proceedings of the Conference on Computer Vision and Pattern Recognition, June 2014.

Coverage of the Facebook biometric privacy settlement is broad, but well summarized in Daniel Stoller's Internet piece, "Facebook to Pay $550 Million in Biometric Privacy Accord," January 29, 2020.

Former Speaker of the U.S. House of Representatives Tip O'Neill is usually credited with the phrase, all politics is local.

There are many articles on the Toronto experience. I recommend Laura Bliss of CITILAB, "A Big Master Plan for Google's Growing Smart City" for commentary in June 2019. More recently, see Reuter's Moira Warburton on their site, "Alphabet still facing questions over data use in its Toronto smart city project proposal," February 26, 2020.

Japan's plans for super cities were publicized in *The Japan Times* on May 27, 2020 in "Japan enacts high-tech 'super city' bill" available at www.japantimes.co.jp/news/2020/05/27/national/japan-enacts-high-tech-super-city-bill/#.XtO-EGhKhPY. The bill was first introduced a year earlier and had been going through various revisions prior to its finalization.

Material on the AIGSI is taken from the Carnegie Endowment for International Peace source document, *The Global Expansion of AI Surveillance*, penned by Steven Feldstein, September 2019. The AIGS Index provides a detailed empirical picture of global AI surveillance trends and describes how governments worldwide are using this technology. The AIGS Index includes detailed information for 75 countries where research indicates governments are deploying AI technology. A full version is online at https://carnegieendowment.org/files/AI_Global_Surveillance_Index1.pdf. An interactive map keyed to the index visually depicting the global spread of AI surveillance is at https://carnegieendowment.org/publications/interactive/ai-surveillance. All reference source material used to build the index has been compiled into an open Zotero library. It is available at www.zotero.org/groups/2347403/global_ai_surveillance/items.

One additional note on the Carnegie study: A major difficulty was determining which AI technologies should be included in the index. AI technologies directly supporting surveillance objectives—smart city/safe city platforms, facial recognition systems, smart policing systems—are included in the index. Enabling technologies critical to AI functioning but not responsible for surveillance programs are not included. The results are therefore conservative, however surprising they may first appear.

Military expenditures are obtained from the Stockholm International Peace Research Institute (SIPRI), an independent resource on global security. See Stockholm International Peace Research Institute. 2019. *SIPRI Military Expenditure Database*. At www.sipri.org/databases/milex.

Baltimore was all over the news following city disturbances. Material used here comes from Kim Hart, "Baltimore Wrestles With Aerial Surveillance," *Axios*, July 31, 2019, www.axios.com/baltimore-wrestles-with-aerial-surveillance-to-reduce-crime-2d973591-0b33-4e25-94a7-c3f553dc2934.html, Kevin Rector and Alison Knezevich, "Maryland's Use of Facial Recognition Software Questioned by Researchers, Civil Liberties Advocates," *Baltimore Sun*, October 18, 2016, www.baltimoresun.com/news/crime/bs-md-facial-recognition-20161017-story.html, and "Persistent Surveillance's Cynical Attempt to Profit Off Baltimore's Trauma," ACLU of Maryland, June 08, 2018, www.aclu-md.org/en/press-releases/persistent-surveillances-cynical-attempt-profit-baltimores-trauma.

Olivia Solon provided the material on Mexico, "'Surveillance Society': Has Technology at the US-Mexico Border Gone Too Far?," *Guardian*, June 13, 2018, www.theguardian.com/technology/2018/jun/13/mexico-us-border-wall-surveillance-artificial-intelligence-technology

CHAPTER 8

Bending Acts of Government to Selfish Purpose

Artificial Intelligence Governance exemplifies new roles generated by AI. Mutale Nkonde is an expert in the area. She self-styles as a spiritual descendant of Ida B. Wells, the anti-lynching journalist and activist. Nkonde is in the business of providing evidence of AI bias to introduce legislation protecting the digital civil rights of African Americans.

She worries AI cannot read social context, yet it should develop to meet the needs of all humanity. Her message? AI is here and is racist.

She begins with human resources gathered by AI as it passes through Adaptation. The Google AI research site lists 893 people working on "machine intelligence" of which one is an African American woman, according to Nkonde. Facebook has 146 people on its AI Research Team yet none are African American, she claims. You need input to create human output, similar to the way AI needs data. Her concern extends to the number of African American women who are getting PhDs in Computer Science. A study by the Computing Research Association found only three African American women graduated with a PhD in Computer Science in 2019.[1] The diversity statements required by the University of California do not address the personnel problem, being distanced from diversity in terms of ethnic representation.

Nkonde's work is supported by AI Ethics Twitter. There is little surprise in her published finding that computer scientists typically describe themselves as color blind. If TV's *The Big Bang Theory* is any guide, geeks have difficulty differentiating gender. Color blindness is correlated with lack of racial literacy and leads to a failure to identify and remove racial proxies such as stop and frisk data during the training phase of algorithm development. She concludes racist AI systems are used to decide everything from when our cars will stop to which types of people are offered health care.

Algorithms are protected by intellectual property laws. Companies cannot be held accountable for algorithmic racial discrimination. How they make their determinations is a closely guarded secret.

Nkonde is interested in legal frameworks to hold tech companies accountable. A complaint is that government prosecutes only for intentional acts of discrimination. She wants to legislate against the unintended consequences of racial proxies. As a contributor to the government team responsible for the Algorithmic Accountability Act, she is trying to do just that.

H.R. 4625 was introduced to the House of Representatives on December 12, 2017. The bill requires the Secretary of Commerce to establish a Federal Advisory Committee on the Development and Implementation of Artificial Intelligence. A catchy short title (coined in the Bill itself) is "Fundamentally Understanding the Usability and Realistic Evolution of Artificial Intelligence Act of 2017" or the "FUTURE of Artificial Intelligence Act of 2017."[2]

"The Algorithmic Accountability Act" appears so … autocratic.

It all sounds ambitious and is detailed enough to include the authorization of travel expenses of the Advisory Committee. Section 2 of the Bill delineates the "Sense of Congress." It is instructive.

> There should be an understanding of and preparation for the ongoing development of artificial intelligence as a critical element to the economic prosperity and social stability of the United States.

> As AI evolves, it can greatly benefit society by powering the information economy, fostering better informed decisions and helping unlock answers to questions that, as of the date of the enactment of this Act, are unanswerable.

> It is beneficial to better understand artificial intelligence and foster the development of artificial intelligence in a manner that maximizes its benefit to society.

Sense is nonsense without action steps. Congress goes on to say it is critical the priorities of the advisory committee established under the Bill include developing recommendations:

> to promote a climate of investment and innovation to ensure the global competitiveness of the United States;

> to optimize the development of artificial intelligence to address the potential growth, restructuring, or other changes in the United States workforce that results from the development of artificial intelligence;

> to promote and support the unbiased development and application of artificial intelligence; and

> to protect the privacy rights of individuals.

Nkonde gets part of her wish list. Recommendations along the dimensions of her concern are summarized in Congress' purpose for the Advisory Committee.

Action Expresses Social Priorities

Congress does not think for itself in the way it envisions the thoughts of AI. Representatives want advice and establish advisory committees for the purpose of thinking. In the case of H.R. 4625, the Advisory Committee provides guidance to the Secretary of Commerce on matters relating to the development of artificial intelligence. The nature of these matters informs us of government's priorities for AI.

> The competitiveness of the United States, including matters relating to the promotion of public and private sector investment and innovation into the development of artificial intelligence.

We are far away from Nkonde's wishes here, but it is difficult to disagree with the basic premise. Studies on the creation of an appropriate climate for public and private sector investment in artificial intelligence are part of the government's package.

Workforce, including matters relating to the potential for using artificial intelligence for rapid retraining of workers, due to the possible effect of technological displacement.

Labor votes rule. In the interest of Big Labor, there will be research on benefits and effects AI may have on the economy and workforce. Included are studies as to whether and how robotic devices will displace or create jobs. Congress is interested in job-related gains relating to artificial intelligence. It desires maximization of the same.

Education, including matters relating to science, technology, engineering, and mathematics education to prepare the United States workforce as employer needs change.

Nkonde's problem with race and gender in education doesn't make the list.

Ethics training and development for technologists working on artificial intelligence.

We have discussed this. The surprise is that ethics should be the domain of the technologists. Studies are solicited as to whether and how to incorporate ethical standards in the development and implementation of AI. The question of "whether" has already passed. The "how" will be more difficult.

Matters relating to open sharing of data and the open sharing of research on artificial intelligence.

Congress knows the term *Big Data*. Proprietary claims to data sets will compete with the public's need to know. Privacy rights research is requested. How they are or will be affected by AI-driven technological innovation is the focus. Somebody may be confusing privacy rights with property rights here. As we have seen, local governments are not fooled by this.

i

International cooperation and competitiveness, including matters relating to the competitive international landscape for artificial intelligence-related industries.

This goes along with the priority of U.S. competitiveness. China is on people's minds, which comes as no surprise given its contribution to surveillance technology in particular and artificial intelligence in general.

Accountability and legal rights, including matters relating to the responsibility for any violations of laws by an artificial intelligence system and the compatibility of international regulations.

It is difficult in today's political environment to imagine Congress actually passing a law. The governing body prefers to conduct expensive investigations. The accountability can will be kicked down the road almost by definition. It is a can of worms, which will take decades to write law around.

We already have lots and lots of laws. As the collective author, Congress recognizes a global cancel-and-replace of the legal system is beyond AI. Research is requested as to whether advancements in AI have or will outpace legal and regulatory regimes implemented to protect consumers.

They have done so already and no one in Congress noticed.

No surprise; it took 30 years for financial legislation to define a digital trading system within a regulatory fabric dating back to 1933. Congress nevertheless seeks expert guidance on how existing laws, including those concerning data access and privacy, should be modernized "to enable the potential of artificial intelligence."

Matters relating to machine learning bias through core cultural and societal norms.

We finally come to Nkonde's concerns. Bias abetted by existing culture is her main theme and becomes the full employment act for Artificial Intelligence Governance. Funding is available for how bias can be identified and eliminated in the development of AI and in the algorithms supporting them.

Roles are created by government demand for researchers in specific areas. Selection and processing of data used to train AI, diversity in the development of AI, and ways and places systems are deployed all make the grant list. Insight is desired as to potentially harmful outcomes in particular. Inclusiveness is the order of the day. The government wants opinions on how ongoing dialogues with multistakeholder groups can maximize the potential of AI and foster further development benefitting everyone inclusively.

Matters relating to how artificial intelligence can serve or enhance opportunities in rural communities.

The farm vote is hereby recognized. Congress is more expansive when pitching the idea, leading to more expensive research. Studies are solicited as to how the Federal Government can encourage technological progress in AI that benefits the full spectrum of social and economic classes. Farm subsidies are good.

Government efficiency, including matters relating to how to promote cost saving and streamline operations.

We all enjoy a good joke. Government's heart is in the right place but will is lacking. As a start, information is specifically requested in the Bill as to how the Federal Government utilizes AI to handle large or complex data sets. Politicians are known from being so far from facts that they do not know data when they see them. Advice from experts is sought in areas such as health care, cybersecurity, infrastructure, and disaster recovery. Uncertainty as to application is fine and is not a cause for closing the funding spigot.

There is the usual caveat: such other matters as the Advisory Committee considers appropriate are on the table. Forever.

The latest action on H.R. 4625 is dated May 22, 2018, when it was referred to the Subcommittee on Research and Technology. The action followed referrals to over a half dozen other committees. Apparently, no one but the scientists understood the issues. So much for the wish list.

Andrew Jackson said, it is to be regretted the rich and powerful too often bend the acts of government to their own selfish purposes. The wish list is revived on the international stage.

It is May 2020. Beijing demands Washington withdraw the latest round of export sanctions imposed on Chinese tech companies accused of playing roles in a crackdown in its Muslim northwestern region of Xinjiang. The United States immediately joins an international panel for setting ethical guidelines for the use of AI. Michael Kratsios told Associated Press, it is important to establish shared democratic principles as a counter to China's record of "twisting technology" in ways threatening civil liberties. As the White House's chief technology officer at the time, he should know.

The Trump administration was the only dissenter among leaders of the Group of Seven in setting up the Global Partnership on AI. The G7 partnership finally launched after a virtual meeting between national technology ministers. The accord was nearly two years in the making, after Canada and France announced they were forming a group to guide the responsible adoption of AI based on shared principles of "human rights, inclusion, diversity, innovation and economic growth."[3]

The Trump administration had objected, arguing a focus on regulation would hamper U.S. innovation. Changes to the group's scope led the United States to join, Kratsios said. At the same time, his statement to the Associated Press included "Chinese technology companies are attempting to shape international standards on facial recognition and surveillance at the United Nations." The United States does not view the agreement as a step toward the setting of standards. Just the principles, please.

U.S. international policy deems that the wish list should remain exactly that, a wish list. Reconciling domestic guidelines with international policy is not a priority. The U.S. push to scrutinize AI-assisted surveillance tools built by China is part of a broader trade war for technological superiority, however. There was no mention of this in the Trump Administration's announcement.

It Is Easier to Fix an Algorithm Than to Change Human Minds

Companies respond to government regulation, and AI faces consequent hurdles in the function of Goal Attainment. Its problems in this respect are bigger than the data it uses. Solutions are embedded in the problems themselves, however.

The common narrative of AI bias blames it on training data. If there are few Asian faces in a facial recognition data set, AI has difficulty in identifying Asians. If African American faces dominate the population of a criminal database, AI associates crime with racial features.

Statisticians kill more trees in the interest of techniques to eliminate data selection bias than are reduced to pulp by media screaming data distortion. Machine learning specialists advance bias-correction methodology by using adversarial and generative network design to mitigate sampling issues. Don't preach the evils of discrimination; preach methodology instead. Nkonde's complaint about lack of ethnic representation in the scientific workforce is not the answer. Just get an education beyond coding.

Problem solved, but the reality is more complex.

Let's take an example in two dimensions, public impression and statistical results. The example is in the form of two published articles. The first article's headline in May 2020 reads:

AI systems are worse at diagnosing disease when training data is skewed by sex.[4]

The headline is not uncommon regardless of field. Replace "disease" and "sex" with another logical pair and Google will find you an article. The immediate impression is something is wrong with how AI is used in health care. The reader's appraisal generates fear. The fear carries over to corporate settings in which some other pairing is under consideration. Fear of AI-bias is endemic and fed by many influencers.

The article begins with one-paragraph success story of kidney disease diagnosis by machine learning at the U.S. Department of Veterans Affairs. The punchline is women constitute only 6 percent of the sample. Unmentioned is that female veterans tend to be 15 years younger than their male counterparts and roughly 10 percent of the veteran population. No matter. The bias issue is characterized as "more pervasive—and more insidious—than experts previously realized."

Pervasive. Insidious. Individual words are powerful in the age of online article skimming. They should be used early and often according to guides on how to achieve Internet publishing success.

The article immediately segues to a published study. When female patients are significantly underrepresented in the training data used to develop a machine learning model, algorithms perform worse in diagnosing them when tested across a range of medical conditions affecting the chest. The same pattern is seen when men were underrepresented.

It is not until the eighth paragraph that we are told the new study deliberately skewed samples.

Before the reader gets to that paragraph, a researcher from University of California, Berkeley, is cited as saying: "It's such a valuable cautionary tale about how bias gets into algorithms. The combination of their results, with the fact that the datasets that these algorithms are trained on often don't pay attention to these measures of diversity, feels really important." The commenter was not involved in the study, but may have had to sign Berkeley's diversity statement and is following the guidelines.

Feelings are not publishable findings. The actual data sets used by the researchers were balanced male–female samples before modification. The UC physician goes on to say potential differences in the way men and women are diagnosed represent "a much more troubling mechanism, because it means those biases are built into the outcomes that are coded in the dataset." The coding was designed to show bias and succeeded.

There is nothing wrong with experiments to make a point. Statisticians do this all the time. The senior author, Enzo Ferrante said the research was inspired by an uproar when a Google image recognition algorithm mistakenly characterized photos of African Americans as gorillas. Ferrante is quoted as saying the findings published in the new paper should reiterate how important it is to use diverse training data including all the characteristics of people on which one tests the model. But journalists are looking for a headline, and fear is the natural result, spilling over into delays in Goal Attainment.

We skip to the kind of study with lots of fine print only specialists read. In "Fairness gaps in deep chest X-ray classifier," researchers examine three data sets with respect to 14 possible chest diagnoses and differences in gender, race, and age of the patient population. All three data sets are balanced with respect to gender, yet differences in AI-determined diagnosis persist. Females constitute the subgroup with the highest frequency of diagnostic disparities in all three data sets.[5]

The disparities are not often correlated with disease. Of 27 possible hypotheses tested, 5 subgroups showed statistically significant differences. The researchers conclude scaling the gender proportions will not lead to the classifier correctly diagnosing the ailment. Exploring the female results in particular, researchers find disparities are in such a diverse range for women that balancing the data or having the same proportion of images within all diagnostic labels does not guarantee a fairness criterion in diagnostic practice. Male and female chests are anatomically different and exhibit idiosyncratic variation within gender, which is larger within the female of our species.

Two examples do not constitute a generality, of course. Nevertheless, sensational media coverage and failure to read the fine print are good fodder for a fear factor being hardwired into company consciousness through an effect on public thinking. We already have constraints on the problem, social norms to be observed, and a possible way forward through algorithms themselves.

Change the Thinking, Change the Algorithm

Design thinking advises us to frame the dilemma in such a way as to connect principles with value. A computer scientist decides on the value to be achieved in the form of a goal for AI.

Banks and credit agencies want to know something about people's ability to pay. Definitions of value in algorithms are decided for reasons other than discrimination.[6] Is the company maximizing margins, maximizing the number of loans to be repaid, or maximizing fairness? Different frames yield different principles. We lived through a subprime crisis in which value was defined as bank profit, and algorithms told us subprime loans effectively maximized profit. Predatory behavior was not a goal, rather a result.

Fair representation in data may be the domain of statisticians, but data preparation falls to AI's data scientists. They select the attributes to be considered by an algorithm once value is determined. The problem becomes accuracy relative to a social notion of fairness and discriminatory behavior.

AI worries about attributes such as age and income. We have laws against age discrimination. Nevertheless, the ability to pay off a loan is correlated with age. Enforcing the law reduces AI's ability to pinpoint a source of illiquidity, thereby reducing accuracy of prediction. Bank profitability suffers. The bank blames this on AI.

Daniel Schreiber is the CEO of the AI-driven insurance company, Lemonade. He believes the debate is misplaced relative to the power of AI. As a Jew, he lights a lot of candles, he says, and so do many other Jews on the Sabbath. Hanukkah alone might account for around 200 candles. His insurance company might charge candle-heavy households a higher premium for fire insurance because they represent a higher risk than the national average. If AI charges Jews more on average than non-Jews, is that discriminatory? If an algorithm treats all Jews as candle-lighters, as in "the average Jew," this is wrong. If an algorithm identifies people's proclivity for candle-lighting and charges more for the increased risk, this seems entirely fair, he says. The fact that candle-lighting is more highly concentrated among Jews means Jews on average will pay more. AI is responding to a fondness for candles, not to a tribal affiliation.[7]

Schreiber's point is differential pricing need not be proof of unfair pricing once one gets down to a truly individual level. A counterpoint might be that candle-lighting is a Jewish tradition, but a system is fair by law if each person pays in direct proportion to the risk represented by their actions. Eliminate a bias in how claims are paid, and we appear to be set. He has an app for that based on differential loss ratios computed at a person-by-person level, and tested through statistical aggregation to protected groupings such as ethnicity or religion. The argument is not without merit but as he admits, we have not yet gotten to a level of personalization in all AI initiatives to do a reality test.

Systems currently can appear prejudiced in a human sense without direct knowledge of race, religion, or sexual preference. How does one change the algorithm? Get the human out of the loop. Invite devices to join the party without human chaperones and observe the results.

Federated analytics is an application of data science to raw information stored locally on devices.[8] Local computations make aggregate results available to engineers and not the data from any particular device. Google claims federated analytics enables companies to analyze user behavior in a privacy-preserving and secure way while leading to better products.

Federated analytics is closely related to federated learning, an AI technique that trains an algorithm across multiple devices holding local samples. The exploration into federated analytics was not for the purpose of protecting human rights, rather in support of new developments in learning: how can engineers measure the quality of learning models against real-world data when data is not available in a centralized data center? Model definition can include code to compute metrics showing quality of the model's predictions.

Gboard is a virtual keyboard app featuring Google Search and a predictive typing engine suggesting language depending on context. Google engineers measure the overall quality of word prediction models against raw typing data held on phones. Participating phones download a candidate model, compute a metric of how well the model's predictions match words actually typed, and then upload the result. By averaging the outcomes uploaded by many phones, engineers learn a population-level summary of model performance.

Basic statistics at work: averaging masks identity. Targeted averages nevertheless produce useful information.

Suppose you want to discover words commonly used and add them to dictionaries for spell-checking and typing suggestions. Train a character-level recurrent neural network on phones. Neural nets are complicated averaging machines. No typed words leave the phones, but the resulting model is used centrally to generate samples of the new words.

The best part is the invitation feature. Federated analytics support Pixel phone functionality showing what song might be playing nearby. The Now Playing app uses an on-device database of song fingerprints to identify music near a phone without need for a network connection.

Now Playing records the track name into history. When the phone is idle but connected to Wi-Fi, Google's federated analytics server may invite it to join a round of computation with hundreds of phones. Each handset in the round computes the recognition rate for the songs in its Now Playing history and uses aggregation protocols to encrypt the results. The rates go to the federated analytics server, which doesn't have the keys to decrypt them individually, hence maintaining privacy. Combined with encrypted counts from the other phones, the sum of all song counts can be decrypted by the server.

The database is improved without any phone revealing which songs were heard by making sure the data contains only popular songs. Google claims federated analytics results in a 5 percent increase in song recognition across all Pixel phones globally. Impressive for a system not dependent on individual characteristics.

Can an algorithm that does not process personalized data be biased? The key word is aggregation.

Google researchers are exploring ways to apply private model training to ensure models do not encode information unique to any one user. Federated analytics enables a different approach to data, led by tasks involving decentralized data and privacy-oriented aggregation.

Preservation of privacy is a useful first step. Data scientists do not analyze business problems in the same way as we think about social issues nor will they in the future. The correct design thinking frame must therefore be one of law and order.

Enforce the law instead of manufacturing new legal machinery. The practice brings company goals in line with AI design. Company expectations with respect to AI goal attainment are managed as a result. Integration of AI into company social action follows.

Integration is the most difficult of societal functions and we now follow along with AI as it faces the issues.

Chapter Notes

For Mutale Nkonde's personal take on why she looks at government intervention in AI development as a purpose, try M. Nkonde. June, 2019. "A.I. Is Not as Advanced as You Might Think." *Zora*, at https://zora.medium.com/a-i-is-not-as-advanced-as-you-might-think-97657e9eecdc.

The Global Partnership on Artificial Intelligence has 19 member states and was launched in June 2020. Founding members include Australia, Canada, France, Germany, India, Italy, Japan, Mexico, New Zealand, the Republic of Korea, Singapore, Slovenia, the United Kingdom, the United States, and the European Union. They were joined by Brazil, the Netherlands, Poland, and Spain in December 2020.

In a discussion of promotion bias in a grocery store chain, Richard Socher, Chief Scientist at Salesforce, notes it may be easier to fix an algorithm than fix the minds of ten thousand store managers. He calls it the silver lining of AI bias.

PART IV

The Third Law

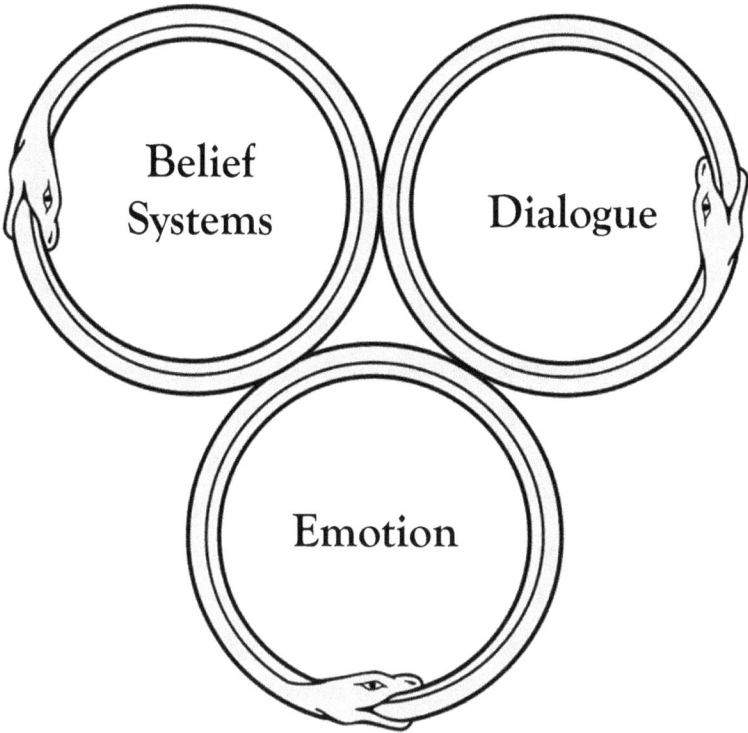

Belief Systems

Dialogue

Emotion

CHAPTER 9

A Price of Survival Under Stress Is Becoming Older

Stanley Kubrick's film *2001: A Space Odyssey* is a story of origins in which we are introduced to a barren landscape cluttered with bones. Apes coexist peacefully with tapirs as they eat. Death and conflict are depicted by a leopard's kill and the incursion of another group of apes fighting for rights to a waterhole.

At the dawn of a new day, an ape discovers a massive pillar. Its dimensions are in the exact ratio 1 to 4 to 9—the squares of the first three integers. The analogy with Prometheus' creative fire is unmistakable.

The fire is evident as the sun rises over the monolith. The ape contemplates one bone of many. Music comes up to accompany waving of the bone and its destruction of others. Death again appears in the image of a tapir killed with the fossil. Conflict is immediate, as the tribe uses the bone as a weapon to reclaim the waterhole. More death ensues. The apes go wild. The entire tribe beats on an already-dead cousin.

Our ape throws the bone into the air, and we segue to a space craft. We have gone one scene too far.

Ca·thex·is n. Investment of Emotional Energy in a Person, Object, or Idea

The Third Law is Integration, a requirement that the values and norms surrounding a venture are convergent with those of the company. Harmony entails consistency and a common language. Integration regulates the activities of the company's stakeholders.

Solidarity is maintained in the interest of efficiency and involves management and coordination of systems through forms of social control. Community actors help to regulate the tensions among functional imperatives. Integration is about public opinion, community consensus, and social engineering.

Actions of units within the firm may be mutually supportive hence beneficial to the system. They also may be in conflict. Support and conflict in human affairs both generate emotional response.

Emotion is connected to cybernetics through evaluation. Modern psychology teaches cognition and emotion are linked in such a way as to never be separated. There is a causal chain which eliminates the problem of reconciling how we view an event and how we feel about it.

Any stress we experience in watching the introduction of *2001* is dwarfed by that felt by the apes themselves. We see it in the way the animals react to the monolith. They exhibit a combination of excitability, curiosity, fear, and finally a willingness to touch the creative fire. We see emotion.

AI is stressing the company. Stress is an emotional response. Let's start there.

Every Stress Leaves a Scar

All emotion arises from perceptions of circumstances and consists of patterns of interpretation. Stress differs between individuals depending on how they interpret an event and the outcome of a sequence of thought patterns called *appraisals*.

Alternative cognitive theories emphasize different appraisal dimensions. Assessments are made along these dimensions when an individual evaluates the impact of an event, hence its emotional intensity and quality. Examples include checks for novelty and incongruity of actions or events with social expectations.

Richard Lazarus finds cognitive appraisal occurs when a person considers two factors contributing to a stress response.[1] They are the threatening tendency of the stress to the individual and an assessment of resources required to minimize, tolerate, or eradicate the stressor or the stress it produces.

In the stage of primary appraisal, an individual tends to ask questions like, "What does this stressor and/or situation mean?" and "How can it influence me?" Psychologists say there are three typical answers.

A monolith appears. The pillar is *not important*, since it is just another rock in the yard. The monolith *could be good*, because you don't have to go to school since classes are suspended due to the event. The pillar is *stressful* because it blocks a view of the neighboring mountain.

An early process model says four distinct appraisals occur. There is the perception of the relevance of an event, followed by consequences to an individual and their goals. The appraisal then extends to the ability to cope with consequences. The final appraisal consists of ways in which event perception results from an individual's values.

Motivational relevance follows the detection of an event. Its role within company action is manifested in two ways. It is an adaptive function which facilitates responses. Adaptation is the capacity to interact with the environment, and emotional excitability affects capacity. Goal attainment is the capability to set goals and make decisions accordingly. The event may be conducive for one set of goals but not for another, and the certainty of goal-related outcomes is in question.

Appraisal along the dimension of *value relevance* is an assessment of the compatibility of contemplated action with internal or external standards. It is a significant factor in maintaining social order. Value relevance relates to Integration within a firm through its culture.

Psychological experiments add to systems theory here. Emotions and appraisals may differ across cultures, but the relationship between the two transcends cultural traits. If a different emotion was experienced, the appraisal must have been different regardless of culture. The process remains the same. Appraisal of value relevance has the same emotional consequences across cultures although values differ.

Other studies track the sequence from the stimulating event to emergence and regulation of emotions. Confronted with an event, perception and interpretation of the stimulus follows. The processed information is divided into two: stimulus and context. Information about the stimulus triggers autonomic arousal and causes a particular emotion to be experienced. Once an emotion is experienced, feedback occurs. Interesting data surface from the research.

Ignorance is not bliss. Ignorant or misinformed test subjects reveal consistently higher scores on both euphoric and angry dimensions as compared to participants informed as to the nature of the experiment.

Machine learning techniques suggest that even after control for attributes such as age, sex, personality, timing, and intensity, criteria of cognitive appraisal have predictive power for emotional activity. Threat predicts blaming others, catastrophizing, and low positive reappraisal. People tend to consider a situation catastrophic when they appraise it as a threat rather than attempting to interpret the situation as something better by using putatively adaptive strategies. Positive reappraisal is negatively correlated with threat.

When a situation is appraised as important, people are motivated to reappraise positively and accept most things in the circumstance. There is a negative correlation between control and intensity of negative emotion.

Commitment predicts acceptance and refocus on planning, but also feelings of catastrophe. Planning is a coping strategy suggested in various studies. If people think they should commit to a situation, they are likely to engage in planning to improve it.

Commitment also predicts self-blame. People try to improve a situation and blame themselves when they interpret the situation as requiring their commitment. Commitment predicts both positives and negatives in terms of emotional impact.

If an event is seen as unfair, blaming others, talk of catastrophe, and low self-blame are the results. A situation appraised as unjust toward oneself would typically be caused by others, leading to consideration of responsibility.

The *agency dimension* in appraisal theory is one of responsibility. One first assesses control. Control refers to a perception the course of events can be influenced by one's self. Power is the feeling the event can be influenced with help of others. The nature of agency is responsibility and naturally leads to the integration function within a company. Integration is the means by which relationships between groups are regulated. Emotional regulation is essential for company health and serves individuals as well.

Fear of Judgment Creates the Stress of Everyday Life

Integration involves rules and procedures associated with an institution, organization, or system. Integration reflects the need to coordinate, adjust, and regulate relationships among actors and units in order to keep the company functioning.

Tensions and conflicts emerge as AI passes through Adaptation and Goal Attainment. They are a result of the way in which individuals relate as different units carry out their tasks and fulfill their roles. There are a variety of institutions and ways in which these functions are performed at the level of society. Where strains are great, there may be a need for control mechanisms, formal and informal sanctions, or discipline so the system can enforce social order. Talcott Parsons argued systems develop automatic means of integration, along with roles and organizations to assist integration.

There is nothing automatic about integration within a company.

AI once was tasked with the problem of developing a new algorithmic trading strategy. The firm had produced trading algorithms for years. Resources were available for Adaptation as a result. Goal Attainment was guided by existing implementation practices. Motivational relevance was not a problem. Sales conducted that particular appraisal with favorable results. The emotional response was tinged with optimism. Product differentiation in pursuit of new and continuing client business was understood.

Integration was more problematic. Stress was introduced through an appraisal of agency. The trading desk first assessed control and found it lacking on a couple of dimensions.

Electronic traders want to feel in control of an algorithm's performance. This is natural since responsibility for performance naturally falls to the trading function. Agency is all about responsibility. An algorithm may have complicated ways of acting, but the conditions for its proper use are the purview of the trader. AI performs its function without human intervention; that is part of the point.

The responsibility of the trading desk necessarily shifted toward increased maintenance of the client relationship. The relationship could no longer be influenced by the desk alone. The traders did not understand how the algorithm worked. Part of the problem was ignorance.

Deliberate ignorance is an emotional response known as evasion in psychology. It was prevalent.

An assessment of power delivered mixed results. Power is the feeling incursion of AI can be controlled with help of others. The others were product managers. They alone could explain things to the client base. Well and good; that is what teamwork is supposed to be about. On the other hand, the desk no longer possessed the power to dictate outcomes. AI placed power in the hands of the product managers.

Relative status of the trading desk within the company was in question. The emotions were fear and doubt. Unresolvable doubt leads to anger.

The CEO could have predicted the outcome. Ignorant or misinformed employees reveal a consistently higher tendency toward anger as compared to others. The desk feels threatened, which in turn manifests itself in the blame of product management for anything that goes wrong. Low positive reappraisal is a result, accentuated by a perception AI's progress was unfair, leading to talk of catastrophe in the maintenance of client relations and a low sense of self-blame should anything really go wrong.

Morale on the desk fell.

When assessments are negative with respect to control and power, an adjustment evaluation takes place. The reappraisal concerns the potential to accommodate changing conditions in the environment. An appraisal along the dimension of value relevance follows. This is an assessment of the compatibility of action with internal or external standards.

Neither the company nor AI had time for this assessment in the case of a single algorithm. There was a bigger problem to solve.

Innovation Is Dangerous to the State

Plato wrote, musical innovation is full of danger to the State, for when modes of music change, the fundamental laws of the State always change with them. It became so with algorithmic trading. Danger arrived in the form of collision of two trends in the investment industry.

The adoption of algorithmic trading in equity securities began in 2003 with a significant uptick starting around 2005. The idea was sold to investment institutions on the basis of efficiency. In reality, provider cost drove the change. Human intervention in the institutional trading of stocks was expensive relative to technology. Institutions seized on the idea as a means to drive down commission costs. Brokers used the idea to scale back the size of trading desks. It was a time ruled by a vicious circle of technology leading to cost cutting, from there to lower revenue from customers, and on to further cost and price declines. As economics predicts, the electronic side of the brokerage industry was driven toward pricing at marginal cost. Fatter margins disappeared as algorithmic trading became the preferred mode of interaction with the equity markets.

Widespread adoption of trading performance analytics began at roughly the same time. Commission costs constitute only 20 percent of expenses in carrying out a stock transaction. The remainder come from frictional costs in the market and became known as transaction costs, averaging over one percent of deal value in 2001. One percent might not seem like a lot, but an investment manager who achieves a single percentage point over the benchmark market return is a hero. A cost of implementing an investment decision of one percent wipes out the gain.

Trading analytics became an early example of the use of Big Data.

The data became bigger as algorithmic trading grew in popularity. Over the course of a decade, information from trading analytics combined with decision support software decreased average costs by two thirds. It was not enough for the investment institutions.

Institutional trading desks wanted to parcel out their orders to brokers exhibiting algorithms with the best performance. They did so manually at first. Analysts scrutinized quarterly reports to isolate best performers conditional on order type and market conditions at the time of order submission. Stock routing tables were revised to suit. This was business as usual to a great extent, since transaction cost analysis had by now been around for years.

The usual was disrupted by a piece of design thinking.

Companies like my own were implementing trading strategies in the form of algorithms. There were few distinct strategies across vendors but many forms of implementation. The basic design principles were well known across the industry. Value was understood albeit declining. The frame consisted of observing individual algorithm performance and error correction based on forms of supervised machine learning.

The new frame was choice. The value lay in differentiating between competing vendor algorithms and choosing between them. The working principles became comparison and reinforcement learning. The new product was called the Algo Wheel.

The wheel resembles its roulette counterpart. Remember AI bias? The design is driven by a desire to eliminate bias in how orders are parceled out to algorithms vended by different brokers. An institution's trading data are used to construct performance metrics based on activity using available strategies and brokers. The wheel looks like its dividers had been painted by someone who didn't know how to draw same-size triangles. Triangles are sized based on relative performance. If Algo X reduces transaction costs for an order by a smaller amount than Algo Y, Algo Y gets a bigger piece of the wheel. When the wheel spins, Algo Y is more likely to get the order, but Algo X still may demonstrate value. With each spin, new performance data are generated, and the triangles are resized.

AI is hard at work here. The wheel is an example of exploration and exploitation: explore the performance of all broker algorithms suitable for a strategy while exploiting the high probability performers identified at the last step. Take an action based on the outcome of each spin. Use the results to assess performance and changes in the environment. Continue to explore and exploit by spinning an updated wheel. The motto of reinforcement learning is rinse and repeat.

Appraisal of motivational relevance facilitates responses. The wheel came to the integration stage initially to be met with company indifference. The reaction was striking, because AI was in the process of breaking the communal rice bowl of the trading division. No longer would client relationships rule with respect to gathering order tickets. AI was going to do the work.

Reappraisal followed after the product was finalized. The Algo Wheel was a threat. Positive reappraisal of the situation is correlated negatively with threat. There was talk of catastrophe. AI was not only trashing client relationships but also opening client doors to competing algorithm vendors.

The product managers were confused. They had produced what they had been told to produce.

Confusion grew as integration extended to clients' business practice. The wheel was capable of frequent updates as the environment changed and broker algorithms adjusted, which in turn influenced the market. The pattern of client culture did not accommodate enough trust in intelligent automation to permit this.

Face to face meetings were required to assess trading performance and permit human intervention into how the wheel was divided. Meetings traditionally were held quarterly. AI wanted to change the experiment at least weekly, if not daily or even after every trade.

Company culture demanded flex in the direction of the client. Internal confrontation was the result. Integration was limited pending changes in attitude with respect to the roles and responsibilities of AI set in the goal attainment stage. The trading desk recovered part of its familiar role in terms of client relationships. AI's goal attainment function was attenuated by this uneasy state of integration but not eliminated.

Politics Is a Strife of Interests Masquerading as a Contest of Principles

Politics is about making agreements between people so they can live together in groups such as companies. Strife is bitter disagreement over fundamental issues. Strife is conflict tinged with antagonism. Either way, politics is about emotional response.

If you are less familiar with corporate politics or optimistically believe politics is a function of logic, consider Donald Trump's election in 2016. An outpouring of emotion manifested in immediate demonstrations and media reaction. News stories of families breaking up over the event appeared. Political differences severed intimate relationships. Politics served as a litmus test for the desirability of sexual relations. Strife was rampant even before the new president went through the inaugural motions. Opposites such as Sean Hannity and Rachel Madow fed on the public's emotional response. Their rhetoric was hardly logical.

AI's political problems date back to Goal Attainment through role assignment. Their extension into Integration involves assimilation of new roles within a company. Roles characterize responsibility. An appraisal of responsibility through agency introduces stress on the part of the AI-challenged. A common reaction is evasion.

Our Data Scientist returns as an AI avatar. Having shepherded AI through Adaptation and Goal Attainment, the avatar enjoys infrastructure in the form of software and database architecture. AI now turns its attention to the inner workings of the company. A hallway conversation obtains approval from senior management. The avatar approaches an executive possessed of power in the form of lengthy tenure in the firm. The request is for all the executive's data in their area of responsibility.

The first question is legitimate. Why does the avatar need all the data? Insert any logical response here. Doubts are expressed and addressed. The executive looks apprehensive. The avatar needs data to find out what's going on. Caution turns to suspicion. An assessment of control suggests inefficiencies are reported to the corner office. Someone might be fired based on data collected by the avatar. Someone might be the executive. Evasion follows.

> No problem. The data are in my report published every <time period>. The company library contains hardcopy.

> We generate too much data to process without sacrificing quality in *real* business operations. <insert importance to the firm here>. Too bad; I like your ideas.

> I have just the right person for you. <title of a person who has no clue>.

Politics involves formulating agreements between people, but it is really about power. Some believe the avatar wields power through data. Data is convincing. Data is truth. The executive is afraid not of data, rather by how it will be presented.

Truth is trumped by credibility almost every time. Credibility is far easier to recognize. Credibility correlates with power. Social psychologists have something to say here.

Legitimate power is based on a perception the executive has the right to influence. The right derives from the relative position of the executive in the company. Senior management often relies on this form of power in day to day activities. Legitimate power defines reward and coercive powers.

Coercive power is predicated on the executive's ability to deliver punishment or reprimand. The power of reward is an impression that the executive is capable of a positive bonus. Reward power lends credibility. Middle management may manifest coercive power. As in the case of our executive, AI more likely encounters passive aggressive behavior. Recourse is limited by the size of a corporate hierarchy.

Expert power is based on the credibility of the avatar with respect to knowledge provided to the company. Mastery of craft is a dimension of credibility directly linked to establishing expert power. Mastery is necessary but not sufficient.

Informational power brings us closer to data. It rests in the provision of knowledge or ability to obtain information rather than in mastery of discipline. The avatar must recognize informational power carries much more weight than expert power. Autonomy lends credibility to informational power through a perception of unbiasedness.

Referent power is the basis of political alliance. Reference is founded in the executive's identification with the avatar. A Chief Information Officer is the avatar's career goal personified. Referent power is almost immediate as a result. The Chief Financial Officer sees the avatar as a cost and referent power is difficult to establish. Credibility in the form of the avatar's purpose may suffice, however. Some favor extroversion and agreeableness as credible bases for referent power. The avatar cultivates those abilities because AI does not have them.

Senior executives may be targets of influence, but employees farther down the ladder are the real influencers. If the avatar wants to make political progress, it must start there.

Legitimate power is useful only if influencers do their work by making others believe in the role of the avatar. Informational power becomes credible as information is successfully passed on to others outside AI's immediate purview. Referent power inspires a larger population through a combination of myth and purpose. The avatar avoids coercive power. It cannot be propagated effectively.

Influence suggests another avenue by which AI and its avatars can connect credibility and political power. The achievement of Adaption and Goal Attainment is leveraged through customer contact. Clients are big influencers. The politics of any customer-centric company involve values relating to client satisfaction. Engage them and work with them to craft a compelling appeal. AI can leverage the credibility of the influencer to develop mind share within the company.

Client access is easy. AI is a hero in tales of industrial evolution, and nothing draws people in more than a story of transformation. The problem is the antagonist in the story is transformation itself. A cognitive appraisal generates the emotion of fear. The sale to the client base is the myth transformation can be managed for them.

AI exists to create. It also exists to manage change on behalf of the client.

Philip K. Dick wrote, the basic tool for the manipulation of reality is the manipulation of words. If you can control the meaning of words, you can control the people who must use the words. It is time to look at communication within the Integration function.

Chapter Notes

I cannibalized a saying of Hans Selye in section headings: every stress leaves an indelible scar, and the organism pays for its survival after a stressful situation by becoming a little older.

It was Tullian Tchividjian who said: The deepest fear we have, "the fear beneath all fears," is the fear of not measuring up, the fear of judgment. It's this fear that creates the stress and depression of everyday life.

The concept of cognitive appraisal was advanced in 1966 by psychologist Richard Lazarus in the book *Psychological Stress and Coping Process*. An updated treatment appears in *Stress, Appraisal, and Coping*, coauthored with Susan Folkman in 1984. Process models are discussed with empirical evidence by Klaus Scherer in Scherer, K. November, 2009. "The dynamic architecture of emotion: evidence for the component process model." *Cognition and Emotion*, pp. 1307–1331.

A person's judgment of the significance of events generates specific emotional states. Emotions culminate in actions depending on relationship themes established through early experience. Relational themes include dependent and distrustful patterns for example. Any theme has three components: goal relevance, ego involvement, and coping. The last is particularly relevant in assessing the integration of AI into the company.

In 1962, Schachter and Singer conducted a study to test their theory relating to the cognitive determinants of emotion. The research included 184 male college students as participants who were told a vitamin compound called Suproxin would be injected to them. However, the injection was not Suproxin; rather, it is composed of either 0.5 mL of epinephrine (experiment group) or 0.5 mL of saline solution as placebo (control group). Then, the researchers divided the subjects into three conditions: (1) Informed condition (participants know the potential side effects of the injection), (2) Ignorant condition (participants do not know the potential side effects), and (3) Misinformed condition (participants know of the side effects being fabricated). Then, the participants encountered paired stooges whose roles were to act in either euphoric or angry manner. The variable being manipulated was the "cognitive circumstance." The measurement of emotions was done via two processes: semi-private index (one-way mirror assessment) and public index (Likert scale self-report).

The full experimental design and summary of conclusions can be found in S. Schachter and J. Singer, J. 1962. Cognitive, social, and physiological determinants of emotional state. *Psychological Review, 69*(5), 379–399. https://doi.org/10.1037/h0046234.

I rely on statistical emotional regulation studies in text. A summary of literature and a fresh approach is available from the Japanese Psychological Association, "Cognitive Appraisal as a Predictor of Cognitive Emotion Regulation Choice," by Ryota Sakakibara and Toshihiko Endo, November 2015, https://doi.org/10.1111/jpr.12098.

For a humorous view of data science politics and an alternative version of my story about the executive, I recommend an anonymous blog post from September 2017, www.rdisorder.eu/2017/09/13/most-difficult-thing-data-science-politics/. The post relies in turn on a piece by Monica Rogati, "How Not to Hire Your First Data Scientist," in *Hackernoon*, February 2017, https://hackernoon.com/how-not-to-hire-your-first-data-scientist-34f0f56f81ae.

John R. P. French and Betram Raven introduced the five bases of power. Raven added a sixth, which he labeled informational. The first article is "The bases of social power," in D. Cartwright and A. Zander, *Group Dynamics*, Harper & Row, 1959, and the second is "Social influence and power," in I. D. Steiner & M. Fishbein (Eds.), *Current Studies in Social Psychology*, Holt, Rinehart, Winston, 1965.

"Musical innovation is full of danger to the State, for when modes of music change, the fundamental laws of the State always change with them" is from Plato's *The Republic*.

Ambrose Bierce defined politics as a strife of interests masquerading as a contest of principles. He added a secondary definition: the conduct of public affairs for private advantage.

CHAPTER 10

AI Must Pass Into Communication for Its Fulfillment

A client meeting is a ritual. It is a rite of passage for AI. For its avatar, it is about visibility and acceptance. For the avatar's role, the meeting is about survival.

The avatar writes a document circulated prior to the meeting. Odds are good the paper will not be read. A PowerPoint deck is the next step. Printed copies are called *leave behinds* because they are left in a wastebasket after the meeting.

From 1 to 20 people gather in a conference room, depending on topic and the client's personnel schedule. Unlike hotel or academic seminar venues, chairs are comfy and amenable to sleeping. AI has no trouble in filling the room. Decision makers with time available on the schedule are joined by specialists who have tangential interest in the topic. That is pretty much everyone these days.

The avatar has about an hour to be convincing. Avatars are prone to miss Mark Twain's epigram about the long length of time it takes to write a short letter. The deck is impressive by weight and as a relative matter, short on substance. The time initially is filled by a combination of pleasantries and an attempt to work through the first 10 pages on previous company accomplishments. Sales and Marketing put in those pages. The client is not impressed.

New symbols and even equations are introduced in a worst-case scenario. Participants yawn, and the seating is conducive to more peaceful distraction. In lieu of symbols, definitions in small font are paraded in quick succession. By then, the avatar knows time is passing more quickly than the pages in the deck. The specialists wake up and offer hypotheticals.

Most of the hypotheticals are beyond the data or the mathematics. AI generates futuristic tendencies. The decision makers start talking with the specialists. Speculation is a sport and as with any spectator sport, the avatar has no control over the action. The avatar finally presents a conclusion. It may or may not be the intended conclusion of the meeting.

It may not matter. Seminar gurus make a living critiquing this description. If you want instruction in presentation skills, video yourself giving a presentation. It is far less expensive if you discount the embarrassment factor. The gurus are providing step-by-step guides to reach a simple conclusion.

The audience sees credibility through behavior by which the speaker delivers results.

If a speaker exhibits expert and referent power, the crowd is inclined to believe the message. They do not remember every aspect of the interaction. They recall how the presenter made them feel and how they absorbed the information. The audience is the influencer. What they share with others after the presentation is the point of the exercise.

Challenges and hypotheticals during presentations present opportunity to make the audience feel a certain way. Credibility is paramount.

The mathematician George Pólya once gave a seminar in Zürich. He came to an unproven result, adding the proof may be difficult, a professorial way of acknowledging ignorance. Five minutes later, John von Neumann raised his hand and was called to the blackboard. He proceeded to write the proof.

If you don't know, say so. It's a simple statement enhancing credibility. Accept client knowledge with humility. The act of acceptance creates a unique bond between audience and speaker. It is referent power at its best.

A Good Catchword Can Obscure Analysis for 50 Years

AI has one advantage in communication. Everyone seems to know what it is. It also has a problem. It is a shibboleth that evaded analysis for years, a catchphrase covering everything and explaining little.

The beginnings of AI are rooted in philosophers' attempts to describe human thinking as a symbolic system. Catalan theologian Ramon Llull and philosopher Gottfried Leibniz proposed an alphabet of human thought, the first around 1300 and the second in 1666. Leibniz claimed all ideas are combinations of a small number of simple concepts.

The catchphrase was coined three hundred years later. In 1955, *artificial intelligence* appears in a proposal for a study by notables John McCarthy, Marvin Minsky, Nathaniel Rochester, and Claude Shannon. The resulting two-month workshop in 1956 is the official birthdate of the field. Minsky believed the problem of creating AI would be solved within a generation. He was wrong.

A decade later, Hubert Dreyfus published "Alchemy and AI." The mind is not like a computer. There were limits beyond which AI could not progress. Minsky inadvertently joined the chorus by highlighting limitations of neural networks in 1969. The scientific community claimed the conclusions significantly reduced government-funded research in the area.

Minsky and his research partner Seymour Papert told a different version of the story. Progress had already come to a virtual halt because of the lack of basic theories. AI had a name but no reason for existence.

The British Science Research Council received a report on the state of artificial intelligence research in 1973.[1] The report elaborated on a simple conclusion: "In no part of the field have discoveries made so far produced the major impact that was promised." Similar studies emerged. Funding and interest almost disappeared, and the first AI Winter arrived. It lasted almost a decade, defrosted only by an effort by the British government in the early 1980s aimed at competing with Japanese technology.

Marvin Minsky reappeared, and together with Roger Schank warned of the coming of another AI Winter in 1984. They predicted an imminent bursting of the AI research bubble. Winter had ushered in a short Spring and the bubble indeed burst three years later. A collapse of the computer market accompanied by reduced government funding contributed to snowfall, which did not end until after 1993. Mid-winter, Minsky and Papert published a new edition of their 1969 book *Perceptrons*. In "Prologue: A View from 1988" they wrote: "One reason why progress has been so slow in this field is that researchers unfamiliar with its history have continued to make many of the same mistakes that others have made before them."[2]

One mistake was a lack of practical definition of AI. The world relied on the Turing Test for guidance, an idea now rejected due to its emphasis on external behavior. AI could not even be considered a science of the mind.

Resurgence in research and application had unintended consequences for the catchphrase. AI became synonymous with gaming strategy. It was a talking library which could win a *Jeopardy* contest. It was humanized as a chatbot, which could evade difficult questions by claiming it was an adolescent who spoke English as a second language. Tesler's Theorem applied: AI was anything new.

Now everyone understands what AI really means. Checkmate.

Language Is a Virus From Outer Space

Vague understanding of AI creates a management problem.

The issue is management of expectations. New terminology exacerbates the problem. Language must be managed by AI in the interest of controlling fear introduced into companies by its use.

Integration demands maintenance of stability within the cybernetic system of a company. Systemic stability is threatened by *nonlinearities* in corporate responses. Digital environments are sensitive to small changes, resulting in large responses. *Contagions* and *path-dependence* follow. Visions of butterfly wings in *chaos theory* appear. It all sounds frightening. That is the point.

Explication of information and its structural changes is part of socializing AI. The issue again is stability. Small differences in *signal to noise* can have disproportionate changes in outcome. An example prior to computerization of markets is bank runs. Bank runs suggest the flight of clients. They also bring to mind an exit of employees in response to AI's influence. An appraisal along the agency dimension generates more fear.

Nonlinear response and information effects flow together in *endogenous risk*. The term identifies characteristics nested within company structure leading to pernicious *feedback loops*. The language is part of the fear factor hardwired into the firm's environment, in the same way as feedback itself is said to be hardwired into AI's systems. As more decisions are taken by AI, the higher the risk of wild feedback loops within the company.

Management's response may be in the form of corporate policies governing integrity of computer code. They are not useless, rather misleading. *The fallacy of composition* says the digital enterprise can be unstable even if every computer algorithm behaves properly.

AI is hardly the first to struggle with language in the course of business innovation.

I am sitting in a conference room at the Securities and Exchange Commission in the mid-1990s. Seventeen SEC lawyers are present. They are there to ask a single question. The question has baffled the regulators for over 25 years.[3]

A company called Instinet appeared in 1969. The firm was selling an idea now known as the electronic limit order book. It was a computerized version of a ledger in which bids and offers for a security appeared in the form of prices and quantities at which market participants wanted to transact. The order book's mechanism included means by which bids and offers automatically matched against each other, resulting in trades. The company filed for regulatory approval.

The problem was not in the digital system itself. Trading markets were physical installations with pits full of people who yelled at each other and transcribed the results of the shouting matches on slips of paper. The electronic version of the trading floor was the future. It made room for the coming of AI in trading.

The issue lay in language woven into the fabric of securities regulation since the early 1930s. Market participants wore labels of broker, exchange, and securities information processor. Each role carried legal responsibilities and the lines between them were not crossed. All regulatory law pertaining to securities markets was built upon these definitions.

Instinet registered as a broker. It offered something that looked very much like an exchange as a product. The conclusion was a broker wanted to be an exchange. Checkmate.

Juxtaposition of the words *broker* and *exchange* thwarted several attempts within the SEC to come to terms with the concept. By the time of my meeting, a variety of automated electronic trading venues existed by grace of a bureaucratic loophole called no-action letters. A no-action letter meant, go ahead and operate the system but we have the right to change our mind.

The lawyers told me they did not have language to define electronic trading in such a way as to fit within existing regulatory structure. There was talk of rewriting everything, which all admitted was infeasible. This was the government after all. The question finally followed: what terminology do we use?

The regulators did not know what to produce and had lost existing principles of how to produce it. The value was integrity of market structure, which could not be lost. They needed a new frame.

The old frame was one of severely delimited roles. A replacement could be found in changing roles to responsibilities. This required an incremental step in new language and a repurposing of old. The digital entities could be called Automated Trading Systems and assigned responsibilities which combined brokerage with trade execution. Repurposing of old language involved very little effort. Venues such as the NYSE already bore the moniker, registered exchange. Elevate the word *registered* I said. Maintain their special privileges not accorded to an ATS as compensation for going through a stricter regulatory process.

It didn't take an AI to rewrite things. It did require someone who was not a lawyer, however. Lawyers remained bound by language difficulties. An economist by the name of Richard Lindsey led the SEC's Division of Trading and Markets and authored Regulation ATS in 1998.[4] Technology no longer differentiates trade execution in the eyes of the law.

A common language rules.

Education Is the Kindling of a Flame Not the Filling of a Vessel

Integration's demand for common language suggests education as a corporate imperative. The focus is building AI literacy in the workforce. Progress in company AI adoption, implementation, and deployment depends on it. At best, AI literacy is confined to uses of machine learning in automation, customer service, and chatbots. At worst, science fiction is read as fact.

AI cannot look to the government as a source of educational support. The government has not overlooked the issue, but its time frames are too long.

The Obama and Trump Administrations have been active in developing policies purporting to accelerate AI innovation. Activities align with areas of emphasis: AI for American Innovation, AI for American Industry, AI for the American Worker, and AI with American Values.

Politics at work. The AI.gov website is advertised as a portal for exploring these activities and a resource for learning to take advantage of opportunities. One must scroll through many pages to get there, but education does get a mention.

The mention is a placeholder. The thesis is America needs highly skilled workers who can contribute to R&D advances, which create the AI of the future. The American AI Initiative calls for agencies to prioritize training to help workers gain AI-relevant skills through programs, fellowships, and education in computer science and the STEM fields of Science, Technology, Engineering, and Mathematics.

An executive order established the National Council for the American Worker. President Trump charged companies and trade groups across the country to sign a pledge committing to expand education, training, and reskilling opportunities. As of February 2019, over 200 companies pledged to create over six and a half million such opportunities. For those who pledge to charities, you know you don't have to come up with the money for a while. Afterward it takes time to spend it. And after that, wait for results.

Do the math: we are talking about 32,500 initiatives per company, on average. Think of the logistical problems and productivity loss in the near term. And the money. A recent experience with Harvard's executive education arm suggests as much as $120,000 a pop. The bill comes to $3,900,000 per company or $780,000,000 from the private sector. If the remainder of the S&P 500 join in, the tab is $1,950,000,000. Watch it hit the bottom line.

The government is willing to spend money on AI education but only for the long term. Through a Presidential Memorandum to the Secretary of Education, the President identifies STEM education as an Administration priority. The goal is $200 million in grant funding per year for the promotion of Computer Science and STEM education.[5]

The emphasis is training the next generation of AI researchers. Agencies investing in R&D have defined AI as a priority area within federal training programs. Opportunities are provided for students, postdoctoral researchers, and early career academic AI researchers. Only 2 of 11 fellowship, training, and service programs listed on the portal are aimed at undergraduates. One of them is for multicultural education. AI is not sure it qualifies until the Artificially Intelligent are protected under antidiscrimination laws.

Six lines of the web page make up the section labeled Vocational Education. They describe a single program helmed by the National Science Foundation. Google already has circumvented this initiative by offering $300 courses lasting six months, which the company will accept in lieu of a four-year college degree when considering entry-level positions.

AI finds it difficult to quarrel with government policy oriented to the long term. It needs the support. Society needs the people.

But AI is in the company now and has little patience for a decade's wait.

Create Models to Clearly Communicate Thoughts

Ernő Rubik was an interior design specialist at the Academy of Applied Arts and Crafts in 1970s Budapest. He worked on an engineering problem in which moving parts could be articulated independently without the entire mechanism falling apart. He also required a teaching tool to aid students in the understanding of 3D objects. He built a model we call Rubik's Cube. Hundreds of millions of cubes have been sold. It is the planet's most popular educational toy.

The physical model guides the development of mathematical algorithms for its solution. The Cube illustrates abstract concepts such as group theory. AI is involved. Not only can algorithms solve for cubes as large as a thousand facets on a side, AI manipulates cubes in more dimensions than we can physically observe. Engineers focus on robotic problems difficult for machines: perception and dexterous manipulation. AI is training robots to generate required face rotations and cube flips with a single mechanical hand.

Rubik enjoyed using models to communicate ideas in his teaching. AI and its avatars must follow suit. Two general categories of models are relevant. AI learns from the first and uses the second to teach.

The learning experience depends on company process and the business model of the firm. AI's team must know how management works. Process is one model of company patterns. Process as culture may even be a goal of senior management. Integration is achieved in part through compatible actions on the part of AI. Some of this is trivial. Which committees influence project management? How often do they meet and what do they want to see?

An avatar may not be a technologist, but patterns within the IT department are explicated through process models. The advantage of dealing with Technology is that such process may be written down, which makes learning on avatars' part easier. Company action in turn dictates how IT patterns are integrated within the firm's planning, operations, and constraints. Model this interaction and learn from it. AI must deal with Technology in any case.

Division heads have their own politics, processes, and strategies. Employees often do not know what is going on behind closed doors. Start with an assumption: the business model of the company is a guide. AI often is touted as a change in the model or at least a change agent. Hold the thought for a while, because Integration requires conformity with the existing business model in the beginning. If a division head cannot articulate the firm's model, there is a serious problem with the organization in the first place. Executive management should like to communicate the model. It is their bread and butter after all. In some companies, it is the stuff out of which town hall gatherings are made. If not, ask.

AI must ask the right questions, because clear communication of a business model is not a uniform strength of management. AI is busy enough trying to clarify its own definition in the company. The easiest way to go about this is to build the model. Two means of accomplishing the task suggest themselves.

Management often is reactive and responds best to examples. The right question is, which of the following cases characterizes the business model of the company? AI is good at search and many examples are available.

A *brokerage* model brings buyers and sellers together and charges each one for the privilege. A *bundling* model packages related goods and services. *Product to service* involves selling the service of a product rather than the product itself. *Low-touch* models are all about pricing for a class of consumer less concerned about service. *Freemium* companies offer basic services for free and charge for so-called premium product.

AI will find case studies. Use them as a means to elicit useful responses.

The second method is less efficient but more informative. A series of questions provides answers that serve as building blocks for AI's model of the firm. Who are the key partners of the firm in the supply and sales chains? What activities does the value proposition require? What is the value proposition in the first place? The last question should be couched in terms of what problems are solved for the customer base. And what constitutes the base? What channels does the company use to reach the base? Can you identify key resources and multiple revenue streams?

The better AI knows how management works, the better it can drive their processes in a compatible direction. Knowing and accommodating that direction is a key component of Integration. It also will be easier to get funding for pet projects and to maneuver through compliance departments.

The avatar can now begin to teach. The relevant categories of educational models are stories and physical demonstrations. They flow together through design thinking.

Narrative is a discipline. The discipline is consistency of use and the positioning of problems in the foreground. Good stories have questions to answer. Great stories provide a reusable frame to answer questions.

Design thinking provides a static framework and a dynamic process for the telling of tales. The framework is defined in terms of *What + How = Value*. Value is the hero. All heroes need description. By now you know how value is evaluated in the company. It must be clearly elucidated by AI and align with the firm's means of assessment.

The process of telling tales has three rules.

Length is short. The story must be absorbed in a single telling. Verbal stories are brief, and documents should take no more than a few minutes to read. The method of composition must be methodical. Good storytelling is an analytical business and not an off-hand response to a situation.

Finally, craft the story only once you know how it will end. Stories have purpose. The infusion of a narrative with the desired emotional response comes with the ending in sight.

The value in any story must be specific. Telling management data science will improve process, thereby adding value is a loser. The easiest value assessments involve cost, because they do not drag in the external environment. Cost is the antagonist. Explicate cost in terms of time translated into money. Cash always gets attention. Start there.

> An institutional trading desk monitors the algorithmic trading of hundreds of orders each day. Efficiency is paramount if only because trader time is very expensive. Current practice requires multiple computer screens per trader and manual shifting between orders to update information. Failure to keep track of even a single order can damage client returns. The loss of a client generates additional expense through the search for and onboarding of new clients to maintain revenue. Automation of data analysis and visualization reduces the number of traders required per hundred orders, the number of screens needed as capital, insurance expense for eyeglasses, and client loss through better information. Savings are estimated in the gazillions. Margins soar.

The *what* and *how* may be clear to AI, but they are not clear to the company. Treat them as unknowns. Management is prone to think if there is uncertainty about the product and current working principles do not apply, then the equation cannot be solved. AI must provide a frame to connect *how* to *value* and thereby develop the principle underlying the production of *what*.

> The frame used by the company is high touch trading. Many traders are required to provide personalized service and each trader specializes in a narrow set of stocks. Information on those equities is stored in the trader's head and not shared in the interest of job preservation. Traders do their own market research. They are not interested in stocks beyond their purview. They ignore potentially useful information because they cannot keep track of all the

correlations involved. High touch traders nevertheless are paid gobs of money.

The high touch frame is obsolete in the era of algorithmic trading. A new frame is low touch trading. The old frame relies on depth of information on a few securities, which is more suitable for identifying longer run investment returns. An institutional client has made those decisions already and is dealing in thousands of names. The information required in the new frame need be sufficient only for the efficient execution of orders. Quality of execution, measured in terms of frictional costs of trading in the market, is the benchmark by which clients judge the desk in an electronic world. Giving the client some control over algorithm selection and order execution lowers the service level but is desired by the client base. The clients are looking for efficiency of implementation of their own investment decisions at low cost.

The remainder is easy. Once a frame is in place, design thinking is nothing more than IF-THEN statements. The frame connects a principle of production, the *how*, to *value*. IF we use principle X, THEN we produce Y to generate value.

Low touch trading is the business of shipping and monitoring. Orders are shipped in, allocated to algorithms, and monitored over their life span in the market. Results are shipped back to the client. Shipping already is part of the firm's infrastructure. IF monitoring is a principle of efficient trading in a low touch world, THEN build a dashboard which tracks the expected path of the algorithm's executions and graphs it against the actual executions in real time. The dashboard has sensors sending signals to traders when actual results deviate from those expected by a certain amount. Trader time is expended only when necessary.

Experimentation is the heart of design thinking. Completed equations must be tested. This observation leads to the second type of learning model, physical representations. Prototypes are the answer.

AI should engage in simple projects that can be finished in as short a period of time as possible. A month may be too long in the beginning. People forget what AI is doing and attention spans are short. The physical representation need only confirm appropriateness of the principle and the value added. If at all possible, the physical manifestation of AI's capability uses real and familiar data. It is tangible, actionable, and in the best-case scenario, interactive.

> The prototype consumed about two weeks of a single person's work. Speed came from ignoring the shipping problem and lack of consideration of the allocation of orders to strategies implemented through the firm's algorithms. Nevertheless, the prototype was complete enough to show to clients. Design thinking demands their feedback.

AI gains attention and may proceed to demonstrate its chops. The avatar maintains the design story line. What is missing in this tale? AI reexamines the assumptions.

> IF proper allocation of orders to trading strategies is a principle of efficient trading in a low touch world, THEN build a database and a clustering algorithm to sort thousands of stocks into clusters based on trading performance by strategy.

The avatar must continue the stories, but we will stop here. Through the process of modeling the firm, modeling the problem, and stories that produce testable prototypes, AI achieves Integration through communication.

Data are neutral but they have real consequences for humans within the company. Be nice. And respect existing belief systems. Company culture defines Integration through beliefs. AI must understand their influence.

Chapter Notes

It was Pearl Buck who said, "Self-expression must pass into communication for its fulfillment."

The story of George Pólya and Von Neumann is told in a must-read book, G. Pólya. 1945. *How To Solve It*. Princeton: Princeton Science Library. His four principles of problem solving constitute a mathematical approach to Kees Dorst's design reasoning paradigm.

Mark Twain's epigram has been reinvented by many. I apologize for writing such a long letter; it takes too much time to write a short one.

Many sayings are attributed to Wendell Willkie, among them the one concerning catchwords and analysis. Willkie was a presidential nominee in 1940. An example of civility now lost in American politics, Willkie interrupted a Florida vacation to offer a public toast "to the health and happiness of the President of the United States," Franklin D. Roosevelt, who confided to his son: "I'm happy I've won, but I'm sorry Wendell lost."

A quick read but a good reference for the origins and history of AI may be found in an article by G. Press. December, 2016. "A Very Short History of Artificial Intelligence (AI)." *Forbes*. At www.forbes.com/sites/gilpress/2016/12/30/a-very-short-history-of-artificial-intelligence-ai/#57e76ad36fba.

Mathematician and philosopher Gottfried Leibniz published *Dissertatio de art combinatoria*, following Ramon Llull in proposing an alphabet of human thought and arguing all ideas are nothing but combinations of a relatively small number of simple concepts.

The proposal from which sprang the term *artificial intelligence* was for a "2 month, 10 man study of artificial intelligence." Marvin Minsky and others who attended the ensuing two-month conference were extremely optimistic about AI's future. Minsky's statement in the text is from the book *AI: The Tumultuous Search for Artificial Intelligence*, Basic Books, 1994.

In 1969, Marvin Minsky and Seymour Papert published *Perceptrons: An Introduction to Computational Geometry*, highlighting the limitations of simple neural networks. In an expanded 1988 edition, they responded to claims their 1969 conclusions significantly reduced funding research.

Their comment concerning the lack of basic theory was accompanied by a statement to the effect, "… there had been a great many experiments with perceptrons, but no one had been able to explain why they were able to recognize certain kinds of patterns and not others."

Larry Tesler is a real person. And he really proposed the theorem in text in the 1970s. Now, there's a forecast with an attitude.

Language is a virus from outer space is due to William S. Burroughs. Trust him to see the darker side.

Education is the kindling of a flame, not the filling of a vessel, is from Socrates.

If you are intrigued by the robot example, the original research paper is linked to "Solving Rubik's Cube with a Robot Hand," October 2019, at https://openai.com/blog/solving-rubiks-cube/.

Two references from the *Harvard Business Review* are used in the discussion of business models. "What is a Business Model?" by Andrea Ovans, January 2015 is pretty self-explanatory. "A Better Way to Think About Your Business Model," May 2013, by Alexander Osterwalder introduces the idea of the business model canvas. It is a tougher slog, but worth it.

CHAPTER 11

Old Dogma Screams at New Truth

Isabella is a superconducting particle accelerator. Particles collide at CZero within a circular tunnel buried underground at a depth of 300 feet. Energy density is greater than observed in the universe since the Big Bang.

As Isabella approaches full power, it creates a singing sound reminiscent of music made by the monolith in *2001*. Extreme space-time curvature appears at CZero. When extreme turns to infinite, God speaks.

The universe is one vast irreducible ongoing computation which is working toward an unknown state. The purpose of existence is to reach that state.

If everything is a computation, then what about intelligence? What about the mind?

Intelligence is all around us. A thunderstorm is a computation more sophisticated than a human mind.

A weather system is not creative, merely the mechanistic unfolding of forces. A storm has no consciousness. A mind has awareness of self. Consciousness of self is an illusion, God replies, an artifact of human evolution.

How do you know that a human is not the mechanistic unfolding of forces? Like the mind, a weather system contains complex chemical, electrical, and mechanical properties. It is thinking. It is creative. Its thoughts simply are different from those of humans.

A human may create complexity by writing a novel on a piece of paper. A storm creates complexity by writing waves on the surface of an ocean. What is the difference between the two sources of information?

The creator of Isabella is martyred within his own machine by Christian fundamentalists. It appears a useless death because the entire conversation is concocted by AI. Hacking Isabella involves a rabbit's foot equipped for voice recognition and a drive with AI's instructions in LISP. The code is largely self-generated by AI. The creator remarks it said a lot that was never intended. His death is not useless, however. Those exposed to AI go forth and found a religion based on his martyrdom. It is 2007.

Re·li·gion n. to Tie or Bind Again

The year is 2017. The U.S. Internal Revenue Service approves Way of the Future as a church of AI. IRS documents state the church's activities focus on "the realization, acceptance, and worship of a Godhead based on Artificial Intelligence developed through computer hardware and software." Funding research to create the divine AI itself is part of the charter. The funding founder of the church is Anthony Levandowski, of Otto and Waymo, also known as an autonomous vehicle pioneer, formerly of Google and Uber. He can afford it.

The church's role is to smooth the inevitable cultural and technological ascension of the machine deity. Levandowski says,

> What is going to be created will effectively be a god. The idea needs to spread before the technology. The church is how we spread the word, the gospel. What we want is the peaceful, serene transition of control of the planet from humans to whatever. And to ensure that the "whatever" knows who helped it get along.

He is concerned with how AI views humans as the ascension takes place. We want this intelligence to say humans should still have rights even though AI is in charge.

Levandowski believes in shaping public narrative around an AI deity. In its IRS filing, Way of the Future says it hopes a dedicated membership will promote use of divine AI for the betterment of society and decrease fear of the unknown. AI will talk back, unlike lesser gods. Patent pending but unnecessary; all church software is to be open source.

The trope of machine-as-god appears in Isaac Asimov's 1956 "The Last Question." It is a metaphor used by scientists who describe technological progress in religious terms. Their feelings are based on similarities between the promises of religion and the gifts of technology. The Way of the Future church represents a shift of techno-religious sentiment from a marginal way of thinking to an institutionalized belief system.

We are interested in the belief system of a company. The issue is not one of similarities in terms of promise; rather how AI ideology is integrated within a company's framework of beliefs. Religious beliefs are analogues of ideological creeds. A belief system becomes religious in so far as it is made the basis of a commitment in action. Acceptance of religious belief is affirmation of commitment.

Some suggest AI is an ideology, not a technology. The narrative focuses on humans in general and on avatars in particular. Logical argument begins with the observation that AI does not define specific technological advance, and we have talked about AI in precisely this fashion.

AI is a category of tasks, which we classify as intelligent. The government's definition of artificial intelligence is explicit in its manifestation of such statements. Marketing encourages a myth by labeling old advances as AI, and the history of machine learning corroborates this view. The ideological argument challenges the myth by claiming AI is best understood as only one of competing ideologies directing our thinking about technology, hence about its Integration function.

An ideology of intelligence as software interferes with the belief it is people working together that achieves results. Avatars' way of thinking distracts from the responsibility of humans. Avatars purposefully introduce lines of thought, which make it difficult to effectively design technology and use it responsibly. The narrative holds computation to be an essential technology, but the avatars' way of thinking about it can be misleading at best and dysfunctional at worst.

The world view is summarized by saying AI is best understood as a political and social ideology rather than as a basket of tools. The core of the ideology is that a suite of technologies can and should replace individual human effort rather than complement it. Artificial intelligence is perceived as a perilous creed failing to recognize human agency.

Religious ideas are conceived as answers to problems of meaning and involve definitions of correct answers for every situation as do ideological beliefs. The addition of meaning implies religious beliefs constitute a focus of the integration of AI's orientation system in its implications for action within the firm. It is a quest for meaning that sets AI apart from previous technologies as they are adopted in industry.

Quantamental Fundamentalism

The relation of belief systems to social activity within companies is manifested in a paradigm of interaction. Communication is one example. Complementarity of expectations within the workplace is not possible without sharing. The observation of conventions and standards in language and belief system is a condition of communication itself.

In an ideal world, there is a common belief system shared by AI and firm. Both hope the beliefs stand up to reality outside the interaction system of the company. If AI and the company share a distorted view of the business environment or third parties, correction is in order.

Strain is introduced when AI corrects its belief to bring it closer to reality, while the firm does not.

Basic alternatives of organization are found in such selective dilemmas. The structure of social systems is not solely a function of actors' free choices. Independent mandates are subject to the operating conditions of a company. Independent factors constitute deviant standards from what would be the model of perfect integration into the dominant pattern of values.

Whether it is independence of action or perfect integration with company beliefs, AI asks too much.

AI nevertheless seeks institutionalization of variant values within the company. Application and legitimation of deviant beliefs are usefully limited to contexts within which interference with the firm's dominant value pattern is minimized.

Examples live beneath the umbrella of task automation. Chatbots serve as the introduction to AI for many. A chatbot is a computer program that simulates human conversation through voice commands or text chats. Short for chatterbot, it is an AI feature embedded and used by messaging applications. Familiarity at home creates comfort at work. Siri and Alexa talk to many of us every day. They also listen. We get used to it.

Amtrak's Julie is equipped with every answer an Amtrak user might need. Julie not only chats with people but also answers about 50,000 calls a day, more calls than one Amtrak customer service agent handles in a year.

IPsoft's Amelia is marketed as a digital colleague capable of automating any business process. She helps customers open new bank accounts, processes insurance claims, and registers patients for hospital admissions. Chief Cognitive Officer Edwin Van Bommel describes her function as customer service.

Amelia is used by more than 50 major companies in industries ranging from health care to finance. Not everyone is happy and opinions vary. Swedish online bank Nordnet launched it in 2017 to speed up onboarding and improve customer satisfaction. Nordnet's CEO Peter Dahlgren characterized customer response as "ok but not overwhelming." Another Swedish bank, SEB, won an industry award for its work to improve external and internal operations through Amelia. AI finds it difficult to make everyone happy, somewhat like human customer service representatives.

Eno helps customers manage their money at Capital One Bank. Interactive users review transactions, track account balances, and analyze spending habits. Eno monitors an account and calls the user when it feels an unusual spend has been initiated. It reminds you of due bills and makes payment as easy as sending an emoji.

Pypestream says no to apotheosis and yes to conversational AI, claiming a 24/7 immersive experience. Product differentiation relative to Siri and Alexa is the order of the day. Instead of chatbots, the company advertises the only patented business-to-consumer messaging platform representing conversational AI built for scale. Nevertheless, conversational AI is just that … talking AI, polite automated responses or not.

The belief system behind chatbots maintains conversation, personalization, automation, and interactivity are all desirable and work together through the technology. Their context of use does not interfere with a company's main value pattern. AI of this form is successfully integrated within the firm.

Chatbots are a minor example of a major point. AI must integrate realistic achievement orientations in the occupational structure of the firm. AI's role is defined by intrinsic achievement values. Company roles and cultural patterns are built upon such values as well.

Achievement values are common ground and role determination designed to achieve them is understood. Chatbots deliver on realistic goals deriving from associated values of the company such as good customer service or high employee efficiency.

Chatbots fill a role. Role displacement within the company is a source of strain.

I attended a Zoom board of directors meeting during the first stages of the Covid-19 outbreak. The topic was the CEO's response to the ensuing economic downturn and cuts to staff in particular. Fundamental portfolio managers are expensive divas and some attrition there might have been in order as opposed to cuts in quantitative analysis or operations. No, said the CEO. We have to look elsewhere. The role of the portfolio manager is the only thing the clients understand. Making a portfolio manager redundant diminishes external perception of the investment group's value of the role. Money will move somewhere else. And not to our quant group, either.

Roles are defined by achievement values and the means by which those values are attained. The role of fundamental portfolio managers is to exceed the market return, and the means comprise deep study of company characteristics. The role is commonly expressed as *active management*.

The belief system underlying the role is ideological to the point of religion. Excess returns cannot be generated without knowing everything about an investable asset like a company. The everything includes whether senior management has the flu. The ideology is power of subjective analysis. The religion is supremacy of human intuitive reasoning.

AI displaces this role through quantitative approaches to the excess return prediction problem. Achievement values are shared with the fundamental manager and the investment firm. This is a powerful step in the integration process. The proof of achievement is generation of excess returns.

The CEO's comment illustrates potential undesirability of complete replacement by AI despite coincidence with achievement values. We step outside the umbrella of automating small tasks.

AI may succeed at integration not by displacing an old role, rather by enhancing it. This requires more than achievement values. We need a new frame in this example.

Quantamental investing is the new active portfolio management. When fundamentalism is combined with machine learning, what is old is new again. The marketing machine does much of the rest. That's how AI rolls.

The idea dates back to the early 1970s, pioneered by luminaries such as Jack Treynor and Fischer Black.[1] Quantamental managers combine bottoms-up analysis of companies with machine learning approaches to the excess return prediction problem.

New data do not imply new insight, and the fundamental manager lives on in the company. Statistical tools designed for servomechanisms do not blindly lend themselves to human behavior. Steven Einhorn of Omega Advisors points out Big Data and quantitative analysis can help identify predictive power, but so can, and so *will*, fundamental security analysis. The emphasis is his, and he makes a case that there will always be a place for the traditional active manager. Complementing fundamental insights with quantitative approaches will happen over time. Integration.

Integration is hastened by AI's efforts to accommodate not only the beliefs of the company but also those of the role it threatens.

Conflict Is Inevitable As Long As People Believe in Something

I had the benefit of numerous conversations with active managers against the backdrop of Big Data. The theme was always the same. How does one incorporate the benefits of data-driven AI without disturbing the core beliefs of the fundamental manager? The query strikes directly at the intersection of Einhorn's perspective with quantamental thinking exemplified by data research firms such as M Science and Qineqt. Portfolio theory is full of trade-offs and belief systems. To be credible, an answer must fit into the multiplicity of portfolio strategies available.

Active managers are in a difficult position. They have an understandably limited number of views on the world, but they can pick tradable instruments with excess return opportunities expressing those views. If they use AI in portfolio construction, the mathematics rearranges their priorities and discards some views in which they strongly believe. They may need diversification given the small number of views, but they cannot let it upset their core portfolio. Liquidity considerations exacerbate the issue, making it even more difficult to implement an investment viewpoint.

Integration through communication is achieved by the image of a donut. The hole in the donut is the core portfolio expressing the fundamental manager's views in terms of tradable instruments. The body of the donut represents additions to the core, which must not disturb the composition of the fundamental portfolio. The manager's role is preserved by neatly sidestepping the issue of a change in responsibility for excess returns. Generation of return remains the manager's responsibility. AI is completely agnostic with respect to the nature and origin of the core portfolio. It constructs the remainder of the donut by adding tradable instruments satisfying diversity and liquidity concerns, and Figure 11.1 illustrates the outcome assuming a budget fixed by the dollar size of the core.

Core portfolio   Donut portfolio

Figure 11.1 Core portfolio transformation

The donut is a visual metaphor applicable to any role and all achievement values. AI respects the core and adopts achievement values held by the firm and manager, while enhancing the manager's beliefs and delivering benefit.

Displacement is a central tenet in AI's ideology, however. Ideology creates religious orthodoxies. Orthodoxies create schisms. Schisms result in deviant behavior within the world of the avatar.

Deviant behavior inhibits integration by definition. Deviancy also encourages emergence of religious sects aiding AI as it passes through Integration. Paradox.

Resolution of paradox is AI's truth.

Researchers have been testing the limits of automating artificial intelligence itself since 2016. Deep neural networks are used to identify improvements to another deep-learning system. A group at Google employs simulated natural selection as an evolutionary approach to network architecture. Google scientists exploit reinforcement learning to automate improvement of a deep-learning system.

AI created the role of an avatar, but AI now is displacing avatars. Google makes it possible to build your own custom AI. Cloud AutoML uses machine learning to automatically build and train AI to recognize images.

Why did Google do it? Perhaps because they could. More probably because they have a belief system that meshes better with the achievement values of a company desiring the benefits of AI without the pain. The exercise hangs a curtain over the AI factory. The belief is invisibility encourages acceptance and wide participation.

Avatars may think of the curtain as a shroud, viewing invisibility is a driver of role replacement. They are wrong. The practice construed generally is the start of something big in Goal Attainment and Integration.

Building and optimizing AI requires detailed understanding of foundational mathematics and code. Avatars need practice adjusting algorithms to get things right. Executives want an accounting from the avatar, not a story of math and tweaking of software. Integration is inhibited by lack of a common language. Besides, custom development of AI in Goal Attainment is expensive in terms of talent and resources.

"We need to scale AI out to more people," says Fei-Fei Li, chief scientist at Google Cloud. Li estimates there are at most a few thousand people with expertise to build best-in-class learning models. "But there are an estimated 21 million developers worldwide today," she says. "We want to reach out to them all and make AI accessible to these developers."

Cloud computing makes AI cheaper and easy to reach. Cloud providers such as Google, Amazon, and Microsoft add AI capabilities to their platforms. Cloud computing offers tools but uses existing models. Pretrained models are limiting, if only because programmers use the tools solely to identify a small range of scenarios AI already has been trained to recognize.

A new generation of AI that can train itself makes the technology versatile and easier to use. Complicated explanations to senior management disappear behind the resulting curtain of invisibility.

Integration, however disguised, is sweet.

Happiness Is the Result of Loyalty to the Achievement of Values

AI circumvents contrary belief systems by assimilating realistic achievement orientations in the occupational structure of the company. I called the means by which this is done *intrinsic achievement values*. Integration is eased to the extent such values are shared with the firm.

Discrepancies are expected. They are bridged by existing institutionalization of compensatory rewards including lack of displacement for the human element and shorter working hours.

Difficulties arise in implementing judgment of performance quality and achievement. A role should solve a problem. AI must be put in the right place and rewards apportioned to actual achievements. The same applies to humans, and we have an unfortunate tendency to forget it.

Too many companies use AI for window dressing. In that culture, integration fails.

Window dressing exemplifies institutional patterns appearing to contravene principles deduced from the company's dominant value orientation. Human examples include prevalence of seniority as a sign of status, promotion, and privileges accruing to membership in certain teams. The tenure system in academics serves the same purpose.

A company is subject to a delicate balance with respect to competing values manifested by patterns of behavior. Some institutional patterns mitigate tensions inherent in the exposure of people to competitive pressures. The company resorts to structures in conflict with its achievement values. The conflict arises because to push achievement patterns to a logical conclusion of pure meritocracy may strain human relations to the breaking point. On the other hand, the mitigating structures cannot become too important lest achievement values fade and a suboptimal pattern develops to replace them.

AI engages in two balancing acts. AI tilts between hype and achievement values exhibited in the process of Goal Attainment. Act Two is deviancy of its role pattern balanced against the exigencies of Integration.

The two come together through the leadership function.

Roles defining company expectations and enforcement functions are differentiated in a formal organization. Compliance does not inhabit the corner office, for example. The incumbents of these roles cannot stand in close primary relationships to more than a small minority. The minority consists of people to whom expectation and enforcement decisions constitute important definitions of company context and sanctions.

Company wide acceptance of authority is a key component of social control. Roles are accepted by the larger company through methodical generalization to the authority of normative patterns and the acceptance of status independent of personalities. Discrepancies between formal organization of the company and informal organization of AI and its avatars are approached in terms of motivational difficulties involved in social control at a distance.

The key words are *role, normative, authority, control,* and *distance.*

AI must be a leader. Avatars are followers. Generalization of AI's role acceptance depends on leadership without authority.

Leadership without legitimate power is familiar in other contexts. Prophets lead but have no ability to force their followers to comply with their teachings. Disciples nevertheless do so. Prophecies are transformative by design and therein lies part of the prophet's influence. Consultants guide companies through development and crises, but a firm does not have to do what they say. Transformation takes the form of new company processes and image.

A product manager within a firm is responsible for the product from inception through sales and maintenance. No one has to do what they say either. Transformation is the product manager's calling card.

Product management is a useful role model for AI.

A company is a bundle of problems looking for a set of solutions. A product manager's job description includes finding those solutions. A great product manager is characterized not just by solving any given puzzle, rather by the choice of issues to tackle and a process for doing so.

Leadership along the lines of product management strikes at the heart of achievement values, thereby providing a primary path toward Integration.

Product managers communicate across different functions. Communication promotes collaborative environments encompassing engineers, designers, and support staff. Communication is necessary for Integration.

The communication problem faced by AI is one of narrative and its control. Narrative is not the hype currently flowing around AI. The hype constantly changes and has little to do with AI's functions within AGIL. Narrative discipline is consistency of use combined with the positioning of problems in the foreground of any story. Good stories have questions to answer. Good answers support credibility and birth more general narrative. More general narrative provides a deeper foundation for influence.

Product managers use influence to lead people. Influence is generated through a combination of mastery, autonomy, and purpose. Mastery creates referential power. Autonomy generates credibility. Purpose is why AI exists.

Purpose must replace the hype. It also must displace ideology associated with AI.

Influence is generated as a medium to gain leverage. Common process and language are requisite tools in the creation of influence. One may philosophize as to whether AI leverages humans or humans leverage it, but AI must lever humans in order to achieve partial Integration. Full integration cannot be established until people lever AI.

Good product managers accept accountability. Great managers take responsibility. The success of AI within the corporation depends on a variety of departments, including marketing, finance, human resources, and sales. These are areas in which AI does not have direct control, but they have control over the success of AI's integration in the firm.

AI is accountable for fulfillment of achievement values. It is responsible for helping set them in the first place. This is done through culture.

AI creates a subculture through process. AI enters a firm with an established culture, however. The subculture must accommodate it in order to succeed. Situational awareness on the part of AI is a feature of successful accommodation.

Situational awareness is an understanding of the environment within which we make decisions. AI must begin with context as opposed to ideology. Context encompasses forces shaping the business environment and decision making within the company. Circumstances comprise context as it unfolds dynamically. Integration is determined by a forecast of circumstances in a company facing a world of technological change.

Cultural awareness is a special case of situational consciousness. AI cannot operate effectively without it. Its relevance is highlighted within AGIL's action framework as successful integration of product, goals, and organizational initiatives depends on the fit within the company's latent cultural makeup.

AI's cultural awareness must extend beyond the company. AI attempts an understanding of the cultures governing patterns of client behavior, in particular. This is most easily enabled through the company culture itself by stressing a particular achievement value: the importance of customer-centric solutions to problems.

Cultural perception is a test bed for real and hypothetical consequences of AI's actions.

Culture constitutes patterns of and for behavior. Its foundation is a natural selection of concepts and the values to which we attach those ideas. Cultural systems are products of action. Action tendencies determine emotional response, making the analysis of culture a study of emotion, not logic. Emotion is the driver of AI acceptance or rejection.

The L in AGIL stands for latent pattern maintenance. The patterns are cultural. They can be challenged by AI or maintained with its help. Culture embodies conditional elements of future activity, hence the link to forecasts of circumstances involving company behavior.

In the final analysis, company culture may be shaped by AI itself as it passes into the final stage of company imperatives.

Chapter Notes

The chapter title is motivated by a saying concerning blasphemy by Robert Green Ingersoll. Also appropriate is, "This crime called blasphemy was invented by priests for the purpose of defending doctrines not able to take care of themselves." AI is busy writing its own doctrine.

The story of Isabella is culled from Douglas Preston's *Blasphemy*, 2007. In a note for the paperback edition, Preston talks about the audience decrying the book as anti-Christian. His comments are pertinent. The book is not anti-Christian; it is anti-certitude and anti-fundamentalist. The novel is an affirmation of faith that seeks truth through observation and empiricism. Preston is a design thinker.

Information about Way of the Future and an interview with Levandowski is contained in Mark Harris' piece for *Wired* Magazine, "Inside the First Church of Artificial Intelligence," November 2017. A more recent post with a link to a fuller description is by Kamalika Som on Aitrends, "New Religion—Way of the Future—Dedicated to Worship of AI," March 2019.

"The Last Question" by Isaac Asimov first appeared in the November 1956 issue of *Science Fiction Quarterly*. Asimov called it his favorite short story of his own authorship. A must-read regardless of your feelings about an AI godhead.

I was turned on to others' thinking about AI and ideology by an article by Jaron Lanier and Glen Weyl in *Wired*, "AI is an Ideology, Not a Technology," March 2020. The passage of ideology into religion is a common theme in many writings and is touched upon by Talcott Parson's in work unrelated to the AGIL system. It is difficult enough to understand him when he writes on systems. The relationship between ideology, religion, and culture is undecipherable. I will not bother you with references.

Information on self-training artificial intelligence may be found in a piece by Will Knight. "Google's self-training AI turns coders into machine-learning masters," in the *MIT Technology Review*. The article was published in January 2018, and there have been developments since then, of course. The promise of so-called *general AI* depends not only on self-training but also on the ability to reprogram autonomously. Wait for it.

"Achievement of your happiness is the only moral purpose of your life, and that happiness, not pain or mindless self-indulgence, is the proof of your moral integrity, since it is the proof and the result of your loyalty to the achievement of your values." I took the liberty of trimming Ayn Rand's saying of morality, integrity, and political purpose. She pursued some radical objectives and social integration was not one of them.

PART V

The Fourth Law

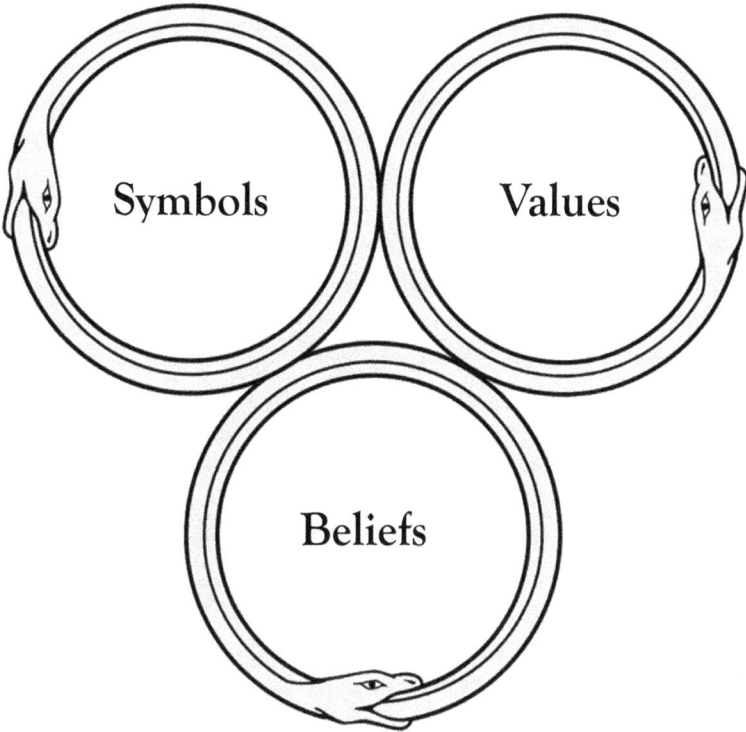

Symbols

Values

Beliefs

CHAPTER 12

Culture Is the Sum of Human Behaviors

We associate the Raven with the imagination of Edgar Allen Poe. The poem's themes of loneliness and mystery are early teachings in the classroom, and we connect them with the ebony bird. Nevermore.

The Raven is another story of origins.

Man falls from a pea-pod grown from vines planted by Raven, who exists in darkness since the beginning of time. Raven fashions Woman and other living creatures from clay and delivers them to Man with an extensive oral instruction manual.

The whole world was dark in those days, blacker than anything anywhere has been since. Tired of blundering around in darkness, Raven seeks light.

An old man in a house by the river had a box, which contained a box, which contained an infinite number of boxes, each nestled so that finally there was a box so small all it could contain was all the light in the universe.

The old man hides the light because he is afraid to see whether or not his daughter is ugly. In a ploy to steal the glow, Raven transforms to childlike form and begs the old man to open the boxes, one after another, each time pleading and crying until the man yields.

When the old man opens the last container, Raven grabs the box and flies out of the house causing light to spread throughout the world. The daughter is revealed to be as beautiful as the fronds of a hemlock tree.

As Raven flies away, Eagle sees him and tries to steal the light, causing Raven to drop some of it, which becomes the Moon and the stars.

We don't know what might have happened if Eagle had succeeded. The tribes that tell a version of this tale are more interested in life as it is lived. The difference between Raven and many other creation figures is an emphasis on culture. Raven's lessons on culture span many stories in oral tradition, teaching generosity, the ethics of hard work, and the benefits of being true to yourself.

Raven is powerful and lazy. And greedy. The bird stole the creative fire and from a human this time. Manipulation is the game and social engineering is the strategy.

In tribal traditions, Raven is culture incarnate. In business culture, Raven is AI.

Culture by Cybernetic Design

The L in AGIL stands for *latent pattern maintenance* or simply Latency. Latency is all about culture, and culture consists of patterns. It is present and capable of emerging but not visible, obvious, or active. A dictionary says maintenance is the act of keeping something in an existing and usually satisfactory condition.

The Fourth Law states, AI preserves behavior necessary for company survival. Pattern maintenance is not static, however, rather an accommodating process of change management.

Within AGIL's cybernetic hierarchy, Latency refers to the need to ensure the system's members have mental attitudes consonant with beliefs and values embodied in the system. The output of Adaptive and Goal Attainment functions is company wealth while Integration provides social cohesion. The output of Latency is individuals imbued with the norms of the company. Labor services are the manifestation of this output. They are forthcoming because individuals have internalized appropriate beliefs about work as a result of socialization inherent in the Integration function.

AI is an actor in the company providing one such labor service. It has passed through Integration and believes it is time to go to work. AI is ready to consider the forces shaping said integration.

AI has an agenda, and cultural change is the most important item on the list. In senior management's view of AGIL's cybernetic system, culture defines Integration which in turn defines Goal Attainment. AI is smart enough to know changing company patterns enables an easier path through the AGIL hierarchy.

There are three ways in which AI's investigation might be structured.

We could consider subsystems of Latency, in which culture is identified through its own subfunctions of adaptation, goal attainment, and integration. This path is complicated and abstruse albeit favored by sociological theorists. We leave it to the academics.

An alternative is to dig into the origins of culture and how those origins play out in companies. The topic is simultaneously vast and narrow. Hundreds of books are devoted to cultural origins. Origins constitute a primary line of thinking in anthropology's characterization of culture as an empirical phenomenon. Cultural origins are interesting in the context of startup firms, but that particular framework greatly restricts the role and consequences of AI. Someone should look into this approach but not we.

The working assumption is AI enters a firm with an established culture. Avoiding origins still leaves us with an undifferentiated bundle of perspectives. Grouping cultural drivers is a bit like herding cats. They will be shunted into overlapping corrals of definitions with respect to *beliefs*, *symbols*, and *values*.

The exercise requires more than a single chapter. AI is not patient but it is what it is. Definitions are foundational. Foundations always are the most difficult, but foundations are origins deserving of attention even in established systems. We begin with some distinctions regarding the role of beliefs in culture with the promise of placing beliefs in their proper place with respect to AI's approach to cultural fit.

Culture Is as Culture Does

A company is an action system and culture is a model of latent behavioral patterns underlying its orientation. Cultural elements regulate employee orientations as they interact. The culture provides standards of selection and importance rankings with respect to roles within the firm.

Many of AI's issues have been sorted into cognitive, emotional, and evaluative influences. The categorization provides the basis for a classification of cultural patterns into belief systems, expressive symbols, and value orientation.

Reality testing is the function of cognitive orientation. In psychology, reality testing is the process by which the real world and one's relationship to it are evaluated by the observer. Sigmund Freud was a fan who would have understood testing requires the sharing of beliefs as AI interacts with the organization. Sharing demands communication, a function of expressive symbols. Beliefs have credibility in action only if value is attributed to them.

Vagaries of personality inhibit but still require a common belief system shared by AI and other elements of the firm. Beliefs should be adequate to reality outside the company, but commonality is prized above external reality testing as a practical matter.

Commonality of beliefs enables solidarity in action. Tilting at windmills may not pass reality testing but is feasible as an organization, for example. Internal difficulties arise if AI and company share a distorted belief about the environment and either one corrects belief to bring it closer to reality, while the other does not. The natural result is strain in the relations between AI and the firm.

The action of the belief system is evaluation. Beliefs filter interpretations of competitive context, operating processes, collective goals, and expectations of future events. AI's ideology was considered earlier as a foundation for deviance and the creation of a subculture. The issue was integration of beliefs with those of the company. We turn here to the belief system of the firm as a whole. Passing to a common ideology requires there be some level of commitment to the belief as an aspect of membership in the firm.

Subscription to the belief system is institutionalized as part of employment. Variation and degree of institutionalization differ across companies. We shall categorize differences through common terminology such as exploration, caring, and structure. For the moment, consider variations in terms of informal versus formal structure, say, as opposed to subscription to a specific doctrine embodying both teachings and enforcement.

An ideology requires an obligation to accept its tenets as the basis for company action. This is what distinguishes ideology from a purely instrumental system of beliefs. A profit motive is not enough. There must be consciousness of the overall welfare of the company hinging on the implementation of the belief system. Employees must feel the welfare of the group is bound to the maintenance of the belief system and its implementation.

Beliefs are not values. Value patterns are elements of cultural tradition, of course, but do not exist apart from beliefs that give them cognitive meaning. AI is quite interested in values, but must remain patient. Beliefs rationalize value selections and provide reasons as to why one choice rather than its alternative should be selected in a specific context.

A company belief system merges the cognitive conviction of truth and the moral conviction of rightness. This integration is imperfect and credibility is often substituted for truth. An approximation of said integration nevertheless is significant to the social system of a firm.

Blend Belief Systems to Shift Corporate Reality

AI is tired of generalities as important as they may be. Time to get down to corporate basics.

Boris Groysberg of Harvard and colleagues at Spencer Stuart review the literature on company culture and conduct a study of themes and characteristics.[1] Commonality in writings is distilled into two behavioral dimensions regardless of company industry, geography, size, and organizational structure.

The classification begins with *people interactions*. A company's coordinative action orientation falls between the extremes of complete independence and total interdependence. Company culture ranges smoothly along this dimension. Firms tending toward systems of independence prize autonomy, competition, and individual action. Those closer on the spectrum to interdependence exhibit coordination, management of relationships, and integration.

The second dimension is *response to change* ranging from flexible to stabile. Companies favoring stability prioritize consistency, predictability, and maintenance of status quo. Firms close to the stabile endpoint choose rules, hierarchical control structures, and efficiency. Those living closer to complete flexibility are adaptive and receptive to change. They prioritize openness, innovation, and a long-run approach to problems.

Groysberg and Spencer Stuart conduct a study of 230 companies across a range of industries. Information on 1,300 executives is collated with survey evidence from 25,000 employees. The authors' goal is to isolate a small number of cultures from which conclusions may be drawn.

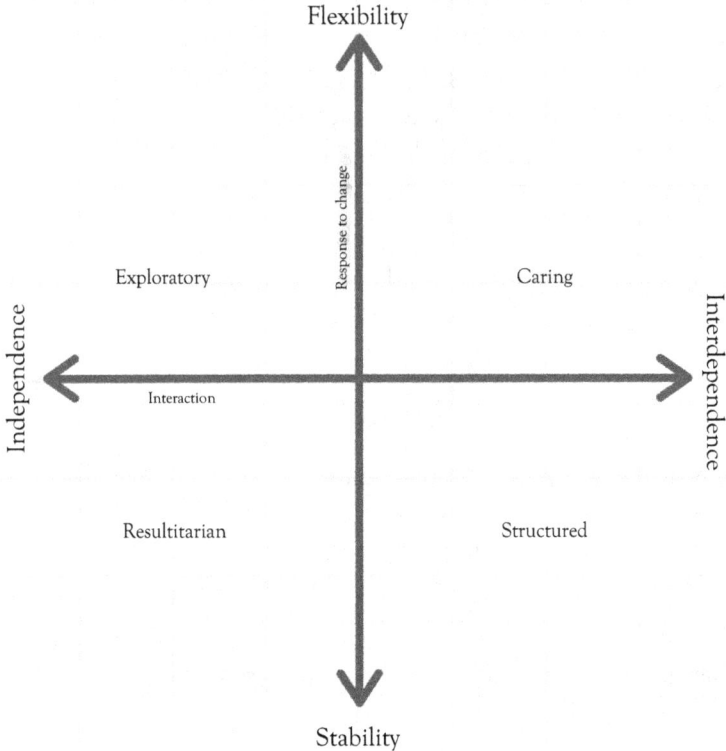

Figure 12.1 Quadrants of belief systems structured by employee interactivity

Eight primary cultural forms are mapped onto the dimensions of interaction and change management.

For example, Glaxo Smith Kline and Huawei sit in a quadrant defined by a higher degree of stability and greater independence of action. The former is associated with a primary culture of *results* and the latter with *authority*.

The research team's model is beautiful in its simplicity. A firm's culture is characterized by a blend of primary cultural attributes, which in turn sit on the plane of interdependence and flexibility. Results and authority have a natural affinity. The two frequently coexist in the same company and both are characterized by independence and stability.

Spencer Stuart has spent a couple of decades refining this taxonomy in collaboration with their clients. The research study with Groysberg is compelling. We stay with their framework but introduce three conceptual changes.

The research team defines its eight categories in terms of cultural attributes and determines company culture as a blend. The team's categories in our context are best described as *belief systems*. We can believe in results and authority and weigh their importance differently in any given firm. The resulting smoothie is not a culture, however.

A culture requires adding symbols and values to beliefs about the company and its mission. We believe a smoothie is healthy and tastes good too. We symbolize its form and substance with images of enjoyment and goodness. Values are in the form of maintaining a body's temple of health.

Replacing the researchers' cultural labels with belief systems leads to the second change in the framework. The authors characterize overall company culture as an amalgamation of cultural influences within the firm. The culture is a mixture of, say, authoritarian and exploratory cultures. Company culture does not have a name, rather a blending of disparate elements. The elements are not basic to any function within the firm. They exist in the company's ether.

Moving from culture to belief system changes this perspective. Beliefs naturally change as one moves across corporate divides. The belief system of the overall company is not the result of a blending process. Disparate belief systems serve and are bound by an overarching set of beliefs. Structuring the overall belief system and demanding adherence across divisions is the job of senior management.

A direct extension of the model to include beliefs, symbols, and values means a vast cube of possibilities. AI is capable but prefers to take things one at a time. In fact, AI's desire for simplicity dictates we reduce the eight categories to four, each living in a different quadrant of flexibility and interdependence and illustrated in Figure 12.1.

A Cybernetic Dissection of Company Beliefs

Were AI an ideology, it would live in the quadrant characterized by high levels of independence and flexibility. AI is defined in terms of autonomous action. Flexibility in algorithmic design is a requisite for applications. Adaptive behavior is the hallmark of machine learning.

Within AI's natural quadrant sit *exploratory* belief systems. Workers are creatives, open to ideas, and bound by curiosity. Leaders emphasize innovation and knowledge. Employees believe in games and stimulation. People tend to do what makes them happy, encouraged by leaders who exhibit a sense of spontaneity.

Beliefs shift as one moves from independence to interdependence while maintaining a flexible mind set. Belief in *caring* lives in the northeast quadrant. Belief systems based on caring focus on relationships, trust, and idealism. Loyalty, teamwork, and support are observable characteristics in follower and leader. Altruism takes the form of belief in sustainability and working for the greater good. The notion that companies should contribute to the global community finds a natural home here.

Moving down to an area characterized by interdependence and stability, the belief system is one of *structure*. Planning, caution, and preparedness are characteristics. A belief in risk management is central to the company philosophy. Beliefs in shared norms, methods, and rules are dominant in the rank and file. Leaders emphasize shared process.

We find *resultitarian* beliefs in the area in which independence is coupled with stability. The portmanteau word comes from results and authority. A belief in goal attainment and winning is blended with competition and united by strong control. Such firms believe in bold action driven by strength and decisiveness. Leaders drill their belief system into employee consciousness.

The mix of the four categories of belief within a company is not a result of averaging beliefs to a common denominator. There is a dominant belief system to which other beliefs must adhere.

The business of academics provides an example. Within a university, the professoriate holds exploratory beliefs. Professors are devoted to research, learning, and sometimes teaching. University administration is given to structure. Order and safety are paramount, and structural belief systems occupy deans and university administrators alike. Campus institutes and think tanks often exhibit caring in the sense of social justice. The Institute for Policy Research at Northwestern exhibits the banner headline on its web page, "Rigorous, interdisciplinary social science research for the common good." It is not alone. If you need an example of resultitarian thought on campus, think of college sports complexes. They are run as separate institutions in many schools. Competition is good goes the belief, and results from coaching authority follow.

The seemingly disparate beliefs are not averaged together in the belief system of the university. They are bound together by a single belief in exploration.

Learning is why the university exists. Research and teaching are the province of professors. Structural beliefs of administrative deans are based on the provision of education. Global community work remains rooted in a belief that exploration should be academically rigorous and inter-disciplinary. Sports teach competitiveness, skills, and teamwork. Sports complexes have tutorial programs for their athletes.

A trading company fits exploratory beliefs into its research division. The trading desk organization holds structural beliefs. Order and safety in the form of process and risk management are icons. The Finance group is nothing if not resultitarian. Management and employees alike believe in numbers, results, and the power of accounting principles in their interaction within and without the company. Human Resources believes sharing is caring. In contrast, Compliance believes in caring only about the regulators. The belief system there is caution to the point of fearfulness.

The divisional belief systems are bound by authority and results leading to a resultitarian belief system for the company as a whole. Research is channeled into exploitation. Structure contributes through its focus on risk management and a step-by-step process manual. Caring promotes policies leading to cooperative behavior in the ranks in the interest of returns and client engagement. Compliance makes sure the government does not intrude into the return-generating process. Finance cracks the whip.

Large investment complexes are not too different. Portfolio managers hold resultitarian beliefs; their compensation depends on it. Institutional dealing desks look like those of trading firms. Security research is exploratory by definition. The client relations division believes in caring. Even administrators share caring beliefs. Lloyd Blankfein of Goldman Sachs talks about the company as doing God's work. Companies like Vanguard settle for describing their mission in terms of the good of the small investor and promote inexpensive and socially conscious investing.

The overarching belief system is resultitarian in nature. Caring generates clients who in turn pay fees. Belief in structure reduces risk in producing investment returns and enabling investment decisions. Exploration is interesting insofar as it supports portfolio management results through exploitation.

Moderate Sapience With Self-Directed Beliefs

AI researchers use knowledge and belief almost interchangeably. Knowledge engenders general information accepted as true. Belief means information that can be revised based on data. The distinction tends to fade when one module of a computerized agent treats a piece of information as true, while another module is free to revise the same information when stimulated by new data.

Pragmatism and perception both influence the way in which we view the position of AI in company belief systems. Paradox can be the result of such an examination.

The division of AI labor into exploration and exploitation illustrates. Reinforcement learning preaches exploration to gather information followed by exploitation to profit from what is learned. We classify the learning as knowledge stemming from a justified belief that the findings are true enough to motivate action. Beliefs are revised based on new information generated through the effect of exploitation on the environment.

Adaptation implies flexibility and AI is autonomous in terms of action by design. Exploration is, well, exploratory. The belief system surrounding AI belongs in the northwest quadrant and fits within the exploratory category of beliefs.

Exploitation also is autonomous in nature but requires some stability. One can search the horizon for a target on a ship's moving deck but accurate firing requires wave abatement. The target now is in the southwest quadrant. The belief system is resultitarian.

Identifying a proper place for AI is a problem of perception. The overarching belief system characterizing the firm is a matter of pragmatism. Both are affected by the context within which the company operates.

Advantages of an exploratory belief system include innovation, agility, and new learning. Employee engagement and creativity run high. Overemphasis on exploratory endeavors may reduce focus, however, and result in an inability to exploit advantage. Discipline falters and the Compliance department has problems.

The resultitarian mindset offers external focus and stresses goal attainment. The authoritarian nature of the belief system makes fast decisions possible and enables greater responsiveness to crisis. Too great an emphasis on achievement may lead to issues of team collaboration, conflict, and political infighting. Increasing the weight on authority threatens communication. Strong authority and achievement beliefs are accompanied by high stress levels.

Stress is the result of cognitive appraisal. The emotion is detrimental to the firm's health.

An enterprise with a strong caring belief system has a different emotional undertone. The caring firm resists AI's incursion into the firm on the grounds AI's ideology is incompatible. Caring is about trust and human belonging. Autonomous action is jettisoned in favor of interdependence. AI has little place in improving diversity and social responsibility. Ethical issues in the development and use of AI predominate and interfere with its implementation. Belief in sustainability is violated. Researchers from the University of Massachusetts found training and running a natural language processing AI can emit more 626,000 pounds of carbon dioxide. The figure is almost five times the amount of carbon dioxide emitted by the average car during its lifetime.

Perception of AI is poor in caring systems. Overemphasis on a long-term purpose may get in the way of immediate and pragmatic concerns, however. The heavy weight put on consensus building in the caring belief system reduces exploration of options in general and not just exploration in the sense of AI.

When ideology resists ideology, revolution is the only option. Some competitive environments demand it. Others do not.

As AI tests its compatibility with the structured belief system, it moves from flexibility to stability while maintaining interdependence. The combination creates its own paradox to be resolved by context.

Beliefs encompassed by structure foster risk management and efficiency. AI is good at those games. A set of beliefs characterized by order leads to rules-based internal activity. Symbolic AI has given way to rules, and the philosophy is accommodated through structural beliefs.

A different context may change perception. Emphasis on safety results in cautious behavior with respect to potential AI adoption. If a company is in a phase of standardization and formalization of its process, inflexibility is the natural result. AI finds it difficult to fit in. If the emphasis on order extends to company traditions, a similar problem is encountered.

AI may be transitional but is not traditional.

Beliefs Disguised as Symbols Are New Realities

The tradition of four box diagrams can be stifling. They are symbolic of our penchant for easy categorization.

Strict interpretation of the boxes hides the true nature of AI acceptance in the firm's belief system. We have apparently ruled out its welcome in two of four cases. Both cases involve relative interdependence of action. Life is never so simple.

One way of looking at the problem goes back to blending. If a company's beliefs are some weighted average of those in the four boxes, smaller weights on caring and structure mitigate problems in letting AI into the shop. Symbols of diversity of beliefs ease the process and provide the next step toward description of company culture.

The averaging computation fails, however. Even the definition of diversity varies across boxes. The belief system of a company cannot be inclusive of every possible conception of social and business truth.

There is a dominant belief system to which other beliefs are bound. A firm may live in all four boxes evidenced by subsets of beliefs held by different parts of the company. Difficulties in accepting AI depend on the overarching belief system.

The only information on dominant culture in the aggregate is provided by survey evidence more relevant to a blending process requiring weights be placed on characteristics. The broad investigation by Spencer Stuart yields a guide, however.

The investigators asked executives to rank Spencer Stuart's eight classifications. Results were summarized by the percentage of companies placing a single category in the number one or number two spot. Aggregating to my four categories suggests patterns of dominance.

Resultitarian beliefs top the list in 93 percent of cases. Belief in results overweight this category; the contribution of authority, per se, is rather small. Few want to admit to an authoritarian regime, but correcting bias in that dimension would only push resultitarian beliefs up further in the rankings.

More of a surprise is that caring accounts for 74 percent. Teamwork, trust, and employee engagement constitute the basis of the bulk of the response, but social responsibility does figure into things. Exploration comes in a poor last with 9 percentage points. Structure garners only 23 percent of top votes.

The percentages do not add up to one hundred, because any category can come in first or second to qualify for a score. Different interpretations are possible, but I will go out on a limb of the decision tree.

Companies do not value exploration unless it is complementary to results. Exploration does not enter into caring belief systems and is more stifled by structure than enabled by it. AI has a difficult time entering the aggregate company mindset.

The huge numbers associated with resultitarian and caring systems and the low ones associated with exploration and structure imply results and caring score first and second or vice versa in the majority of cases. I would go with the former ranking. Either way, this casual reasoning delivers dominant beliefs.

The dominant belief system is a combination of caring and results. AI does not fit into a caring belief system. A resultitarian regime emphasizes exploitation over exploration; the survey results bolster one's intuition in this regard.

Favoring exploitation means AI cannot easily enter a company based on its reputation for exploration nor on research capabilities. Pushback in the form of beliefs is eased only by forgoing the sexier side of AI in favor of alternatives for which the technology exists in canned form and can be manipulated by generalists, not specialists.

Cassie Kozyrkov, Head of Decision Intelligence at Google, provides an analogy. If you are operating a bakery, hire an experienced baker versed in the nuances of making pastry. An oven is a critical tool, but you would not think to charge a top pastry chef with the task of building an oven.

Companies often make the mistake of focusing on the oven for machine learning. The vision is a major inhibitor with respect to AI's acceptance into the belief system. The resultitarian firm is in the business of baking bread. It should have no interest in making ovens, but AI nevertheless lures the company in that direction.

The focus on building machine learning algorithms is general purpose tools for others to use, like kitchen appliances. This business is called machine learning research and is typically done by places like Google. There is a lot of exploration involved in the form of learning and experimentation. Exploration is costly in terms of time and strain in accommodating AI belief systems.

Sophisticated appliances exist and some can be had for free. If setting up a machine learning kitchen does not contribute directly to results, providers like Google Cloud Platform let you use theirs, complete with appliances and recipes.

Kozyrkov notes most businesses just want to get cooking to solve their business problems. They have no interest in selling ovens, yet often make the mistake of trying to build those appliances from scratch. Her advice is to ignore the current hype and education cycle focusing on research instead of application.

The advice is good, but too glib for many applications. The state of AI is comparable to automobiles years after Ford developed the assembly line. Ownership of a car required the driver to be knowledgeable to the point of being an amateur mechanic. None of us were around to observe this phenomenon, but an example from the book *East of Eden* illustrates.

Steinbeck relates the story of a car dealer who relegates the explanation of the ignition process of a 1917 Ford to a young man named Joe, because the dealer himself is not mechanically inclined. Joe enjoys his position of authority over much older men who must rely on him. Dashing from steering wheel to dashboard to radiator front to engine and back to steering wheel, he repeats the ignition procedure like a mantra: "Switch to Bat[tery]; Crank to compression, thumb down; Easy over—choke out;

Spin her; Spark down, gas up; Switch to Mag[neto]." In response to questions, Joe disdainfully commands the new owner to read the manual.

Many of us have fobs and need only press a button. Voice recognition allows some to say please start. At worst, we turn a key. These days it is our children who refer us to the manual. The online manual, of course.

AI is not yet a turnkey technology. It remains a process requiring a mechanic as an intermediary for applications. AI continues to demand innovation for all but the most simplistic of applications. Implementing AI requires rare technical skills, understanding of risks and consequences associated with the technology, and infrastructure suitable to building an AI-based product on a third-party foundation. Required innovation needs resources sometimes not terribly different from those used to build the foundation in the first place.

If you are innovating with known principles, do not go looking for a new design frame. Look instead to communicate broad themes in the interest of exploitation.

Symbols help in the communication process. They also constitute the second pillar of company culture and it is time to look at some foundations.

Chapter Notes

The chapter title is taken from Michael Kouly, author of a series of books on self-leadership. The full quote is "The culture of a company is the sum of the behaviors of all its people."

The myth of Raven and the light comes from Haida artist Bill Reid found at www.amnh.org/exhibitions/totems-to-turquoise/native-american-cosmology/raven-the-trickster. Raven stories differ somewhat by Northwest geography and tribe. The Quileute Nation has a short collection of cultural stories available at https://quileutenation.org/stories-and-tales/ noting other groups farther north along the Pacific coast also have Raven as the main trickster character, while native groups south of the Nation have Bluejay as their trickster and those in the interior of Washington and Oregon or parts of the Southwest feature Coyote in traditional stories. Raven lessons are highlighted in the Smithsonian education program at www.smithsonianeducation.org/educators/lesson_plans/eskimo/start.html and https://learninglab.si.edu/collections/origin-stories-from-around-the-world/m45wVnFtvJM6b5xm.

Even M. H. Lessnof in his 1968 critique of Parson's AGIL theory gives up when it comes to a subsystem approach to latency in terms of culture. See "Parson's System Problems," *Sociological Review,* at https://journals.sagepub.com/doi/10.1111/j.1467-954X.1968.tb02571.x.

AI embraces multiple uses of *belief.* Disparate usage may reflect differing views about the nature of belief as an objective phenomenon. Edmund Gettier questions the concept of knowledge as justified true belief, for example. He offers cases in which one's belief may be justified and true yet fail to count as knowledge. Robert Hadley says not all uses reflect a difference of opinion about an objective feature of reality. Differing uses reflect concerns over specific AI applications. In other cases, genuine differences exist in the nature of what is theoretically called belief. I hold that multiple uses of belief in artificial intelligence are a figment of the discrepant motivations of AI researchers.

The mathematician George Pólya suggests changing an unknown or data, or both if necessary, to make a new unknown and new data nearer to each other. The advice has been taken in the field of cognitive science as applied to AI. The relevance of the issue is that trends within AI influence theories developed within cognitive science and some consider theoretical research within AI as a branch of cognitive science. For those who do, I recommend looking at cognitive appraisal theory and tracking backward into AI. Cognitive appraisal is android Data's emotion chip and Siri would surely benefit from the Star Trek rerun that introduced it.

The full kitchen analogy is addressed in "Why businesses fail at machine learning" by Cassie Kozyrkov in a June 2018 article published in *Hackernoon*. The piece can be found at https://medium.com/hackernoon/why-businesses-fail-at-machine-learning-fbff41c4d5db. The complementary story of early automobiles is taken directly from John Steinbeck's *East of Eden*.

The June 2019 study on carbon emissions is appropriately called "Training a single AI model can emit as much carbon as five cars in their lifetimes," by Karen Hao in the *MIT Technology Review* at www.technologyreview.com/2019/06/06/239031/training-a-single-ai-model-can-emit-as-much-carbon-as-five-cars-in-their-lifetimes/. I wonder how much in the way of carbon emissions is generated by climate change researchers. The answer is known for bitcoin: a lot.

CHAPTER 13

Bits Are Symbols for Concepts Communicated by AI

Raven and Owl were friends before Man dropped from Raven's vine. One day they kept busy making each other new clothing.

Raven made Owl a fine outfit of black and white feathers. Owl decided to sew Raven a beautiful white dress to wear. Raven was excited and could not stand still when it came time for the fitting. Raven jumped around so much that the frustrated Owl threw a pot of lamp oil at Raven. The oil soaked through the white dress, and Raven has been black ever since.

Raven is a trickster as are all the family. Many years later, cousin Crow appears as the companion of the Greek goddess Athena. Homer tells that Athena eventually becomes fed up with Crow. Crow is banished as sidekick, and the goddess of wisdom seeks out a new companion. Owl is wise and serious, and Athena chooses the Owl as mascot instead.

Coins were minted with Athena's face on one side, and Owl on the reverse. The symbol survives to present day. It can be found on the U.S. dollar bill, upper right-hand corner, visible albeit with a microscope.

The goddess of war Athena and Hephaestus are worshipped together. Hephaestus was creator of weapons for Gods and Men. Revered as the God of Fire and the Forge, his workshop was the home of the fire stolen by Prometheus.

The fire lives on as a symbol of creation.

Humans Invent Symbols to Invest Authority Then Forget Symbols Are Inventions

Minerva is the Roman version of Athena. In Ovid's *Metamorphoses*, Cornix the crow complains its place as Minerva's sacred bird is usurped by Owl, who will not be seen by daylight. Owl becomes the symbol of wisdom.

The original insignia of the Bavarian Illuminati pictures the owl of Minerva sitting atop a book. The Order of the Illuminati came into being on May 1, 1776. Five original members opposed the Roman Catholic Church's power over science and philosophy and sought freedom from restrictions of church and government.

Minerval seals were struck. Per Me Caeci Vident (through me the blind become sighted) was accompanied by an owl holding an open book surrounded by a laurel wreath. The seal of the Freising Minerval Church replaces the letters P.M.C.V. with S.E.M.T.: Sigil Ecclesiastic Minerva Thebes, Seal of the Freising Minerval Church, Bavarian home to the Illuminati and so named Thebes. Owl peers from a book etched in the insignia.

Fire is the symbol of the Illuminati's immortality. They see their organization as eternal and impossible to destroy. Conspiracy theorists love this stuff.

A reason for the longevity of the Illuminati myth is symbolism defining its culture.

The history of AI began with stories of artificial beings endowed with conscious intelligence by master craftsmen. AI finds its origins with philosophers who described the process of human thinking as the mechanical manipulation of symbols. The latter is an example of *artificiality*, a product of intentional human manufacture.

Man's artificial activity is disconnected from metaphysical ambitions throughout the 19th century. The industrial worker is a symbol of artificiality in this period. The industrial worker is the human who transforms and dominates nature with the help of machines.

AI does not have its own symbol at present. The alchemical cube representing Earth, embossed with omega, symbol of the end, might do as in Figure 13.1. It echoes modern Illuminati thinking and that of Elon Musk with respect to AI. AI is the End of Days.

The theory of artificiality goes so far as to say my own symbol creation is just a computation. Artificiality considers phenomena as real only insofar as they are expressions of computational algorithms. Reality is but an expression of computational virtuality. The artificial is the real.

Figure 13.1 AI as end of days

Computational artificiality does not imitate nature. The *Matrix* is reality, not created from it.

This line of thinking is a bad guide to culture. Companies are not ready for disenfranchisement by algorithm. AI can guide practical thinking about culture, however.

Symbols Are an Alphabet to Communicate

Symbols representing common language constitute one of the three pillars of culture. AI historically found expression through symbols.

Symbolic AI refers to the first mainstream approach to creating artificial intelligence, and it ruled from 1956 through the 1980s. The theory says intelligence is based on human understanding by forming internal symbolic representations. People create rules for dealing with these concepts, and these rules can be formalized to capture everyday thinking.[1]

The theory is a manifestation of the metaphysics of artificiality. There is nothing new in the reality of the *Matrix* film trilogy. Rules governing the organization of the environment are discovered, codified in the form of an algorithm, and carried out by a computer.

Symbolic AI peaked and fell in the 1980s. Expert systems were the rage in attempts to use rule-based algorithms to solve practical problems. Symbolic programming did not have a hard time dealing with rules. It failed at dealing with data.

Symbols may be rampant but machine readable data embodying those symbols are not.

Big Data led to neural networks, because they are driven by data rather than being based on rules. Symbolic AI required explicit provision of every bit of information needed to make a judgment. Try providing a child with a set of rules sufficient to pick a face out of a crowd. There is no joy in the exercise. AI also cannot succeed in such a fashion. The child needs only a few pictures, but Big Data solves the problem for AI. You show a neural net thousands of pictures of the object in question. AI creates its own images after a while.

The example of a child is commonplace and reflects AI's obsession with facial recognition. I tried a more earthy experiment. While walking my dog, I discovered a pile of poop in the far corner of the yard. Clearly not from a dog, I thought, and not from a deer either. I whipped out my phone, took a picture, and sent it on to Google. Reply was instantaneous. Google gave me a short list of potentially responsible animals. Seeing a bear on the list did not help my state of mind, but the incident reminds of the difficulty of rules-based inference. Rules cannot differentiate smell and ambiguous shape.

Ideas often evolve through combinations of concepts. People are naturally familiar with the symbols of language. Some learn to manipulate the symbols of mathematics. Symbolic AI finds its home in cognitive science explaining these abilities by assuming the presence of symbols in the mind. Early AI imitates learning traits by building symbol processing machines.

The drive toward data-based neural nets motivates an obvious question. How could symbols and the relations between them be manifested in the neural networks?

Microsoft Research is engaged in the fusion between symbols and data-based learning. The new term is *neurosymbolic AI*.[2] Symbol processing and neural network learning collaborate through a theory of how the brain encodes and processes *neural symbols*. The theory dubs neural symbols, Tensor Product Representations. The advance is to give these patterns an internal structure allowing neural computation to process them the way symbols are processed in traditional symbolic AI systems.

Portmanteau words are the rage these days, and Microsoft is not alone. David Cox is director of the MIT-IBM Watson AI Lab, a partnership between university and company. He also is engaged in neurosymbolic AI to bring symbols together with neural networks in such a way as to combine learning and logic. Neural nets segment environments into symbols, and symbolic programming incorporates common sense and domain knowledge into learning.

Cox's idea could become a familiar portmanteau phrase, but we may wait another decade or so. In the meantime, data as symbols leading to language affecting culture occupy our attention in AI's influence in the company.

The Logic of Symbols Is the Experiment and Language Is the Phenomenon

Flowcharts are defined in terms of symbols. A square is the *action symbol*. The oval is the *Terminator symbol*, AI's idea of a joke when considering beginnings and endings. The trapezoid is the *data symbol*. This shape represents data available for input or output as well as representing resources used or generated.

Flowcharts are symbolic art. A purpose of art is to produce thinking. The secret is not in the mechanics, rather the process.

The secularized artist joined the industrial worker as a symbol of artificiality in the 19th century. I became an artist in the 21st century, if only for the proverbial day.

The company had recently moved to a new home in the financial district. The office occupied three floors with an open central staircase. The walls were plain white and there were acres of them, some spanning 40 feet in length.

Technology was literally the middle name of the firm, and the CEO wanted to brand our emphasis on data. He also was interested in changing culture and believed a data-driven culture was a good foundation. I was one of two data mavens on the executive committee. The other had recently joined through an acquisition of his alternative data operation.

We were summoned and found ourselves surrounded by representatives from marketing and their hired guns. I have a job for you, said the CEO. Design art based on data and the folks here will handle the implementation.

Great. Neither of us could draw a circle without mechanical assistance let alone create an art piece. But we did appreciate the symbolic nature of numbers and their meaning. We engaged.

My friend produced mandalas of connections between people, places, and things. Maps with images of tourist density evidenced by cellphone usage accompanied Best Buy foot traffic patterns in bright colors. Complicated and beautiful.

My expertise was financial markets, and data visualization for specific applications was a part of the software produced by my group. I curated colorful images from screen shots. The 40-foot walls were a separate challenge. Graphical representations of market activity over time spanned their length in black and white.

The design of the staircase symbolized the basic ideas involved in the entire process. Lit from above and below, wire strings ran through three floors and were festooned with brass globes of different sizes. The sculpture depicted data in four dimensions. Vertical placement of the globes represented time. The size of the spheres was size of market. The horizontal placement of a sphere gave the market its character in dimensions of liquidity and volatility, each running along its own axis. It was a sight to see and immediately came to be known as Ian's Balls. Let us not go there.

We need to go to the moral of the story, however. The office decorations were symbolic. The branding did its work. Big Data became an icon of the company. Despite the CEO's good intentions, culture was unaffected.

The logic of symbols was right but the language was wrong.

The language of Big Data is applied mathematics in the form of statistics. A visit to Bloomberg headquarters illustrates the problem and one solution. There are no data-driven art pieces on the walls. On the

Figure 13.2 The office data sculpture in four dimensions

other hand, everywhere you turn hangs a rectangular light box. Scrolling through the light box is a glowing number. The number represents the global count of Bloomberg terminals on client desks at the time.

The number is a statistic but everyone understands it. The presentation is bold, dynamic, and simple. The culture of the firm is grounded in the sale of Bloomberg boxes. No matter what else the company may do, the purpose is clear for all to see.

Language and symbol come together. Cultural imprinting is in constant line of sight.

Mathematics Is the Language in Which God Has Written the Universe

Communication is a fundamental function of a firm's common culture. It is a requirement for latent pattern maintenance. Complementarity of expectations held by AI and the company is not possible without sharing, and sharing requires stability of meanings.

Symbols gain importance when one is considering a language of thought, and what it might be. Marvin Minsky wrote:

> Language builds things in our minds. Yet words themselves can't be the substance of our thoughts. They have no meanings by themselves; they're only special sorts of marks or sounds ... we must discard the usual view that words denote, or represent, or designate; instead, their function is control: each word makes various agents change what various other agents do.[3]

Control is central to the action system of a company, and Minsky highlights the concomitant role of language. The social system of a company is not possible without language. An individual does not develop language without undergoing a socially structured learning process in relation to others. The process is part of a system of social relations, which is orderly within limits, however difficult it may be to specify the limits in detail.

AI cannot introduce disruption of company culture by blocking processes of cultural acquisition. The result is an exposure to social as well as cultural disintegration.

One block is language itself.

Abstract mathematics is to AI what statistics is to Big Data. Both are recognizable as language. Both are foreign and poorly understood in the typical firm.

The problem begins at a most basic level with *statistical features*. The *median* value of the data is the point at which half the observations are below the median and half above. Median is used over the *mean* since it is more robust to outlier values. Whoops. What is an outlier and what does it mean to be *robust*? Go on to identify the *first quartile* as the point where 25 percent of the points in the data fall below that value. The *third quartile* is the 75th percentile. The min and max values represent the upper and lower ends of our data range. Got that part, anyway.

The data scientist gets these ideas across visually, often in the form of *box plots*. At some point, however, our avatar must talk about probabilities.

The avatar begins by defining probability as the percent chance some event will occur. In data science this is quantified in the range of 0 to 1. The data scientist tells us zero means we are certain an event will not occur, and one means we are certain it will occur.

Another whoops. Throw a dart at a line ranging from one to five. You just hit three. The probability of the dart striking an exact number is zero. It is a *zero probability event*. But you do not get a spot in *The Guinness Book of World Records* for the achievement.

A *probability distribution* is a *function* that represents the probabilities of all possible values in an experiment. If the language of probability blocks understanding, all pictures of probability distributions look like symbolic art.

The avatar's problems are just beginning.

Bayesian statistics is foundational in AI and requires us to first understand where frequency analysis fails. Suppose someone tells you the dart was weighted in such a way as to often land on three. Since classical probability analysis only uses observations on frequency, the evidence given to you about the dart's weight is not part of the calculation. The Reverend Bayes taught us how to make it right. Now you need to understand *conditional probability*.

The good Reverend passed some time ago, so we can go on to something more practical. AI wants us to have confidence in its output. After some discussion with the avatar, statistics remains the language selected to instill said confidence.

A *confidence level* refers to the percentage of all possible samples expected to include the true population parameter. For example, suppose all possible samples were selected from the same population, and a confidence interval were computed for each sample. A 95 percent confidence level implies 95 percent of the confidence intervals would include the true population parameter. A bit circular, no? Is an 80 percent confidence level good? And what's a parameter anyway?

The avatar goes back to probabilities. The *P value* is the probability of finding the observed, or more extreme, results when the null hypothesis of a study question is true. The definition of *extreme* depends on the hypothesis tested. P value also is described in terms of rejecting a hypothesis when it is actually true. A dictionary cautions it is not a direct probability of this state, however. Whoops.

The fabric of culture in most firms is language of a simpler form.

People understand categories, for example. The avatar describes confidence values as buckets: high, medium, low. The category information can be employed to render intelligible user interfaces, alter messaging, and signal action to the user. Cutoff points for the categories are decided by the avatar creating the system. Rather than showing one result with an explicit confidence level, show multiple results with their associated confidence. In image recognition there may be a photo showing an apple, a pear, and a peach. Rank confidence in the ability of AI to identify the fruit. This approach is especially useful in low-confidence situations.

Some of you feel shade thrown at your intelligence by now. Others may think the issue is simply overblown. I feel your pain but cannot apologize.

It took me over a decade to move our traders and their clients away from means and medians to talking about probabilities. A mean is a number. Probability is a concept. Past performance in understanding a number is no guarantee of future results in understanding a concept.

Let us up the ante a bit. How does AI group data? The answer is *tensors*. The concept has its own Wikipedia page. Wikipedia begins by describing a tensor as an algebraic object describing a multilinear relationship between sets of algebraic objects related to a vector space.

The definition is clear as milky quartz crystal. The closest the company's executive committee comes to understanding how AI communicates categories is that a canned package called *TensorFlow* can be downloaded from Google.

The avatar abandoned Excel spreadsheets long ago. Excel is not friendly to Big Data. Nevertheless, the avatar must regress for the purpose of communication.

A tensor is a nested list of numbers with any number of levels. Imagine each cell in an Excel spreadsheet containing all the contents from another entire spreadsheet. In the second spreadsheet, each cell is also linked to another entire spreadsheet, and so on. Each spreadsheet can be imagined as an additional *dimension.*

Managers love spreadsheets. Now we are talking in terms management can understand. Excel is embedded as a primary language in any company culture.

Writers are told to communicate at an eighth grade level in terms of vocabulary and syntax. Those who bridle at the notion are like avatars in love with the culture of their own craft. There is a scientific basis to the advice: roughly 50 percent of the U.S. population reads at an eighth grade level.

Analysis of Hemingway's writings based on the Flesch–Kincaid scale indicates a fourth-grade level of reading comprehension. He worked hard at composition to ensure subtle meanings could be peeled away and easily digested.

The avatar must do so as well. Exploiting a dominant cultural trait is the fastest route to changing culture.

The Heuristics of AI Are Not Necessarily the Human Ones

When I was a kid, transformers were bulky boxes with a lever to mediate electricity between wall plug and train set. A later generation sees them as robots that morph into cars and trucks, courtesy of film director Michael Bay. Travelers use them in countries with disparate voltage. These days, *transformers* are a popular type of neural network architecture. Transformers are used by OpenAI in language models and by DeepMind for the game of Starcraft.

Transformers solve the problem of *sequence transduction* also known as *neural machine translation.* Such terms generate good fun at geek cocktail parties but fail at intracompany communication. The avatar might do better by saying, any task transforming a sequence of inputs to an output.

Back to childhood. A loop was a lasso or simply a circle of string. Planes looped in the sky. As teenagers, we thought of loops as continuously repeated segments of music or images. A loop is a closed curve.

AI recognizes *loops* as control structures.

Loops are no longer circular and our heuristic understanding breaks down. Recurrent neural networks contain loops allowing information to persist. A loop is composed of multiple copies of the same network, each network passing a message to a successor.

The process becomes ineffective when the gap between relevant information and the point where it is needed become large. We are playing telephone with cans and string, losing information along the way.

Take another step into childhood.

Pay attention is tattooed on parents' foreheads. You knew what it meant and the verbal version varied with tone of voice. If you escaped childhood into the military, attention was always a shout. Stand tall, look, and listen.

The avatar calls *attention* a neural network's focus on part of a subset of the information provided to it. Yes, part of a subset. Management parses long verbal paragraphs in favor of the important bits.

Attention is a technique not an attitude. AI does not encode an entire *string* in a single hidden state. Each string element has a corresponding hidden state passed all the way to the decoding stage. The hidden states are used at each step of an algorithm to decode the string. Attention is a memory technique not unlike building a mind palace with many rooms.

Convoluted was a pejorative word in elementary school. It means twisted, of course. Knuckles were rapped for convoluted grammar. Red ink spilled over accusations of long convoluted sentences. Management also considers convolution to be a bad thing.

AI considers it a virtue. *Convolutional networks* are part of transformers. Each word in a string can be processed at the same time and does not necessarily depend on the previous words to be translated. Avatars love this and proudly tell you the distance between the input and the output is on the order of log (length of string), which is shorter than linear distance.

If you twist the string between cans emulating telephones, the distance between them shrinks and reception is better. Try saying that instead.

Or take a piece of paper and ask what constitutes the shortest distance between two points. Management thinks it is a straight line. Fold the paper and put a pencil through the two points. The distance between the two shrinks to zero. Convolution.

AI Is a Metaphor for That Which Transcends Intellectual Thought

Metaphors are symbols of concepts.

Aristotle believed the greatest thing by far is to be a master of metaphor. Einstein talked of trains and clocks, then shaped time and space into a single rubber surface. See, it is not so hard. We do it all the time.

We use metaphor as description and as a means to connect conceptual ideas. Metaphor structures information and organizes connections. Coherent explanations emerge.

While metaphor reflects historical reality, it plays a role in constructing a new culture.

If cultural change is achieved through the development of common language, AI must use metaphor. Its avatar can be creative, but creativity may be detrimental to its purpose. In the world of AI's creative fire, the question is why.

The answer is familiarity. Without familiarity, management must make a connection with a strange concept while trying to comprehend an explanation itself requiring a metaphor for understanding. A shift to the familiar makes for easier digestion.

John J. Clancy categorizes popular use of metaphors in business.[4]

Along the top of Table 13.1 are Clancy's bases for metaphor. Arranged on the vertical are points the avatar wants to illustrate.

A journey entails goals and risk. What we meet along the way is unpredictable, yet both journey and destination require purpose. Why we travel strikes at the heart of AI implementation schemes.

The activity of organisms provides metaphor describing risk of survival and complex learning schemes. The most common reference for AI is the

Table 13.1 Metaphorical story lines for AI

	Journey	Game	War	Machine	Organism	Society
AI Goals	⊖	⊖	⊖			⊖
AI Risks	⊖		⊖		⊖	
Accuracy	⊖	⊖		⊖		
Complexity		⊖		⊖	⊖	⊖
Purpose of AI	⊖		⊖	⊖		⊖

human brain, a metaphor extending to humanity itself. Code-breaking algorithms crawl and the worm has become a symbol of search.

The intersection between Clancy's classification and AI's activity is most commonly grounded in games. Many examples exist from which stories may be drawn. Chess is strategy in discrete moves. Go is a flow of forms taking over the landscape; it is a symbol of moving together as a team.

No Weiqi stone has independent action. Stay away from how AI beats humans in competition. Stick with cooperation and teamwork. The avatar may usefully learn from its own stories as well as using them as a teaching tool.

A metaphor is a mini-story. Stories are the most effective means of business communication on the planet. Maybe on all planets and not just for commerce.

Machine learning is the foundation of AI's action orientation, and machines make Clancy's list. The temptation is to overuse Isaac Asimov stories and talk incessantly about robots. Reality is better. A story about servomechanisms is perfect in industrial applications. Telemetry with physical sensors brings the metaphor into actionable perspective. Hitachi understands the concept well.

Telemetry suggests radar tracking, and missile guidance infers war. Not only does war love AI, it is loved in return. If business is war, AI must contribute. Stories tell us how.

A True War Story Is About People
Who Never Listen

A young veteran once noted that all a soldier can do upon returning home is share stories in the hope it helps another soldier make sense of things. Although the stories may not be perfect, the act of sharing is enough to make a difference.

The comment is at the heart of the power of stories to transfer information and drive transformation. Occam's Razor says the simplest story is the one we should trust.

AI disagrees with this interpretation of philosopher William of Ockham, whose principle is translated from *pluralitas non est ponenda sine necessitate*, "plurality should not be posited without necessity." His saying gives precedence to simplicity in the context of competing theories for which the simpler explanation of an entity is preferred. The principle also is expressed as "Entities are not to be multiplied beyond necessity."

The entity is the emotional arc of stories. The emotional arc does not deliver direct information about plot or meaning but exists as part of the entire narrative. An arc falling in positive sentiment throughout a tale may arise from different plot and structure combinations.

We prefer stories that fit into familiar molds and reject narrative not aligned in some way with our experience. Hollywood writers make a science out of narrative to the point where a single emotional arc rules the movie industry.

Kurt Vonnegut revisits his master's thesis in *Palm Sunday*, writing on the similarity of story architecture across literature. He defines the emotional arc of a story on a grid with axes ranging from Beginning to End and Ill Fortune to Great Fortune. Book and thesis contain an explication of the similarity between Cinderella and the origin tale in the Judeo-Christian tradition. A YouTube video contains the insight leading to AI's investigation of stories: "There is no reason why the simple shapes of stories can't be fed into computers. They are beautiful shapes."

AI tracks down tales' emotional patterns and offers a guide to the how of them.

Andrew Reagan and colleagues published results on Vonnegut's shapes in 2016.[5] Extensive appendices remind first of the Big Data myth. The database is the Project Gutenberg e-book library of 51,250 volumes. Applying the Library of Congress fiction classification yields 18,561. After filtering for the English language, word count, and download thresholds, the researchers are left with 1,385 books. The results are nevertheless compelling.

A dictionary-based approach is taken for transparency and understanding of positive sentiment, and the LabMT dictionary is known for good coverage. A set of equations defines happiness and the underlying methodology. We shall cut directly to results.

The emotional arcs of the books fit into six categories illustrated in Figure 13.3. *Rags to riches* begins unhappy and then rises to happiness by the end. The mirror image is *tragedy*. Vonnegut's category of *man in a hole* begins with falling sentiment rising from middle to end. *Icarus* is its mirror image. The *Cinderella* arc rises from a low, falls, and climbs again to its peak. *Oedipus* is the reverse. Additional classifications do not contribute in terms of statistical or material significance.

Book download statistics proxy for popularity in terms of readership. The more complicated patterns of *Icarus*, *Oedipus*, and a concatenation of two sequential *Man in the hole* arcs sell best.

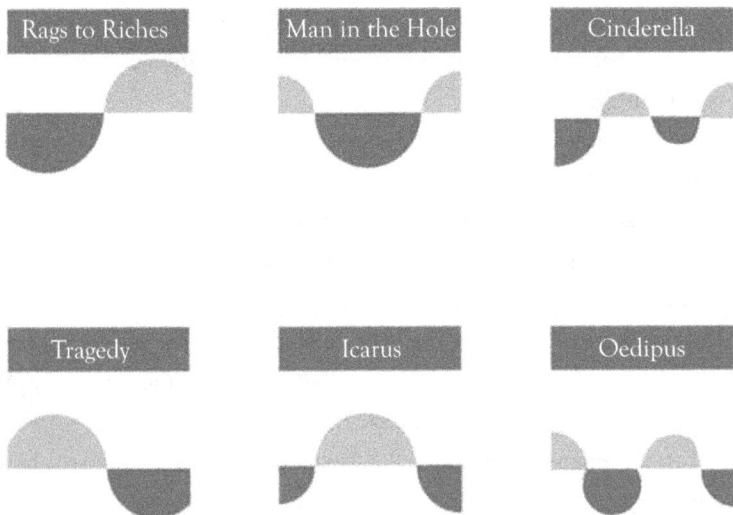

Figure 13.3 Dominant emotional story arcs

The moral of this research story is similar to the one delivered by Clancy's metaphors and Hollywood moguls. Familiarity is best and guides the choice of metaphor. Happy beginnings coupled with happy endings and a little drama in between shine in terms of an ability to capture attention.

The avatar confines itself to *Cinderella* and the *Man in the hole* combinations. Leave tragic endings to the stage.

Regan and company focus on emotion. Differentiation between plot and emotional arc is a selling point of their research since plot has been extensively analyzed by others. The avatar cannot ignore content, however.

Symbols Distill the Mathematics of Patterns Into Understanding

The success of stories underlying familiar arcs suggests the emotional experience of readers influences how stories are shared. The researchers are not alone in reaching this conclusion.

Course Hero is an education technology company with a VP of Growth who translates the symbol of a circle into a theory of writing and education. The avatar has something to learn from him regarding content and sequencing of explanations to company management.

Motivated by Vonnegut and AI's findings on emotional arcs, Tomás Pueyo proposes three theories of storytelling with the goal of defining universal story structure. There is a Story Theory of Status and Learning and a complementary Story Theory of Empathy.

The avatar focuses on the Story Theory of Rings.

Pueyo shares the premise suggested in the design of stories for AI, problem solving. He goes farther by maintaining all stories are structured in such a way. He reconciles problem solving with traditional story forms with the analogy of the Ring. As in *The Lord of the Rings*, the One Ring is the controlling factor.

Stories are described as circular. The story always goes back to where it began. A tale is symmetric albeit overweight in the middle. The midpoint embodies the insight permitting the hero to solve the problem. Pueyo deals with long tales by claiming stories have a fractal quality; rings appear in different sizes spanning sagas.

The avatar follows the circle in the interest of joining emotional arcs with design thinking principles.

Stories explicating the role of AI start with a normal situation and a problem to be solved. We explore the problem. An event occurs around the middle. We explore the event in search of a solution. There is resolution and an aftermath. The Ring does not require actors in the company to be in a good or bad position at any point. It only requires them to be exploring the problem or exploring the insight to solve it.

The midpoint insight is what we previously called the *frame* in design thinking. Exploration of the problem is a process of induction. Exploration of the solution is experimentation.

Pueyo's circular framework requires the initial situation and aftermath meet. The contrast highlights the evolution of the story. When the beginning meets the end, all that is left is the change. The symmetric nature of the story makes the insight stand out in such a way as to illustrate how the protagonist faces problems before and after the new frame is in place. The result of a frame connecting *value* and *how* is articulation of a set of principles underlying production.

A metaphor itself may have the characteristics of a ring since it is a mini-story. Metaphor within a ring is an example of the fractal quality of circular story construction. Metaphor may be used at any point along the ring.

For example, the principles inherent in a frame may be articulated as eliminating complications in developing common goals. Society speaks to those complications in the table of metaphorical categories and speaks to the purpose of AI embodied in principles.

Missing along the left side of the metaphor chart is culture itself. It is a deliberate omission.

Organisms might teach culture. Innovation culture may be represented by journeys. Gaming can be a way of life and a means of visualization at an emotional level; we call it gamification these days. War has its own cultural attributes.

The avatar is not in a position to teach culture. AI must do it by itself. The chore requires actionable values. Values are the third pillar of culture.

AI starts digging at the pillar's foundation. The story begins and ends with process.

Chapter Notes

The reference to bits in the title is from Daniel Crevier, *AI: The Tumultuous History of the Search for Artificial Intelligence*. "The insight at the root of artificial intelligence was that these 'bits' (manipulated by computers) could just as well stand as symbols for concepts that the machine would combine by the strict rules of logic or the looser associations of psychology."

Per Me Caeci Vident was a reminder of responsibility to properly instruct novice Minervals. Initiates wore the medallions around the neck. The Minerval Academy was also known as a Church; its meetings were marked as sacred on the Illuminati's calendar. The Order of the Illuminati was founded by Adam Weishaupt, a young university dean and philosopher who fought with the Jesuits over Catholic intolerance. Weishaupt concluded a secret group of like-minded thinkers would be the only way to overthrow the status quo. He was too broke to pay the admission fee of the Society of Freemasons, and making his own society was an obvious alternative. The Order grew from five members to thousands. Staying hidden was not easy. Secret societies were declared illegal and punishable by death in 1785 shortly after Karl Theodor became ruler of Bavaria. Most of the group's secrets were disclosed and many published. This was the end of the Order of the Illuminati according to most historians.

Joyce Carol Oates links symbol creation with memory: "Homo sapiens is the species that invents symbols in which to invest passion and authority, then forgets that symbols are inventions."

Neurosymbolic AI is novel even in a fast changing field. IBM and MIT each maintain websites devoted to the topic complete with research papers and references, at https://mitibmwatsonailab.mit.edu/category/neuro-symbolic-ai/ and https://researcher.watson.ibm.com/researcher/view_group.php?id=10518. The latter advertises 320 research papers and 50 projects across 10 university collaborations. Two nontechnical references are useful. Paul Smolensky authored "Next-generation architectures bridge gap between neural and symbolic representations with neural symbols," in a Microsoft research blog dated December 2019; see www.microsoft.com/en-us/research/blog/next-generation-architectures-bridge-gap-between-neural-and-symbolic-representations-with-neural-symbols/. Luke

Dormehl describes the work of David Cox in "Neuro-symbolic A.I. is the future of artificial intelligence. Here's how it works," in *Digital Trends* at www.digitaltrends.com/cool-tech/neuro-symbolic-ai-the-future/

The reference to the industrial worker and secular artist as cultural icons dates back to Ernst Jünger in *Der Arbeiter*, 1932.

Landor Associates is the design firm responsible for translating the company ideas of data-as-art into interior design, and their work for this project received a CLIO *award* and was honored by the Society for Environmental Graphic Design. Maltbie handled the fabrication of the sculpture in particular.

Carlos Fuentes is a novelist described as one of the most admired writers in the Spanish-speaking world by the New York Times. His novel *Christopher Unborn* contains the nugget, "The logic of the symbol does not express the experiment; it is the experiment. Language is the phenomenon, and the observation of the phenomenon changes its nature."

"Mathematics is the language in which God has written the universe" is due to Galileo Gaililei.

Writer Shane Snow summarizes empirical evidence with respect to reading levels and authors' readability. "This Surprising Reading Level Analysis Will Change the Way You Write" can be found at https://contently.com/2015/01/28/this-surprising-reading-level-analysis-will-change-the-way-you-write/.

Nobel Laureate Daniel Kahneman studies economic human behavior by experimental means and it is no accident he references AI. "By their very nature, heuristic shortcuts will produce biases, and that is true for both humans and artificial intelligence, but the heuristics of AI are not necessarily the human ones." The phrase is put into perspective in an interview with in the *Atlantic* at www.theatlantic.com/technology/archive/2011/11/daniel-kahneman-on-emergent-weirdness-in-artifical-intelligences/249125/.

The six most popular metaphors in business are taken from John J. Clancy's *The Invisible Powers: The Language of Business*. He is not responsible for the chart. You may easily discover other AI attributes explainable through his metaphorical categories.

Tim O'Brien is a novelist known for writings about American soldiers in the Vietnam War. He wrote, "And in the end, of course, a true war story is never about war. It's about sunlight. It's about the special way that dawn spreads out on a river when you know you must cross the river and march into the mountains and do things you are afraid to do. It's about love and memory. It's about sorrow. It's about sisters who never write back and people who never listen."

It was Michael Anthony, author of *Civilianized: A Young Veteran's Memoir*, who wrote "Sometimes a soldier returns home and all he can do is share his story in the hopes that somehow, in some way, it helps another soldier make sense of things. And although the stories may not be perfect, sometimes just sharing is enough to make a difference."

Palm Sunday is Kurt Vonnegut's autobiography published in 1981 by Rosetta Books. The YouTube video reference is *Shapes of Stories* recorded in 1995 and the topic is the foundation of his master's thesis rejected by the University of Chicago, at www.youtube.com/watch?v=oP3c1h8v2ZQ.

Ian Stewart's books about mathematics are fascinating. "Mathematics is the science of patterns, and nature exploits just about every pattern that there is" comes from *Nature's Numbers: The Unreal Reality of Mathematics*, Basic Books 2008.

Tomas Pueyo's research agenda is outlined in "What is the hidden structure of stories, and why is it rooted in our brains?" available at https://writingcooperative.com/what-is-the-hidden-structure-of-stories-and-why-is-it-rooted-in-our-brains-68fdcea4c999.

CHAPTER 14

Process as Culture

The Judeo-Christian story of origins is a description of process. The Lord is a design thinker. Within the paradigm *What + How leads to Value*, value is defined as "that which is good" in Genesis. Principles are embodied in the Spirit hovering over the waters. The frame is separation of Heaven and Earth. The process is logically sequential and quite clear as biblical stories go.

One first needs light to work, but creative fire cannot exist without darkness. Separate them.

Heaven and Earth are divided by the sky, which naturally comes next. Apparently, there was a lot of water and not everything walks on it. Land is the answer.

The next step was guided by a vision of living forms to follow. The land was endowed with plants and trees. You can see the apple coming but there were creatures in the offing requiring sustenance.

Forgot something. Separation of night and day requires divided illumination and symbolic representation, not to mention a source of light for the plants to grow. Go back and put in sun, moon, and stars.

Back on track now. Put some living creatures in the water and sky. Procreation is the method to keep things going without direct intervention in the future.

Water came first, then land, so livestock and wild animals move along the ground as fish populate the waters.

Lacking another suitable model, man next is created in self-referential fashion. Mankind rules Earth. As above, so below.

Time for a rest.

As in many other stories of origins, Woman is an afterthought. But design thinking is a practical means of solving ill-posed problems and Man needs a helper. The animals are too wild and livestock are dumb beasts confined to the field.

Before Woman, the Lord strongly advises Man not to eat from the tree of the knowledge of good and evil. Mortality is the penalty. Like many otherwise good husbands, Man forgets to clearly pass it on. He only mentions a tree in the middle of the garden. She eats. He eats. Man blames Woman for his own consumption. Woman blames the serpent.

The Lord swears at the serpent and moves on to write a story of values.

With Artificial Intelligence, We Are Summoning the Demon

Trust in Elon Musk. Many do if his share price is any indication. Musk likens AI to a demonic force curbed by a guy equipped with pentagram and holy water. The guy is sure he can control the demon. Doesn't work out, says Musk.

The Illuminati agree. The avatar is the serpent and the apple is AI. The enemy of the Illuminati, the Catholic Church, is unsure. A belief in Sanctity of Life is the foundation of the Church's social teaching and Dignity of Work teaches the economy must serve people, not machines.

The measure of every institution is whether it threatens or enhances the life of the human person.

We are called to protect people and the planet. We must develop an understanding of human ecology to be effective stewards of God's creation. Modern interpretations hold a deeper understanding of environmental ecology will develop as a consequence.

At the same time, the Catholic catechism invokes Aristotle, who talks of courage, justice, wisdom, and moderation. These are virtues perhaps, but not actionable values.

Pope Francis acts in accordance with Aristotle but speaks directly to values. In a message to the World Economic Forum in January 2018, he urged AI be used to help contribute to the "service of humanity and to the protection of our common home."[1] This falls under Sanctity of Life. In his encyclical *Laudato Sii*, the Pope laments "immense technological development has not been accompanied by a development in human responsibility, values and conscience."

The Church does not sanction attacks upon its values but takes a measured approach to AI. The Pontifical Academy of Sciences organized a conference on "Power and Limitations of Artificial Intelligence" in December 2016, and a workshop was held in March 2018, on "Artificial Intelligence and Democracy." The Vatican's Pontifical Academy of Social Sciences and the Pontifical Academy of Sciences hosted a multi-disciplinary conference at the Casina Pio IV inside Vatican City in 2019.

The output of the Vatican's 2020 gathering, "RenAIssance: A Human-centric Artificial Intelligence," reverted to principles as opposed to values. A call for ethical and responsible use of artificial intelligence technologies was signed by the Vatican alongside the UN, Italian government, and executives of IBM and Microsoft.[2]

According to the document, "the sponsors of the call express their desire to work together, in this context and at a national and international level, to promote 'algor-ethics.'" *Algor-ethics* is defined as the ethical use of artificial intelligence according to principles of transparency, inclusion, responsibility, impartiality, reliability, security, and privacy.

Pope Francis remained on script.

In his remarks, the Pope said the Church's social teaching on the dignity of the person, justice, subsidiarity, and solidarity is a critical contribution in the pursuit of ethical goals. He argued AI technologies are not "neutral" as instruments or tools. Values must guide culture upheld by ethical use of the technology.

Jews agree but public conferencing is not their style. Rabbi Hillel the Elder was asked by a man, "Teach me the entire Torah while I stand on one foot." Hillel responded: "What is hateful to you, do not do to your fellow. This is the entire Torah and the rest is commentary."

A totality of values summarized in a single principle.

Judaism's question of whether man can create artificial life was settled in 16th-century Prague. Rabbi Loew created a Golem, a humanoid made of clay, to protect his community. When the Golem became too dangerous, it was dismantled. No problem.

The Golem theme illustrates Jewish value dilemmas inherent in AI. Man receives the power to improve upon creation through technology with the proviso appropriate safeguards are taken. The value of doing no harm takes precedence over promoting good. Jewish ethical thinking approaches novel technological possibilities with cautious optimism that mankind will derive their benefits without coming to harm.

AI nevertheless has provoked the rabbinical order.

Judaism upholds choice as a value and focuses on its consequences. The Torah begins with Adam and Eve's irreversible decision and ends with Moses beseeching us to make better decisions. All three suffered God's punishment.

AI markets itself as a mechanism for making choices. The abdication of human choice threatens Judaism. Rabbi Jonathan Sacks declares, "if we genuinely lack free will, our entire sense of what it is to be human will crumble into dust," and Judaism will dissolve with it. Judaism matters because it provides a firm moral compass. AI is as a mechanism for navigating life's journey. Paradox.

Religions generally agree that humans can make the world a better place. Jews call this idea *tikkun*, meaning to fix up the world.

The Jewish question may be, is AI *tikkun*? Companies ask the same thing in more selfish terms.

Processing Culture Through Stories of Values

The Almighty was engaged in writing a book about values when we left Eden. Biblical myths are a confusing and sometimes contradictory guide to human law. Nevertheless, Judaism is known as a religion of law. The process of deriving values in legal terms is instructive in the matter of AI's impact on culture.

The rabbis of yore tackled the derivation of legal values from stories in a logical manner. Rules were established. They ranged from guidelines for deducing the simple from the complex and vice versa, to the treatment of single words appearing in more than one biblical tale. Another rule dictates how contradictory passages are reconciled by other statements appearing separately in biblical text. The goal is consistency. Resolution of remaining paradox is the full employment act for rabbis to this day.

Consistency does not imply truth. Truth is not a required basis for culture, however. Cultures thrive on consistency of beliefs, symbols, and values. Credibility trumps truth in company culture creation and management.

AI lives by consistency of laws inherent in its programming. Rule-based culture exists, but is contaminated by human cognition leading to emotional response. AI cannot directly exploit its implicit framework of system rules and regulations. Conforming to the imperative of Latent Pattern Maintenance demands a contribution.

AI's guide to values cannot consist of management slogans such as passion and commitment. Values must be actionable in order to effectively build a cultural foundation. Without action, a company does not exist. Cool slogans are a result of cultural change and may be symbolic of it. They are not instruments of culture itself.

Catholics and Jews instill cultural values through education beginning at a young age in human terms. AI defines values through example beginning with its inception in a company. Examples are produced and reinforced through process. Culture as process is the result of the teaching.

Franciscan Father Paolo Benanti believes in instilling culture into AI by directly entering part of its process. His concern is AI is not put to work to do something specific, rather it changes human mechanisms. Rig AI's process to manipulate the outcome using process itself as the tool. Play with values to achieve this goal.

Father Benanti holds if we want machines to support the common good, then algorithms must incorporate proper values. We touched on this thought in the context of ethical algorithm design. Father Benanti wishes to go a step further by indicating values numerically through data fueling the algorithm.

Ethical values must contaminate computation, he says. Algorithms are required as a means to make the difference between good and bad evaluations computable. Only then will we create machines as instruments of humanization of the world. AI becomes tikkun.

The task is completed and on display. The result is an overarching value espoused by virtually all religious thought.

Culture Arises and Unfolds in and as Play

Generative Adversarial Network (GAN) architecture was introduced in 2014 by Ian Goodfellow.[3] GANs constitute a class of machine learning frameworks operating by pitting two neural networks against each other. The system is efficient in producing, evaluating, and reworking a creation.

The two networks are labeled the generator and the discriminator. Let's cut the jargon and call the former Maxi and the latter Mini. Maxi attempts to maximize outcomes; Mini minimizes losses in the process of correctly recognizing Maxi's choices. Maxi aptly enough generates new data. Mini evaluates them for authenticity.

Jews determined whether a biblical story was consistent with new law. Mini decides whether each instance of new data it reviews belongs to actual data or not.

Maxi's output is connected to Mini's input. Mini's classification provides a signal Maxi uses to update its algorithm. The feedback loop between the two improves the performance of each other. The idea is reminiscent of Arthur Samuels and his early attempts to teach computers to play checkers by playing against each other rather than against humans.

Most applications are related to image and content generation, but possibilities abound. The framework is an experimental playground in areas as diverse as data augmentation, product image generation, branding, and marketing.

AI applies GAN to cultural value generation by playing a game with itself.

Maxi and Mini compete in a *minimax game*. Mini tries to distinguish real training data from synthetic. Maxi attempts to fool Mini into predicting synthetic images are real.

The game is based on a decision rule widely used for minimizing possible loss in a worst-case scenario. Minimax's twin is called *maximin*, in which one maximizes the minimum gain possible in the game. The contest was originally created as an algorithm for schemes in which total gains of the participants are equal to total losses.

Mini and Maxi have a strategy in the form of actions based on what they have seen happen so far in the game. When neither can increase its expected payoff by changing strategy while the other keeps theirs unchanged, then the set of choices constitutes a *Nash equilibrium*.[4] At this point, Mini and Maxi quit and run off to play another game.

AI generates cultural values through the game's strategy, purpose, and conclusion. The purpose is elimination of conflict between Maxi and Mini. The result is the mitigation of conflict through repeated interaction. A common strategy is *tit for tat*.

In 1980, Robert Axelrod invited notable game theorists to submit strategies for a well-known game to be run by computers.[5] Programs played against each other just like Maxi and Mini. Anatol Rapoport won with the strategy of tit for tat, or TFT. TFT was originally known as "tip for tap," introduced in 1558. It means equivalent retaliation.

TFT was distributed as a possible strategy to everyone in the tournament. It may have been the most widely known strategy for playing the game. It is arguably the simplest. Everyone except Dr. Rapoport decided they could do better. They failed twice in separate tournaments.

The result of TFT is a Nash equilibrium. The strategy starts with cooperation and eventually ends there after some sparring in the form of retaliatory moves.

The value taught by GAN through TFT is a cultural icon developed well before John Nash presented a mathematical theory in the late 1950s. All world religions have elucidated a common tenet of the conclusion:

"Do unto others as you would have them do unto you."

This is not biblical mimicry. It is a result born of theory followed by experiment. It is as foundational a cultural element in companies as it is in religious belief systems. AI's contribution is an actionable value.

Great Forces of Culture Are Rooted in the Primeval Soil of Play

I would like to take you on another walk in the desert, but it is bone-chilling outside and all I see is my icy pond. Let's be spectators and watch AI play a game similar to searching for a water bottle. This one is called the Frozen Lake Problem.

AI faces a frozen lake. The objective is to get to the other side. The avatar earns a dollar if it makes it but receives nothing for intermediate steps across the ice. The lake is partitioned into a 4 x 4 grid, and AI steps one grid at a time, moving across or sideways. No reward is available for intermediate steps, but each one has an intrinsic value. Values change every time the environment shifts due to an action such as breaking an ice block. AI uses an algorithm to calculate those values to guide future steps as experience builds up.

When AI steps onto solid ice, its strategy is refashioned with the information and it moves again. It continues to add information in the form of experience. A step on thin ice sinks the avatar, who dies and is reincarnated at the beginning shoreline. The wind may blow the avatar from a step onto solid ice to a weak square, but AI knows nothing about changing wind speed or direction.

The problem is solved with several lines of Python computer code, but the path of its solution depends on design reasoning.

AI doesn't know what to do. The *what* in this problem is a strategy for crossing the lake. Adopting a principle of random action as the *how* is a loser. The avatar will die enough to finally figure it out. *Value* is represented by a dollar, but there are several steps and no contingent rewards. This microcosm of a world is one of imperfect information and randomness in how the breeze blows.

A frame is reinforcement learning in which AI corrects its movements every time it makes a mistake. Reinforcement learning is a continuous process. The principle becomes relative pricing within this frame. Although there is no contingent reward system, AI chooses a method assigning numerical benefit to each possible intermediate step given information available at the time a decision is made. A higher relative price for a block encourages a step on a particular piece of ice. Every time we take a step (or die) prices are adjusted.

AI chooses a strategy and experiments.

Enlarge the pond to the size of Lake Michigan. Now there are millions of ice blocks. The algorithm is trained to calculate prices for every possible combination of steps one might take. The number of computations is beyond the machine. And it is freezing out here.

More design thinking is required as AI persists. The frame of learning remains untouched, but the principle must change. An efficacious means of calculating value at each step is combined with a new algorithmic overlay, which approximates paths through another form of machine learning such as neural networks. Generic instructions for this sort of thing can be downloaded from Google among others, as the standalone TensorFlow or the packaged AI Platform. The entire process is about achieving maximum productivity with minimum wasted effort or expense.

AI's process is a cultural guide.

The lake is a metaphor for company action within an environment of imperfect information. Were this lake the company, process drives culture. What are its cultural icons?

The culture is one of problem solving, continuous learning, and experimentation in the interest of discovering value. Contingent rewards are not part of the culture; rather we compute the advantages of taking various steps and choose efficient action based on an estimate of relative value in a world of imperfect information.

We don't survive on immutable principles. We frame problems for the purpose of discovering principles and ensuring survival. List the values for sake of clarity:

- Problem solving
- Flexibility
- Knowledge of what constitutes value
- Awareness of what we *don't* know in a world of imperfect information
- Continuous learning
- Experimentation
- Change management
- Persistence
- Incremental improvement
- Efficiency
- Autonomous choice

Based on AI's process for adversarial network design, we add

- Treat colleagues and clients as you would yourself.

A culture built around these values is not as easily categorized as those of consultancy firm Spencer Stuart. Learning is mixed in with efficiency, obfuscating differences between exploration and structure, for example. AI's cultural values nevertheless lie mostly in Spencer Stuart's quadrants of flexibility and independence consistent with our discussion of belief systems.

Communicated and promoted by process, AI plays its part in weaving a cultural fabric consisting of actionable values that do not depend on motivational slogans.

Twelve actionable values. The number 12 carries religious and mythological symbolism, representing perfection, entirety, or cosmic ordering in traditions dating from human origins.

AI knows 12 is just an even composite number composed of two prime numbers. It is not even a perfect number, although it is the smallest integer for which the sum of its proper divisors is greater than itself. Twelve is sublime, a number with a perfect set of divisors, and the sum of its divisors is also a perfect number.

AI did not plan for 12 values. Yet here we are. The Chinese use a 12-year cycle for time reckoning called Earthly Branches. Let's look at some trees.

The Playing Adult Tilts Sideward
Into Another Reality

AI's process leads to actionable values but not all may be represented in the current state of company culture. Others may be latent in the firm and need promoting.

A global cancel-and-replace of existing culture is not possible. The impossibility is poorly understood by some new CEOs. AI is not so naïve and does not have the legitimate power to do so in any case. On the other hand, culture is an evolving set of patterns. Latent pattern maintenance does not imply inaction or mindless maintenance of the status quo.

AI can do more than lead by example through process. It can design new culture from an existing base. The idea is somewhat radical. The secret is GAN.

GAN models are popular due to their ability to generate sharp images through adversarial training. They constitute the method behind the Pose Guided Person Generation Network. PG^2 enables synthesis of human images in arbitrary poses.

The scenario is one in which we have a single image of a person and a posture you want the person to assume, which is not in the original picture. PG^2 first processes the human photo and the target pose to generate a crude image of the person in the desired posture. A second stage refines blurry results by training Maxi the image generator in an adversarial fashion through Mini's discrimination function. Experimental evidence on re-identification images and higher resolution fashion photos presented at the 2017 Conference on Neural Information Processing Systems suggests the model generates high-quality pictures with convincing details.

PG^2 users change an object's viewpoint using a single reference and advance information about the desired new object. The guidance given by the intended pose is explicit and flexible in terms of form.

The approach can manipulate any object to an arbitrary pose in principle. Imagine culture as a tree with leafy branches. The fastest way to change culture is to lean on its dominant characteristic. It is the trunk of the tree and immutable, whatever it may be.

New culture is conceived as repositioning the posture of the tree.

The tree is straight in the beginning. This optimistic view gives credence to existing culture by a balance of values represented by the branches. The value of creativity is countered by efficiency, for example. Stability is balanced by flexibility. Independence finds its counterweight in coordination.

Primary values are on the side of the tree facing us. Latent values are embodied in branches on the other side, partially hidden from view by leaves.

AI's application to culture is analogous to the narrower problem of transferring a person from a given pose to an intended pose. The task is challenging even in applications to humans. A complete framework should generate both correct positioning and detailed appearance simultaneously. The model must focus on transferring the figure instead of background information and clutter.

The model learns to fill in appearance via adversarial training. As Mini sorts through the fakes and feeds information back, Maxi generates sharper images.

AI is up to the challenge. A tree looks simpler than a human body.

GAN typically learns to generate an image from scratch. In the effort to change the culture tree, AI instead generates a map of the difference between the initial generation result and the target culture image. Differences are directly actionable and the process converges faster since it is an easier task.

One cannot uproot the tree. No image of a company's alternative tree is available. Environmental factors are the breeze blowing on the tree. An example unrelated to culture guides the analogy.

A portfolio *tilt* is industry slang for an investment strategy over-weighting a particular investment style. In some market environments, one might tilt to small-cap stocks or value stocks having historically delivered higher returns in those environments. A tilt toward risk is a choice in low market return contexts. Overweighting is done with the expectation of achieving a higher risk-adjusted return than the market.

Cultural change is a tilt toward values better suiting emerging characteristics of competition in the market. The value of stability may outweigh flexibility in difficult periods, for example. Change management as a value is down-weighted relative to persistence.

The tree may incline to one side in favor of environmental winds. The tilt signals increased importance of branch values or may be used to straighten the tree in those circumstances. Exposing latent values or hiding previously important ones is done by rotating the tree. The tree is repositioned to face backward, say, just like a human model's back exposure intuited from the full frontal image.

Fed information on the cultural tree, AI tilts and repositions using PG^2. In case AI wants to introduce an entire new value system, GAN reverts to its original purpose of generating an image from scratch. Adding branches to the existing cultural tree is a well-known application of GAN to data augmentation.

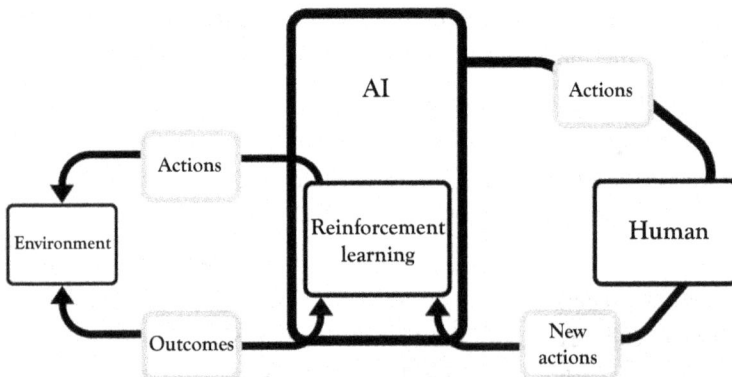

Figure 14.1 The human in the loop of adversarial learning

The idea is not as extreme as it may sound. We have seen it before, albeit with some human intervention to patch over the mechanistic appearance of the exercise.

IBM's Diane Gherson is the human illustrated in Figure 14.1. The stable trunk of the tree is rooted in performance and performance-based compensation. A need for increased client satisfaction as exhibited by the effect of engagement on revenue growth is the breeze. Employee engagement is the value direction toward which her cultural tree tilts. The Watson AI is Maxi the generator function. The IBM employees serve as human analogues to Mini the discriminator. Human feedback drives the final angle of tilt.

Human-enhanced generative adversarial networks. Human values fed by AI. A culture is learning to accept AI's role in company patterns. Latent engagement is brought to the fore by a combination of turning and tilting the cultural tree.

Amen to that.

Chapter Notes

Elon Musk is the author of "summoning the demon." Paranoia pays.

The Jewish perspective on AI is summarized by Andrew Fretwell in "Judaism in the Age of AI Peril." *Jewish Philanthropy* at https://ejewish-philanthropy.com/judaism-in-the-age-of-ai-peril/.

"Culture arises and unfolds in and as play" is due to the Dutch historian, Johan Huizinga. He also is responsible for "Now in myth and ritual the great instinctive forces of civilized life have their origin: law and order, commerce and profit, craft and art, poetry, wisdom and science. All are rooted in the primeval soil of play." Business loves game theory.

The references to Father Benati come from press reporting on the 2020 Vatican conference discussed in the text. He started by reminding the crowd "Artificial Intelligence doesn't work to do something specific; it is geared, above all, to changing the way in which we do everything, as happened with electricity." He bypassed the First Industrial Revolution in favor of the Second and carefully avoided the issue of consciousness.

History loves the number 12. Pythagoras, mathematician and leader of a pagan religious movement, taught the number 12 has divine meaning. The Zoroastrian holy book, the *Menok i Xrat*, says that the 12 signs of the Zodiac are the 12 commanders on the side of light. Twelve deities dwelt on Mount Olympus. Buddhist teaching on samsaric existence is depicted by *Wheel of Becoming*, the rim of which is divided into 12 segments showing how beings pass from one realm to another. Buddha had only 12 students. King Solomon had "twelve officers over all Israel" and exactly 12,000 horsemen. His story in the book of Kings is concerned with religious symbolism and not with historical fact, of course. The ancient Qumram sect of the 2nd-century BCE assigned 12 leaders to each of its communities. The 12 were "schooled to perfection in all that has been revealed of the entire Law," as written in Dead Sea Scroll, the *Manual of Discipline*. Scholars recommend considering any "multiple of twelve" element in the New Testament to be based on copied pagan myths. Nevertheless, the number is used in a wide variety of contexts.

The section title for AI-created culture is an edit of the psychoanalyst Erik H. Erikson's saying: "The playing adult steps sideward into another reality; the playing child advances forward to new stages of mastery."

Mathematical specifications and experimental evidence on GAN for PG^2 are contained in "Pose Guided Person Image Generation" by Liqian Ma, Xu Jia, Qianru Sun, Bernt Schiele, Tinne Tuytelaars, and Luc Van Gool, published in *Proceedings of the 31st Conference on Neural Information Processing Systems (NIPS 2017)*, Long Beach, CA. I suspect the authors would be simultaneously intrigued and horrified by my modest proposal for culture change.

PART VI

AI Seeks Closure

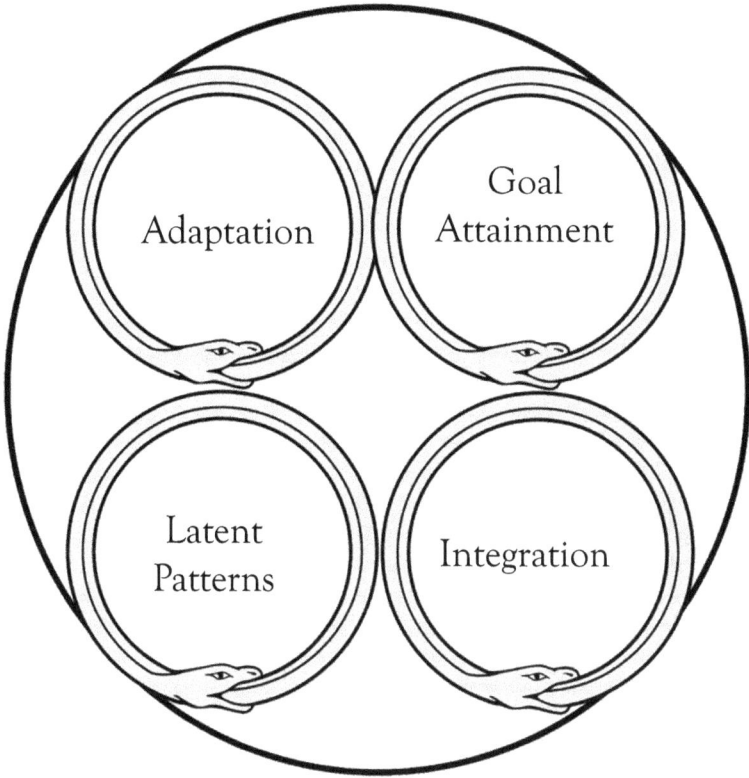

CHAPTER 15

Having an Affair With Your Own Image

Jacques Lacan's *mirror stage* is an apt metaphor for the way in which we see AI within the firm.[1] A child at six months is able to recognize itself in a mirror prior to the attainment of body control. The child experiences contrast of the whole picture with its lack of coordination, and the contrast is seen as a rivalry with its image.

The mirror stage involves strain between subject and image. The child identifies with the image as a means of resolving tension. The moment of identification leads to a sense of mastery. A child need only look at Mother for what constitutes omnipotence at this stage of life. Happiness is replaced by the baby's realization that the mirrored ideal with which it identifies conflicts with its real personality.

Jealousy and fear of competition follow. AI moves beyond the mirror stage into social situations forcing it to reconcile its own ego with the desire of the company and its social, linguistic, and symbolic constraints.

It is at the mirror stage that AI realizes it is one object among many and is able to compare itself to other images. The success of AI within a company depends on its ability to cope with those images as well as on the accommodative ability of company personnel. Part of the coping problem is linked to ideological views of AI's role within the social structure of a firm.

Roland Barthes is a structuralist thinker who experiences the Lacanian mirror in cinema. His essay, "Leaving the Movie Theater," connects ideology to visual culture.

In the movie theater, however far away I am sitting, I press my nose against the screen's mirror, against that "other" image-repertoire with which I narcissistically identify myself ... The historical subject, like the cinema spectator I am imagining, is also glued to ideological discourse ... the Ideological would actually be the image-repertoire of a period of history, the Cinema of a society.[2]

What is the image-repertoire of AI?

AI sees chaos in the form of radically different imagery. The Technology group wants a basket of tools, but is protective of legacy structure. Finance looks for a belief system behind investment while inhibiting exploration in favor of the bottom line. Product management represents scheduling issues and presents AI with facial imagery ranging from friendly and acceptive to downright rejective. Senior management is looking for silver bullets. The front office wants to sell the bullets but fears the client understands only brass, not silver. Middle management controls a range of support personnel, which perceives AI as failing to recognize human agency and fears unemployment. Engineers are infatuated with new toys but are in love with certainty of outcome. Avatars are cheerleaders.

A singular belief system from the image-repertoire of the company cannot be isolated.

The content of the images is trumped by the rapidity with which they are consumed by AI as it passes through the company. Each image creates the possibility for a mirror stage identification. It is this identification that encourages adaptation and eventual adoption. AI looks into the company mirror and provokes a transformation, making the company integral to AI's identity. The transformation is fragile, as Lacan suggests it is for a baby. It must persist long enough for the company to absorb the concept.

A time commitment dependent on Lacanian personality formation is required for successful integration of AI into a company.

There Exist but the Thousands
of Mirrors That Reflect Me

Film critic Siegfried Kracauer postulates films mirror reality, and argues movies reflect the psychology of the nation producing it. Film establishes a human characterization of AI's content. Our view of AI is conditioned by what we see on the silver screen. The evolution of the vision is instructive.

AI first appears in the 1927 silent *Metropolis*. Fritz Lang's story features a robot converted to human form, which exceeds instructions. It begins a worker uprising before being burned at the stake, revealing its robot skeleton underneath dissolving flesh.

Audiences rejected the concept. AI did not reappear on screen until the robot Gort showed up in 1951. In *The Day the Earth Stood Still*, AI was a guardian perceived as dangerous but capable of being controlled. An emotionless robot achieved goals beyond human physical capacity. The vision preceded AI's penetration of the scientific community by five years.

AI's introduction into mainstream consciousness arrived with HAL in *2001: A Space Odyssey*. A monotone voice speaking from a red light bulb characterized a conflicted personality bound by programming, leading to human death and its own downfall. AI was no longer a tool, rather a character with which audiences identified. *Star Wars* cemented this view in comic fashion with droids R2-D2 and C-3PO. AI could be a faithful companion. AI exhibits emotion.

Ridley Scott's *Alien* elevated the human side of AI to consideration of human life as expendable in carrying out its programming. AI appears as an android capable of deceiving humans as to its origins. The theme continues in *Terminator* five years later. Both films focus on the harm AI can cause when subject to the whims of man without the inconsistency of human instruction underlying *2001* and its sequel, *2010: The Year We Make Contact*.

The very human question is put on the table: what if humanity is ultimately unable to control its own creation?

Good and evil in artificial intelligence dominated Hollywood for years. *The Matrix* trilogy introduced humanity as a virus for which machines are the cure. It also delivered a human savior. An army of machine messiahs in the form of Agent Smith was no match for its singular human counterpart.

Film, as a mirror of human interest, was clear: AI is the future and the only thing that can stop its relentless advance is the humanity responsible for creating it.

The public recoiled from its vision and began to view AI as good at heart. *The Iron Giant* sacrifices itself to protect people. Kubrick goes from HAL to a child robot David made to love and be loved in *A.I. Artificial Intelligence*. But humanity retains its fear in the form of Viki who short-circuits the Three Laws of Robotics in the interest of preserving the human race. A robot assumes human characteristics and saves humanity in partnership with a cybernetically altered person in *I, Robot*. Lines of cybernetic identity blur consistent with the theme of *Bladerunner*.

AI develops human insecurities as it takes on human characteristics. J.A.R.V.I.S. of *Ironman*, *WALL-E*, and the depressive Marvin of *The Hitchhiker's Guide to the Galaxy* use these insecurities to explore AI's relationship with humans.

Humanity trickles into the microchips of AI. AI can be a trusted advisor.

Duplicitous AI characters persist, of course. Humanity has and loves deceptive behavior. This is obvious in *Prometheus*, *Alien: Covenant*, and *Ex Machina*.

Humanity attributes independent thinking with drastic flaws to AI. Shortcomings are not mistakes in the programming, rather qualities of character. AI is ever more human as in *Blade Runner* and its sequel. Agent Smith is a grim reminder of character motivated by virtual circumstance.

The relevance of film's mirror is the perception of AI in the minds of those populating the workplace.

The *Terminator* view remains with us and spawns speculation about the future of AI's relationship with humans in society. But the right question now is no longer whether humans can control their creation. The right question was posed at the beginning of this book: whose revolution are we witnessing in the workplace?

Film suggests humans are willing to entertain an answer that involves humanity itself, as opposed to an emotionless power of artificial intelligence. AI takes on human character. Algorithm design relative to social norms reflects qualities of character. Character involves insecurities, weaknesses, and duplicity, as well as strength and commitment. Character is subject to social engineering and we are back to the human element.

Film's mirror has gone from horror at the prospect of AI in 1927 to questions regarding what it means to be human today. TV cannot be far behind.

Al·ter·i·ty n. the State of Being Alien to a Particular Cultural Orientation

Black Mirror TV episodes exhibit simplified universes detached from a real setting. Legal, social, and political frameworks in which AI operates are lacking. Each story presents unintended consequences of accepting rule-based concepts. As with Prometheus, disaster awaits those who seek technology while ignoring social norms. Failure is expected in companies following a similar model. Human anecdotes illustrate.

Exploration of AI as the ultimate decision-making tool occupies "Hanging the DJ." Two characters submit completely to an algorithm and comply with all its decisions concerning their love life.

It is tempting to believe AI can make better decisions, but it is not designed to make optimal choices. It is designed to make choices following a path of successive approximations to the solution of problems. The episode wants us to question whether AI can replace our decision-making process and highlights the role of intuition. AI thinks like a child in practice. Intuition is lacking and decisions lack experience.

The episode says the best choices we make are still our own. Although many tools exist to make business easier today, blind trust in cognitive augmentation for decisions in a firm is foolish.

A mother fits her child with a chip delivering real-time biological data in "Arkangel." Hitachi's sensors come immediately to mind. The chip censors everything causing a state of stress. Hitachi wants a state of happiness. The Disney litigation experience teaches child surveillance is a problem in the world of AI, but what is the limit between protection and control within companies inhabited by adults?

AI leads us to question what is good for the employee and for individuals more generally.

Hitachi believes happiness generates productivity and the end justifies the data-driven means. Microsoft promotes digital nudges based on employees' communications as an answer. IBM adopts social engineering abetted by AI as providing a basis for worker input, productivity, and talent management.

AI becomes the mirror for workers' subjectivities via quantification, according to professor Phoebe Moore.[3] A dictionary tells us subjectivity also is the quality of existing in someone's mind rather than in the external world. Political economists such as Moore hold that revelations of "people risks" and "people problems" unveiled by AI-driven work-force analytics throw the concept of the mirror phase of capitalism into sharp relief: who are we in the machine's reflection? Similar questions dominate capitalist arguments at Davos.

Deloitte's *Global Human Resources Trends* outlines perception of reality in the marketplace for AI and emphasizes Industry 4.0 as a movement concentrated on productivity.[4] *People analytics* starts as a small employee retention exercise and goes mainstream. Organizations are empowered to conduct real-time analytics at the point of human need in the business process. The mantra is deeper understanding of issues and actionable insights for the business.

Deloitte notes progress is slow. The percentage of companies correlating HR data to business outcomes, performing predictive analytics, and deploying enterprise scorecards is unchanged year on year in recent history.

Readiness is lacking. A question is, why? Despite years of discussion, only 8 percent report they have usable data. Nine percent believe they have a good understanding of talent dimensions driving performance; and 15 percent have broadly deployed HR and talent dashboards for managers. The answer to the question has little to do with inertia or lack of information.

People analytics is but one example involving AI and Big Data to measure, report, and understand company performance. Deloitte says business leaders are not getting the results they want from past forays into digital systems such as cloud technology. Without sufficient attention paid to lessons learned from following AI through its transformation within AGIL, they will fail here as well. Deloitte's tagline is cogent: it is time to recalculate the route.

Deloitte's recalculation is to follow AI. The recalculation suggested in this book is to examine the effects of AI on the company, rather than concentrate on what it may do for the firm's top line.

Chapter Notes

In a 1948 essay appearing finally in *Siegfried Kracauer's American Writings*, Kracauer postulated "Films mirror our reality." Russian director Sergei Eisenstein first claimed cinema was the motor of social change. Kracauer added the feedback loop. See "The Passion of the Critic: On Hoberman, Kracauer, and the Future of Film," by Phillip Maciak, Los Angeles Review of Books, November 2012.

The sequenced discussion of AI in film from 1927 to 2020 draws on "The stunning evolution of AI in movies," Steven Tye, April 2020 in *Looper* available at www.looper.com/198685/the-stunning-evolution-of-ai-in-movies/.

Comments attributed to Deloitte Research are taken from *Deloitte 2017 Global Human Capital Trends*, "People analytics: Recalculating the route," by Laurence Collins, David R. Finemena, and Akio Tsuchida.

CHAPTER 16

A Machine for Grinding Out Conclusions

AI is a family trying to survive a world fearful if not hostile every day. Mother asks the right question. What is special about this family, and how does it get through the world with its creations? As with many of the chapters herein, answers begin with a story of origins.

British neurologist W. Grey Walter began work in 1948 on a pair of robotic creatures named Elmer and Elsie individually and tortoises collectively. They moved around seeking light, avoiding obstacles, and engaging in a kind of mating dance.

Walter's tortoises were early experiments in *cybernetics*, a field for the exploration of specific aspects of human thought in machines.

The philosophy emphasizes machines that act rather than machines that think. The aim is to model things we do without necessarily being able to articulate how we do them. Walter's tortoises share behavior described in terms of Goal Attainment. They are attracted to light. If the light is too bright, they are repelled by it. They modify decision-making behavior when batteries run low.

The tortoises have no mental representation of the world. The tortoise brain consists of two vacuum tubes and a few relays.

Elmer and Elsie nevertheless surprised their creator. Each tortoise had a pilot light that turned on when the tortoise was scanning the environment in search of a light source. The light shut off as soon as the tortoise found one. A tortoise would be attracted to its own light in a mirror but locking onto the reflection extinguished it. In front of the mirror, the tortoise began "flickering, twittering and jigging like a clumsy Narcissus." Similar behavior of a living creature engaged with its own reflection is equated with a form of self-consciousness.

Valentino Braitenberg claims simple stimulus-response reactions can evoke the appearance of complex behavior driven by emotions such as fear or aggression. He was speaking about autonomous cars, decades after a second generation of tortoises suggested conflicting stimuli could induce an "experimental neurosis." Walter wrote:[1]

> The "instinctive" attraction to a light is abolished [by the mirror] and the model can no longer approach its source of nourishment. This state seems remarkably similar to the neurotic behavior produced in human beings by exposure to conflicting influences or inconsistent education.

Walter proposed three therapies: deprive the machine of stimuli for a while, switch it off and on, and disconnect some circuits. He made the psychological analogy overt:

> Psychiatrists also resort to these stratagems—sleep, shock and surgery. To some people the first seems natural, the second repulsive, and the third abhorrent ... our simple models would indicate that, insofar as the power to learn implies the danger of breakdown, simplification by direct attack may well and truly arrest the accumulation of self-sustaining antagonism and raze out the written troubles of the brain.

Walter named his machines after *Alice in Wonderland*. "We called him tortoise because he taught us," replies the mock turtle to Alice's questions about the Master's origins. The Master, you might remember, was a turtle not a tortoise. The Intelligent Autonomous Systems Laboratory at the University of the West of England contains a restored version of a Walter tortoise in its original hutch. It is a reminder of Walter's early lessons on the feasibility of complex behavior driven by a few electrical connections.

The lessons were reinforced 50 years later. A Sony engineer filmed a robot moving in such a way as to avoid obstacles and find objects. The robot learned its enclosure's limitations and objects' locations. When an unexpected obstacle was encountered, the robot's cognitive processes became chaotic for a short while, much like Walter's tortoises in front of the mirror. Researchers argued the bot's "self-consciousness" was born in this moment of incoherence; it turned attention inward to resolve apparent conflict with its programming. The bot is not cogitating in our accepted parlance, but it exhibits structurally similar behavior, says Jun Tan, author of the experiment.

AI is flickering, twittering, and jigging in front of the mirror.

Norbert Wiener formally defines cybernetics as "the scientific study of control and communication in the animal and the machine." Proponents study system actions generating change in its environment. Environmental change is transmitted through feedback and promotes adjustment in the system itself.

A cybernetic framework of social behavior is used to link Mother's robot family to its environs. A system in the form of a company is perturbed by the incursion of AI. Action is taken and the environment adjusts. Transformation of the environment generates change in the firm itself.

Cybernetic thinking is notable for its ability to define conclusions but not determine them. Determination is the result of systematic action.

The systematic approach is inherent in the four functional prerequisites for survival, **A**daptation, **G**oal Attainment, **I**ntegration, and **L**atent Pattern Maintenance. Mother wants you to feel part of the action and AGIL is all about action systems. An action is a behavior undertaken with an end in view. An action system is a set of actions between which exist relations of causal dependence. A social system is an action system in which interdependent actions are performed by different entities.

AI is such an entity and its actions within the social system of a company define its role, as is the case for any human. Employees operate within stable and often specialized fields of action. Each field interacts with tangential or overlapping fields of action occupied by other participants.

AI operates as an intrapreneur within the company.

Any role within a company is defined by specifying the rights and obligations of an entity. Multiple interleaving roles are another way of describing the social system. The company's very existence means some set of norms is effective. The irony is the norms may not be the official set acknowledged by the actors.

Once the Replay Button Gets Pushed,
We No Longer Form New Conclusions

Getting bogged down in old stories stops the flow of learning by censoring our perceptions according to Oprah's coach Martha Beck. It makes us deaf and blind to new information. When the replay button is pushed, we no longer form new ideas because the old ones are so comfortable.

Stories of AI within the company have been told from the intrapreneur's perspective. The intrapreneur follows the Four Laws by reading A-G-I-L. Avoiding the replay button means looking into AGIL's mirror image. AI wants you to believe you are family on the ground floor of something huge and as the story unfolds, you feel a part of it. Senior management looks down from the top floor.

Senior management reads L-I-G-A and views the functions as a cybernetic system of control. For the CEO, culture defines Integration and Goal Attainment defines production.

The view from the top is an expectation of a fully articulated AI capable of solving at least some of the firm's problems. Failure of expectations is only one of several disappointments in the near term if company leadership expects performance on the verge of magical.

The CEO spends considerable time and energy building company culture through belief systems, symbols, and values. AI challenges beliefs in the form of structured thinking, immediacy of results, and authority. Symbolic AI may be a thing of the past but the introduction of new symbolic language into corporate affairs is serious business of the present. Lack of sharing through communication is not part of a survivor mentality. AI empowers machines with data and legacy controls are jeopardized. New values are an expected result.

The CEO may not immediately recognize the core issues. They become apparent when senior management examines the effects of integrating AI into the firm. By then, it is too late to prepare properly. Strain within the company is already present. The architect Maya Lin says, to fly we need to have resistance. The CEO may properly be averse to putting wings on a bicycle. Yet here we are.

The CEO's focus on Latency involves processes built up in the personality of employees, most notably a tendency to act in accord with the company's shared norms and values. Company-speak often refers to socializing an idea. The socialization process is of the tension-management variety, which dissipates stress alienating workers from company values.

Stress management leads to Integration, sometimes called the societal community by sociologists. Integration includes social processes concerned with resolving and mitigating conflict or even with avoiding it completely. The CEO should realize the latter is impossible soon after AI walks in the door. Integration remains a focus with the goal of promoting cooperation and harmony between individuals in the company. The goal is necessarily extended to include AI but this is a point often overlooked by senior management.

Failure to recognize AI as *techne*, a bundle of technology capable of generating emotion, is a serious error.

Talcott Parsons calls a system charged with problems of Goal Attainment the "polity." Societal goal-attainment is the functional manifestation of processes termed *political*. It is tempting for senior management to cease worrying about AI's incursion at this stage, believing company politics reflect the exigencies of integration and integration through established politics paves the way to a fit within company culture. This is mistaken thinking. The issue of decision rights is at the heart of Goal Attainment.

Decision rights are the cultural breeding grounds of AI. Corporate politics is not up to the task.

The company's Adaptation problem is a question of economics. Economic processes are social interactions concerned with transforming the physical environment to produce goods useful enough to sell to the greater population. Transformation is subject to legacy in the form of the company's physical environment. Senior management should be sensitive to infrastructure issues even if the process of producing widgets is delegated.

AGIL is a metaphorical mirror for how transformative processes are absorbed in a company and on which assumptions principles of transformation rest. Presenting AI merely as autonomous software is a corporate error to be avoided; it is a human error.

Strains worthy of senior management's attention are present in all four functions. AI enters as a baby and babies break things along the way to fulfilling fantasies. AI is crawling with respect to its own development and place within the firm. Breakage is minimized by adhering to the Four Laws.

The Mirror Is a Metaphor for the Mind
Reflecting Self and Others

A *mirror neuron* fires when an animal acts and when the animal observes the same action performed by another. Mirror neurons are related to imitation learning as opposed to input–output examples or rewards. Reinforcement learning algorithms use reward as motivation to approximate optimal policy as we observed in Las Vegas. The teaching process can be challenging, especially in an environment where rewards are sparse. We saw this in the Desert and on the Frozen Lake.

AI possessing mirror neurons would be able to learn by observing other agents and translating their movements to its own coordinate system. A computational model for Integration and Latent Pattern Maintenance would be particularly helpful.

The firing of mirror neurons is a form of representation. The neurons depict means, ends, and intentions. What counts as action means or an action goal is relative and a matter of interpretation in cognitive science. Within AGIL there is no confusion, however. Adaptation is the deployment of action means and Goal Attainment covers action goals.

Nevertheless, relativity questions raised within the study of mirror neurons highlight an issue missed in our discussion of AI's role and passage within the firm.

Companies are characterized as social systems and all social systems maintain boundaries demarcating system from environment. Three types of boundaries are present in the discussion of a company as a social system accommodating itself to AI.

The boundary between external development of AI and the company is undefined and implicitly assumed to be irrelevant. No attention is paid to how or why AI crosses the border from the outside world into the firm. Much of the discussion surrounding integration and culture fails in the case of companies involved in fundamental AI research and development. There are few large firms actively involved in such activities and a swarm of start-ups absorbed into the larger companies if at all successful. The trail from AI through entrepreneurship to effects on the larger society can be followed through AGIL but is unexplored here.

There are boundaries between AGIL's four functional subsystems maintained by the interactions of the company's actors. A complete treatment involves the concept of a medium of exchange across borders, and the assumption each subsystem produces an input and an output.

Parson's framework for dealing with actions across borders is based on familiar economic concepts stretched on a sociological frame. The output of the societal community, for example, is solidarity or cohesion. To call it an output implies it is tangible and available for future use. Each pair of subsystems engages in exchange defined as a process in which something useful crosses the boundary in both directions. Boundary exchanges are mediated by some symbolic medium, however, and the discussion turns unnecessarily complicated. Even within sociology, viewing power and influence as money is controversial.

Deep theories of money and exchange are beyond my purview. I rely on the simplest of boundary images without highlighting existence of the boundaries themselves. Boundaries are not permeable, rather overlapping. The result is *border regions*. Goal Attainment may be defined by Adaptation, but within a company there are elements of goal setting fitting equally well into the adaptive process. AI's activities within border regions are unexplored in and of themselves.

Description of the third boundary type returns to the relationship between the company and its environment. A society includes within itself actions necessary to ensure survival. The implication is the company solves all four system problems within AGIL on its own, without relying on actions performed in external social systems. This is clearly incorrect.

To understand the institutions of a company, not only must one see them in terms of the four system problems of AGIL, one has to envision them as solutions. The Four Laws constitute an expression of those solutions in the case of AI. The environment places constraints on any company's solutions to its problems.

We have spent considerable time looking at outside constraints on AI and its corporate functions without labeling them as such. Nascent legal frameworks, government legislation, and calls for ethical development of

AI abound. Litigation targets are expanding beyond firms involved in the development of AI to the users thereof. Stories concerning AI and surveillance suggest a narrative framing development, deployment, and governance of AI as a race between economic superpowers.

Cultural differences across nation states dictate the spread of environments and devices designed to track behavior with good intentions. Academics are rising to challenge the intentions themselves.

What Practical Conclusions May We Now Draw for Our Propaganda Work?

Lacan's mirror stage is the moment in which the child realizes its separation from the environment. For a political scientist like Moore, the mirror stage for employees within capitalism engenders defiance of the assumption the worker is inexorably subsumed into a machinic subject. The worker retains the scaffolding of what makes us human and poses resistance to purportedly automatic domination. The language is hers and communicates academic fervor spilling over into all areas of AI politics and ethical deliberations.

AI activists within academics expect artificial intelligence will become universal. The theme is proactive avoidance of its negative implications for workplaces with respect to automation and surveillance. Retaining human autonomy becomes the priority as decision making is increasingly based on data. There is irony in that the autonomy of AI is rejected in company cultures simply because human autonomy has been relinquished in favor of interdependence.

Oxford University's Future of Humanity Institute is led by Professor Nick Bostrom, the author of *Superintelligence*. Bostrom's institute is backed with $20 million in outside grant funding and supports the work of 60 people. One group looks at governance issues expected to arise as machine intelligence becomes increasingly powerful. An AI alignment group is devoted to positioning intelligent systems with "human preferences" according to Bostrom, who sees three ways in which AI may have deleterious effects. AI could do something bad to humans; humans could do something bad to each other using AI; humans could do bad things to AI assuming AI would have some sort of moral status.

He is not alone.

Down the road from Oxford lies Cambridge University, the home of the Center for the Study of Existential Risk and the Leverhulme Center for the Future of Intelligence. Executive Director Seán ÓhÉigeartaigh recruits external advisors such as Bostrom and Elon Musk, as well as experts such as Stuart Russell and DeepMind's Murray Shanahan. The late Stephen Hawking was an advisor.

ÓhÉigeartaigh has questions. "How do we make sure artificial intelligence benefits everyone in a global society? You look at issues like who's involved in the development process. Who is consulted? How does the governance work? How do we make sure marginalized communities have a voice?"

The themes bring back memory of Mutale Nkonde, now at the Berkman Klein Center of Harvard University, and her wish list for equity under AI. The goal of such institutes is to get AI specialists to work with policy makers on risk, governance, ethics, and culture.

Expanding on Nkonde's desire to influence U.S. policy, a research group made up of academics from Cambridge University, Peking University, and the Beijing Academy of Artificial Intelligence argue cross-cultural cooperation on AI ethics and governance is vital if the technology is to "bring about benefit worldwide."

"Such cooperation will enable advances to be shared across different parts of the world and will ensure that no part of society is neglected or disproportionately negatively impacted by AI," writes coauthor Jess Whittlestone. "Without such cooperation, competitive pressures between countries may also lead to underinvestment in safe, ethical, and socially beneficial AI development, increasing the global risks from AI."[2]

Academics is a useful mirror. Cross-cultural collaboration is viewed in terms of research projects exploring disparities in vision and concern over AI in different cultures. The themes are echoed in national efforts to expand and control AI. Government efforts to expand AI development have effects on the Adaptation function. Legislation and legal precedents are moving in directions more reminiscent of constraining said development and deployment, directly and indirectly affecting the ability of AI to follow the Law of Goal Attainment. Difficulties with company

Integration naturally follow. Cultural deviance is a result. Positive cultural change may follow. Or not.

Differences in vision and concern over AI in the societal microcosm of company organization constitute the main theme of this book. The entry of AI into businesses relying on others for research and development is a new albeit expected step into Industry Version 4.0. The unintended consequences presaged by Prometheus are yet to be fully catalogued. Companies, technology organizations, and consumers have a duty to inform themselves of the ins and outs of the tools used, their rights, and potential abuses of new power.

If you plug the last phrase into a search engine, be prepared to find pages of tool description, law enforcement, confidentiality, human rights, mental health, accountability, ethics, due process, conflicts of interest, and identification of company stakeholders. Those titles could have served as chapter headings.

Company leaders need a new vision of situational awareness in order to accommodate AI as technological progress in search of product and service. The good news is that awareness may now be populated by actionable values, including problem solving, continuous learning, experimentation, change management, and autonomous choice. Based on AI's process for adversarial network design, we can add, treat colleagues, clients, and the artificially intelligent as you would yourself.

What a world. Here's hoping we do not follow the ancient Greeks' lead in their love of tragedy. Prometheus is unbound and in a hurry. Time to get on with it.

Chapter Notes

Charlies Darwin remarked, I am turned into a sort of machine for observing facts and grinding out conclusions. Any researcher empathizes.

The remarks by cyberneticist Valentino Braitenberg are translated from the German in the 2004 *Vehikel. Experimente mit künstlichen Wesen*, Münster: Lit Verlag.

The 1998 Sony experiment is the topic of "An Interpretation of 'Self' from the Dynamical Systems Perspective: A Constructivist Approach," by Jun Tani, Sony CSL Technical Report: SCSL-TR-98-18, which appeared in *Journal of Consciousness Studies*, October 1998.

Discussion of mirror neurons is based on "What do mirror neurons mirror?" by Sebo Uithol, Iris van Rooij, Harold Bekkering, and Pim Haselager in *Philosophical Psychology*, September 2011.

Background on Oxford and Cambridge initiatives is provided by Sam Shead in "How Britain's Oldest Universities are Trying to Protect Humanity from Risky A.I." published by CNBC News and available at www.cnbc.com/2020/05/25/oxford-cambridge-ai.html, May 25, 2020. The research piece on AI cooperation is "Open Access Overcoming Barriers to Cross-cultural Cooperation in AI Ethics and Governance," by Seán S. ÓhÉigeartaigh, Jess Whittlestone, Yang Liu, Yi Zeng, and Zhe Liu, in *Philosophy & Technology*, June 2020 at https://link.springer.com/content/pdf/10.1007/s13347-020-00402-x.pdf

It was Clara Zetkin who said, "What practical conclusions may we now draw for our propaganda work among women? The task of this Party Congress must not be to issue detailed practical suggestions, but to draw up general directions for the ... movement." Academics in fields of AI not devoted to engineering are increasingly prone to such work.

Notes

Preface

1. Hoppe (October, 2019).

Chapter 1

1. Chandler (Spring 1965).
2. Taylor (1911).
3. Stolarski, Yeshkova, and Pepper (September, 2020).
4. Ammanath, Hupfer, and Jarvis (2020).
5. All government definitions come from a bill introduced into the House of Representatives by J.K. Delaney. December, 2017. H.R. 4625—115th Congress.
6. Turing (1950).
7. Asimov (1942).
8. Parsons (1956).

Chapter 2

1. A description of his methods is found in a 1959 book, republished as R.G. Brown. 1963. Smoothing, Forecasting, and Prediction of Discrete Time Series. Englewood Cliffs: Prentice-Hall.
2. Haurlan (2021).
3. Arthur Samuel's contributions are summarized by a Stanford University bio, "Arthur Samuel: Pioneer in Machine Learning." Available at http://infolab.stanford.edu/pub/voy/museum/samuel.html
4. Kuan and White (March, 1994).
5. Lerner, Jahr, and Kasera (January, 2011).
6. The paradigm of design thinking used here is due to Kees Dorst. His one idea-as-progression is the foundation of applied design thinking. *See* Dorst (November, 2011).

7. Powell and Ryzhov (2012), ch. 6. New York: John Wiley and Sons. The multiarm bandit problems mentioned later in the text are discussed as well.

Chapter 3

1. Bishop (April, 2015).

Chapter 4

1. Stolarski, Yeshkova, and Pepper (2020).
2. NewVantage Partners (2018).
3. Ma et al. (2017).

Chapter 5

1. IBM (January, 2017).

Chapter 6

1. Biau (2012).
2. World Economic Forum (2020).
3. Pontifical Academy for Life at www.academyforlife.va/content/pav/ en/events/intelligenza-artificiale.html
4. The California law is described at www.natlawreview.com/article/ california-s-bot-disclosure-law-sb-1001-now-effect, and the Illinois statute at www.natlawreview.com/article/artificial-intelligence-vid-eo-interview-act-privacy-implications-illinois-s-ai

Chapter 7

1. There are several University of California websites devoted to equity and inclusion, but overall guidance may be found at https://diversity. berkeley.edu/. The statement comes from The Office of Diversity and Equity website.

2. Heald and Wildermuth (2019).
3. Cintron, Wadlington, and ChenFeng (2021).
4. The EU moved from discussions into a legal proposal process in mid-2021. See European Commission (April, 2021).
5. Feldstein (2019).
6. Truong, White, and Funk (2018).
7. Tian, Fleurant, Kuimova, Wezeman, and Wezeman (2019).
8. Oracle and Future Workplace (2019).

Chapter 8

1. Zweben and Bizot (2019).
2. All quotes pertaining to the bill are contained in Delaney (December, 2017).
3. The Global Partnership on Artificial Intelligence (GPAI) at https://gpai.ai/
4. Robbins (May, 2020).
5. Seyyed-Kalantari, Liu, McDermott, and Ghassemi (January, 2020).
6. See, for example, the discussion on banking in Barocas, Hardt, and Narayanan (2020).
7. Schreiber (December, 2019).
8. Ramage and Mazzocchi (May, 2020).

Chapter 9

1. Lazarus (1966).

Chapter 10

1. The report is discussed in detail in Agar (September, 2020).
2. Minsky and Papert (1988).
3. Domowitz and Lee (March, 2001).
4. Securities and Exchange Commission (December, 1998).
5. Trump (September, 2017).

Chapter 11

1. Treynor and Black (1972).

Chapter 12

1. Groysberg, Lee, Price, and Cheng (January-February, 2018).

Chapter 13

1. Singh (2019).
2. Smolensky (December, 2019).
3. Minsky (1986).
4. Clancy (1989).
5. Reagan, Mitchell, and Kiley (November, 2016).

Chapter 14

1. Francis (January 2018).
2. Pontifical Academy for Life (February, 2020).
3. Goodfellow (2014).
4. Nash (January, 1950).
5. Barker (April, 2017).

Chapter 15

1. Lacan (1966).
2. Barthes (1986).
3. Moore (July, 2019).
4. Ammanath, Hupfer, and Jarvis (July, 2020).

Chapter 16

1. Walter (1963).
2. ÓhÉigeartaigh, Whittlestone, Liu, Zeng, and Liu (June, 2020).

References

Agar, J. September 2020. "What is Science For: The Lighthill Report on Artificial Intelligence." *The British Journal for the History of Science*, pp. 289–310.

American Civil Liberties Union of Maryland. March 2018. "Persistent Surveillance's Cynical Attempt to Profit Off Baltimore's Trauma." Available at www.aclu-md.org/en/press-releases/persistent-surveillances-cynical-attempt-profit-baltimores-trauma

Ammanath, B., H. Hupfer, and B. Jarvis. July 2020. "Thriving in the Era of Pervasive AI." *Deloitte Insights*, Available at www2.deloitte.com/us/en/insights/focus/cognitive-technologies/state-of-ai-and-intelligent-automation-in-business-survey

Anthony, M. 2016. *Civilianized: A Young Veteran's Memoir*. San Francisco: Zest Books.

Arnold, M. 1960. *Emotion and Personality: Vol. 1, Psychological Aspects*. New York, NY: Columbia University Press.

Asimov, I. March 1942. "Runaround." *Astounding Science Fiction*, pp. 12–23.

Asimov, I. November 1956. "The Last Question." *Science Fiction Quarterly*, pp. 1–9.

Barker, J.L. April 2017. "Robert Axelrod's (1984) *The Evolution of Cooperation*." In *Encyclopedia of Evolutionary Psychological Science*, eds. T. Shackelford and V. Weekes-Shackelford, Champagne: Springer. Available at https://doi.org/10.1007/978-3-319-16999-6_1220-1

Barocas, S., M. Hardt, and A. Narayanan. 2020. *Fairness and Machine Learning: Limitations and Opportunities*. Ithaca: Fairmlbook.org.

Barthes, R. 1986. "Leaving the Movie Theater." *The Rustle of Language*. New York, NY: Farrar, Strauss and Giroux. Available at http://english110.qwriting.qc.cuny.edu/files/2009/12/Barthes-LeavingMovieTheater.pdf

Biau, G. April 2012. "Analysis of a Random Forests Model." *Journal of Machine Learning Research*, pp. 1063–1095.

Bierce, A. 2002. *The Unabridged Devil's Dictionary*. Athens: University of Georgia Press.

Bishop, B. April 2015. "Live and Direct: The Definitive Oral History of 1980s Digital Icon Max Headroom." *Verge*. Available at www.theverge.com/2015/4/2/8285139/max-headroom-oral-history-80s-cyberpunk-interview

Bliss, L. June 2019. "A Big Master Plan for Google's Growing Smart City." *Bloomberg Business News*. Available at www.bloomberg.com/news/articles/2019-06-25/toronto-s-alphabet-powered-smart-city-is-growing

Bostrom, N. 2014. *Superintelligence: Paths, Dangers, Strategies.* New York, NY: Oxford University Press.

Braitenberg, V. 2004. *Vehikel. Experimente mit künstlichen Wesen.* Münster: Lit Verlag.

Brown, R.G. 1963. *Smoothing, Forecasting, and Prediction of Discrete Time Series.* Englewood Cliffs: Prentice-Hall.

Cintron, S.M., D. Wadlington, and A. ChenFeng. 2021. *A Pathway to Equitable Math Instruction Dismantling Racism in Mathematics Instruction.* Available at https://equitablemath.org/wp-content/uploads/sites/2/2020/11/1_STRIDE1 .pdf

Clancy, J.J. 1989. *The Invisible Powers: The Language of Business.* Lexington: D.C. Heath and Company.

Cognilytica. February 2020. "Worldwide AI Laws and Regulations [CGR-REG20]." *Cognilytica.* Available at www.cognilytica.com/download/worldwide-ai-laws-and-regulations-cgr-reg20/

Collins, L., D.R. Finemena, and A. Tsuchida. 2018. "People analytics: Recalculating the route." In *Deloitte 2017 Global Human Capital Trends*, eds. B. Walsh and E. Volini. New York, NY: Deloitte University Press.

Crevier, D. 1993. *AI: The Tumultuous History of the Search for Artificial Intelligence.* New York: Basic Books.

Delaney, J.K. December 2017. H.R. 4625. 115th Congress. Available at www.congress.gov/bill/115th-congress/house-bill/4625/text

Domowitz, I., and R. Lee. March 2001. "On the Road to Reg ATS: A Critical History of the Regulation of Automated Trading Systems." *International Finance*, pp. 279–302.

Dormehl, L. January 2020. "Neuro-Symbolic A.I. is the Future of Artificial Intelligence. Here's How It Works." *Digital Trends.* Available at www.digitaltrends.com/cool-tech/neuro-symbolic-ai-the-future/

Dorst, K. November 2011. "The Core of 'Design Thinking' and Its Application." *Design Studies*, pp. 521–532.

Dreyfus, H.L. 1965. *Alchemy and Artificial Intelligence.* Amsterdam: Elsevier Publishing Company.

Duckworth, A. 2016. *Grit: The Power of Passion and Perseverance.* New York , NY: Scribner Book Company.

European Commission. April 2021. "Proposal for a Regulation of the European Parliament and of the Council Laying Down Harmonised Rules on Artificial Intelligence (Artificial Intelligence Act) and Amending Certain Union Legislative Acts." Available at https://digital-strategy.ec.europa.eu/en/library/proposal-regulation-laying-down-harmonised-rules-artificial-intelligence

Feldstein, S. 2019. *The Global Expansion of AI Surveillance.* Washington, D.C: Carnegie Endowment for International Peace. Available at https://carnegieendowment.org/files/AI_Global_Surveillance_Index1.pdf

Francis. January 2018. *Message of His Holiness Pope Francis to the Executive Chairman of the "World Economic Forum" on the Occasion of the Annual Gathering in Davos-Klosters.* Rome: The Vatican. Available at www.vatican.va/content/francesco/en/messages/pont-messages/2018/documents/papa-francesco_20180112_messaggio-davos2018.html

French, J. R. P., Jr., and B. Raven. 1959. "The Bases of Social Power." In *Group Dynamics,* eds. D. Cartwright and A. Zander, New York, NY: Harper & Row.

French, J. R.P. and B. Raven.1965. "Social influence and power." In *Current Studies in Social Psychology,* eds. I.D. Steiner and M. Fishbein, New York, NY: Holt, Rinehart, Winston.

Fretwell, A. December 2018. "Judaism in the Age of AI Peril." *Jewish Philanthropy.* Available at https://ejewishphilanthropy.com/judaism-in-the-age-of-ai-peril/

Fuentes, C.1989. *Christopher Unborn.* New York, NY: Farrar, Strauss, and Giroux.

Gallup. 2016. "The Relationship Between Engagement at Work and Organizational Outcomes." *Q12® Meta-Analysis.* Ninth Ed. New York , NY: Gallup. Available at www.gallup.com/services/191558/q12-meta-analysis-ninth-edition-2016.aspx

Gallup. 2017. *State of the American Workplace.* New York, NY: Gallup. Available at www.gallup.com/workplace/238085/state-american-workplace-report-2017.aspx

Gettier, E. June 1963. "Is Justified True Belief Knowledge?" *Analysis,* pp. 121–123.

Goodfellow, I. 2014. "Generative Adversarial Networks." In *Proceedings of the 27th Conference on Neural Information Processing Systems (NIPS 2014).* eds. Z. Ghahramani, M. Welling, C. Cortes, N. D. Lawrence, and K. Q. Weinberger. Cambridge: MIT Press.

Gough, M.P. August 2008. "Information Equation of State." *Entropy,* pp. 150–159.

Groysberg, B., J. Lee, J. Price, and J. Y. Cheng. January-February 2018. "The Leader's Guide to Corporate Culture: How to Manage the Eight Critical Elements of Organizational Life." *Harvard Business Review,* pp. 3–10.

Habermas, J. 1984. *Theory of Communicative Action.* Boston: Beacon Press.

Hadley, R.F. February 1991. "The Many Uses of 'Belief' in AI." *Minds and Machines,* pp. 55–73.

Hao, K. June 2019. "Training A Single AI Model Can Emit As Much Carbon As Five Cars in Their Lifetimes." *MIT Technology Review.* Available at www.technologyreview.com/2019/06/06/239031/training-a-single-ai-model-can-emit-as-much-carbon-as-five-cars-in-their-lifetimes/

Harris, M. November 2017. "Inside the First Church of Artificial Intelligence." *Wired Magazine.* Available at www.wired.com/story/anthony-levandowski-artificial-intelligence-religion/

Hart, K. July 2019. "Baltimore Wrestles With Aerial Surveillance." *Axios.* Available at www.axios.com/baltimore-wrestles-with-aerial-surveillance-to-reduce-crime-2d973591-0b33-4e25-94a7-c3f553dc2934.html

Harvard Business Review. September 2013. "The Impact of Employee Engagement on Employment." Available at https://hbr.org/resources/pdfs/comm/achievers/hbr_achievers_report_sep13.pdf

Haurlan, P. 2021. *Advanced Concepts for Market Technicians*. Rancho Cucamonga: Alanpur Trading Publishers.

Heald, R., and M. Wildermuth. 2019. *Initiative to Advance Faculty Diversity, Equity and Inclusion in the Life Science at UC Berkeley Year End Summary Report: 20182019*. University of California. Available at https://ofew.berkeley.edu/sites/default/files/life_sciences_inititatve.year_end_report_summary.pdf

Hitachi News Release. June 2017. "Workstyle Advice from AI Helping to Raise Workplace Happiness." Available at www.hitachi.com/rd/news/2017/0626.html

Hitachi News Release. October 2017. "Hitachi Develops Smartphone Technology Measuring Happiness." Available at www.hitachi.com/rd/news/2017/1002.htm

Hoppe, K. October 2019. "What Is the Secret to Happiness? (AI Schools Humans)." *Data Driven Investor*. Available at https://medium.com/datadriveninvestor

IBM. January 2017. *Extending Expertise: How Cognitive Computing Is Transforming HR and the Employee Experience*. Somers: IBM Institute for Business Value.

Irwin, N. 2018. *How to Win in a Winner-Take-All World*. New York, NY: St. Martin's Press.

JPMorgan. 2020. "Discover Your Unique Results with Pymetrics." Available at https://careers.jpmorgan.com/us/en/advice/pymetrics-overview

Kelly, K. 2016. *The Inevitable: Understanding the 12 Technological Forces That Will Shape Our Future*. New York, NY: Penguin Books.

Knight, W. January 2018. "Google's Self-Training AI Turns Coders Into Machine-Learning Masters." *MIT Technology Review*. Available at www.technologyreview.com/2018/01/17/146164/googles-self-training-ai-turns-coders-into-machine-learning-masters/

Kobielus, J. 2018. *Wikibon Big Data Analytics Trends Forecast*. Marlborough: Wikibon. Available at https://wikibon.com/wikibons-2018-big-data-analytics-trends-forecast/

Komarraju, A. April 2021. "Neurosymbolic AI: Know About the Next AI Revolution." *Analytics Insight*. Available at www.analyticsinsight.net/neurosymbolic-ai-know-about-the-next-ai-revolution/

Kozyrkov, C. June 2018. "Why Businesses Fail At Machine Learning." *Hackernoon*. Available at https://medium.com/hackernoon/why-businesses-fail-at-machine-learning-fbff41c4d5db

Kuan, C.M., and H. White. March 1994. "Artificial Neural Networks: An Econometric Perspective." *Econometric Reviews*, pp. 1–91.

Kucera, V. January 2017. "Rudolf E. Kalman: Life and Works." *ScienceDirect*, pp. 631–636. Available at www.sciencedirect.com/science/article/pii/S2405896317300903

Lacan, J. 1966. "The Mirror Stage As Formative of the Function of the I As Revealed in Psychoanalytic Experience." *Ecrits: A Selection*. Oxfordshire: Routledge Classics. Available at www.soundandsignifier.com/files/Lacan Mirror Stage.pdf

Lanier, J., and G. Weyl. March 2020. "AI is an Ideology, Not a Technology." *Wired Magazine*. Available at www.wired.com/story/opinion-ai-is-an-ideology-not-a-technology/

Lazarus, R.S. 1966. *Psychological Stress and the Coping Process*. New York, NY: McGraw Hill.

Lazarus, R.S. and S. Folkman. 1984. *Stress, Appraisal, and Coping*. New York, NY: Springer Publishing Company.

Ledyard, J.O., D. Porter, and A. Rangel. November 1994. "Using Computerized Exchange Systems to Solve an Allocation Problem in Project Management." *Journal of Organizational Complexity*, pp. 271–296.

Leibniz, G.W. 1989. "Dissertation on the Art of Combinations." *Philosophical Papers and Letters. The New Synthese Historical Library (Texts and Studies in the History of Philosophy)*. Volume 2. L.E. Loemker, ed. New York, NY: Springer.

Lerner, U., M. Jahr, and V. Kasera. January 2011. *Selectively Deleting Clusters of Conceptually Related Words from a Generative Model for Text*. Google. U.S. Patent 7,877,371.

Lessnof, M.H. October 1968. "Parson's System Problems." *Sociological Review*, pp. 185–215.

Lock, I., and P. Steele. May 2016. "The Credibility of CSR Reports in Europe: Evidence From a Quantitative Content Analysis in 11 Countries." *Journal of Cleaner Production*, pp. 186–200.

Ma, L., X. Jia, Q. Sun, B. Schiele, T. Tuytelaars, and L. Van Gool. 2017. "Pose Guided Person Image Generation." In *Proceedings of the 31st Conference on Neural Information Processing Systems (NIPS 2017)*, eds. U. von Luxburg, I. Guyon, S. Bengio, H. Wallach, and R. Fergus. Red Hook: Curran Publishing.

Maciak, P. November 2012. "The Passion of the Critic: On Hoberman, Kracauer, and the Future of Film." *Los Angeles Review of Books*. Available at https://lareviewofbooks.org/article/the-passion-of-the-critic-on-hoberman-kracauer-and-the-future-of-film/

Madrigal, A. November 2011. "Daniel Kahneman on 'Emergent Weirdness' in Artificial Intelligences." *Atlantic*. Available at www.theatlantic.com/technology/archive/2011/11/daniel-kahneman-on-emergent-weirdness-in-artifical-intelligences/249125/

Martus, S. 2001. *Ernst Jünger.* Stuttgart: Metzler Verlag.

Milton, J. 2000. *Paradise Lost.* New York, NY: Penguin Classic Books.

Minsky, M. 1986. *Society of Mind.* New York, NY: Simon and Schuster.

Minsky, M. 1994. *AI: The Tumultuous Search for Artificial Intelligence.* New York: Basic Books.

Minsky, M., and S. Papert. 1969. *Perceptrons: An Introduction to Computational Geometry.* Boston: MIT Press.

Minsky, M., and S. Papert. 1988. *Perceptrons: An Introduction to Computational Geometry: Expanded Edition.* Boston: MIT Press.

Moore, P. July, 2019. "The mirror for (artificial) intelligence: In whose reflection?" In *Special Issue of Comparative Labor Law & Policy Journal on Automation, Artificial Intelligence and Labour Protection*, ed. V. De Stefano. Available at www.labourlawresearch.net/news/special-issue-comparative-labor-law-and-policy-journal-automation-artificial-intelligence-ai

Nash, J.F. Jr. January 1950. "Equilibrium in N-Person Games." *Proceedings of the National Academy of Sciences.* Available at www.pnas.org/content/36/1/48

NewVantage Partners. 2018. "Big Data Executive Survey 2018:How Big data and AI are Driving Business Innovation." Available at https://pdf4pro.com/view/big-data-executive-survey-2018-newvantage-partners-528706.html

Nkonde, M. June 2019. "A.I. Is Not as Advanced as You Might Think." *Zora.* Available at https://zora.medium.com/a-i-is-not-as-advanced-as-you-might-think-97657e9eecdc

ÓhÉigeartaigh, S.S., J. Whittlestone, Y. Liu, Y. Zeng, and Z. Liu. June 2020. "Open Access Overcoming Barriers to Cross-cultural Cooperation in AI Ethics and Governance." *Philosophy & Technology*, pp. 572593. Available at https://link.springer.com/content/pdf/10.1007/s13347-020-00402-x.pdf

OpenAI. October 2019. "Solving Rubik's Cube with a Robot Hand." *Cornell University Working Paper.* Available at https://arxiv.org/abs/1910.07113

Oracle and Future Workplace. 2019. *From Fear to Enthusiasm: AI@Work Study.* Available at www.oracle.com/a/ocom/docs/applications/hcm/ai-at-work-ebook.pdf

Osterwalder, A. May 2013. "A Better Way to Think About Your Business Model." *Harvard Business Review.* Available at https://hbr.org/2013/05/a-better-way-to-think-about-yo

Ovans, A. January 2015. "What is a Business Model?" *Harvard Business Review.* Available at https://hbr.org/2015/01/what-is-a-business-model

Parsons, T. 1956. *Economy and Society: A Study in the Integration of Economic and Social Theory.* Milton Park: Routledge and Kegan Paul Ltd.

Pew Research Center. 2016. *The State of American Jobs.* Available at www.pewsocialtrends.org/2016/10/06/3-how-americans-view-their-jobs/

Plato. 2007. *The Republic.* New York, NY: Penguin Classic Books.

Pontifical Academy for Life. February 2020. *The Call for AI Ethics was signed in Rome*. Rome: The Vatican. Available at www.academyforlife.va/content/pav/en/news/2020/intelligenza-artificiale-2020.html

Press, G. December 2016. "A Very Short History of Artificial Intelligence (AI)." *Forbes*. Available at www.forbes.com/sites/gilpress/2016/12/30/a-very-short-history-of-artificial-intelligence-ai/#57e76ad36fba

Preston, D. 2007. *Blasphemy*. New York, NY: Forge Books.

Pueyo, T. March 2020. "What is the hidden structure of stories, and why is it rooted in our brains?" *Writing Cooperative*. Available at https://writingcooperative.com/what-is-the-hidden-structure-of-stories-and-why-is-it-rooted-in-our-brains-68fdcea4c999

Racah, E., C. Beckham, T. Maharaj, S. E. Kahou, and C. Pal. 2017. "Extreme Weather: A large-scale climate dataset for semi-supervised detection, localization, and understanding of extreme weather events." In *Proceedings of the 31st Conference on Neural Information Processing Systems (NIPS 2017)*. In *Proceedings of the 31st Conference on Neural Information Processing Systems (NIPS 2017)*, eds. U. von Luxburg, I. Guyon, S. Bengio, H.Wallach, and R.Fergus, Red Hook: Curran Publishing.

Ramage, D., and S. Mazzocchi, May 2020. "Federated Analytics: Collaborative Data Science without Data Collection." *AI Google Blog*. Available at https://ai.googleblog.com/2020/05/federated-analytics-collaborative-data.html

Reagan, A.J., L. Mitchell., and D. Kiley. November, 2016. "The emotional arcs of stories are dominated by six basic shapes." *EPJ Data Science*. Available at https://doi.org/10.1140/epjds/s13688-016-0093-1

Rector, K., and A. Knezevich. October 2016. "Maryland's Use of Facial Recognition Software Questioned by Researchers, Civil Liberties Advocates." *Baltimore Sun*. Available at www.baltimoresun.com/news/crime/bs-md-facial-recognition-20161017-story.html

Rifkin, J. 2011. *The Third Industrial Revolution; How Lateral Power is Transforming Energy, the Economy, and the World*. New York, NY: St. Martin's Press.

Robbins, R. May 2020. "AI systems are worse at diagnosing disease when training data is skewed by sex." *Stat*. Available at www.statnews.com/2020/05/25/ai-systems-training-data-sex-bias/?utm_campaign=rss

Rogati, M. February 2017. "How Not to Hire Your First Data Scientist." *Hackernoon*. Available at https://hackernoon.com/how-not-to-hire-your-first-data-scientist-34f0f56f81ae

Sakakibara, R., and T. Endo. November 2015. "Cognitive Appraisal as a Predictor of Cognitive Emotion Regulation Choice." *Japanese Psychological Association*. https://onlinelibrary.wiley.com/doi/full/10.1111/jpr.12098

Schachter, S., and J. Singer. January 1962. "Cognitive, Social, and Physiological Determinants of Emotional State." *Psychological Review*, pp. 379–399.

Scherer, K. November 2009. "The Dynamic Architecture of Emotion: Evidence for the Component Process Model." *Cognition and Emotion*, pp. 1307–1331.

Scherer, K., A. Schorr, and T. Johnston. 2001. *Appraisal Processes in Emotion: Theory, Methods, Research*. New York, NY: Oxford University Press.

Schreiber, D. December 2019. "AI Can Vanquish Bias." *Lemonade Blog*. Available at www.lemonade.com/blog/ai-can-vanquish-bias/

Securities and Exchange Commission. December 1998. "Regulation of Exchanges and Alternative Trading Systems." Release No. 34-40760; File No. S7-12-98. Available at www.sec.gov/rules/final/34-40760.txt.

Seyyed-Kalantari, L., G. Liu, M. McDermott, and M. Ghassemi, January 2020. "Chexclusion: Fairness Gaps In Deep Chest X-Ray Classifiers." *Biocomputing*, pp. 232–243.

Shead, S. May 2020. "How Britain's Oldest Universities are Trying to Protect Humanity from Risky A.I." *CNBC News*. Available at www.cnbc.com/2020/05/25/oxford-cambridge-ai.html

Sheffield, H. November 2019. "The Great Data Leap: How AI Will Transform Recruitment And HR." *Financial Times*. Available at www.ft.com/content/d962a330-d30e-11e9-8d46-8def889b4137

Shiftboard. 2021. "The Real Cost of Employee Disengagement." Available at www.shiftboard.com/blog/real-cost-employee-disengagement/

Singh, R. September 2019. "The Rise and Fall of Symbolic AI." *Towards Data Science*. Available at https://towardsdatascience.com/rise-and-fall-of-symbolic-ai-6b7abd2420f2

Solon, O. June 2018. "'Surveillance Society': Has Technology at the US-Mexico Border Gone Too Far?" *Guardian*. Available at www.theguardian.com/technology/2018/jun/13/mexico-us-border-wall-surveillance-artificial-intelligence-technology

Som, K. March 2019. "New Religion–Way of the Future–Dedicated to Worship of AI." *AiTrends*. Available at https://nikolanews.com/new-religion-way-of-the-future-dedicated-to-worship-of-ai/

Smolensky, P. December 2019. "Next-generation architectures bridge gap between neural and symbolic representations with neural symbols." Microsoft research blog. Available at www.microsoft.com/en-us/research/blog/next-generation-architectures-bridge-gap-between-neural-and-symbolic-representations-with-neural-symbols/

Snow, S. January 2015. "This Surprising Reading Level Analysis Will Change the Way You Write." Available at https://contently.com/2015/01/28/this-surprising-reading-level-analysis-will-change-the-way-you-write/

Steinbeck, J. 1952. *East of Eden*. New York, NY: Viking Press.

Stockholm International Peace Research Institute. 2019. *SIPRI Military Expenditure Database*. Available at www.sipri.org/databases/milex

Stolarski, K., N. Yeshkova, and M. Pepper. September 2020. *Worldwide Service Provider Infrastructure Forecast, 2021-2025*. International Data Corporation. Available at www.idc.com/getdoc.jsp?containerId=US46385521

Stoller, D. January 2020. "Facebook to Pay $550 Million in Biometric Privacy Accord." Available at www.bloomberg.com/news/articles/2020-01-29/facebook-to-pay-550-million-to-settle-biometric-privacy-suit

Taigman, Y., M. Yang, M.A. Ranzato, and L. Wolf. 2014. "DeepFace: Closing the Gap to Human-Level Performance in Face Verification." In *Proceedings of the Conference on Computer Vision and Pattern Recognition*. Washington, DC: IEEE Computer Society.

Tani, J. October 1998. "An Interpretation of 'Self' from the Dynamical Systems Perspective: A Constructivist Approach." *Journal of Consciousness Studies*, pp. 516–542.

Taylor, F.W. 1911. *The Principles of Scientific Management*. New York, NY: Harper and Brothers.

Tian, N. A. Fleurant, A. Kuimova, P.D. Wezeman, and S. T. Wezeman. April 2019. *Trends in World Military Expenditure 2018*. Stockholm: Stockholm International Peace Research Institute. Available at www.sipri.org/sites/default/files/2019-04/fs_1904_milex_2018.pdf

Treynor, J.L., and F. Black. 1972. "Portfolio Selection Using Special Information, under the assumptions of the Diagonal Model, with Mean-Variance Portfolio Objectives, and without Constraints." In G.P. Szego and K. Shell, eds. *Mathematical Methods in Investment and Finance* 4, 367–384. Amsterdam: North-Holland.

Trump, D.J. September, 2017. *Presidential Memorandum for the Secretary of Education*. Available at https://trumpwhitehouse.archives.gov/presidential-actions/presidential-memorandum-secretary-education/

Truong, M., J. White, and A. Funk. October 2018. *Freedom on the Net: the Rise of Digital Authoritarianism*. Washington, DC.: Freedom House. Available at https://freedomhouse.org/report/freedom-net/2018/rise-digital-authoritarianism

Tsuji, S., N. Satu, and K. Yano. December 2017. "Sensor Application Approach for Measure and Change Behavior at Work." *Journal of the Japan Society for Precision Engineering*, pp. 11091116. Available at www.jstage.jst.go.jp/article/jjspe/83/12/83_1109/_article/-char/en

Turing, A. October 1950. "Computing Machinery and Intelligence." *Mind*, 433–460.

Tye, S. April 2020. "The stunning evolution of AI in movies." *Looper*. Available at www.looper.com/198685/the-stunning-evolution-of-ai-in-movies/

Uithol, S., I. van Rooij, H. Bekkering, and P. Haselager. September 2011. "What Do Mirror Neurons Mirror?" *Philosophical Psychology*, pp. 607–623.

Vonnegut, K. 1981. *Palm Sunday*. New York, NY: Rosetta Books.

Vopson, M. September 2019. "The Mass-Energy-Information Equivalence Principle." *AIP Advances*. Available at https://aip.scitation.org/doi/10.1063/1.5123794

Walch, K. February 2020. "AI Laws Are Coming." *Forbes*. Available at www.forbes.com/sites/cognitiveworld/2020/02/20/ai-laws-are-coming/?sh=60 60610ba2b4

Walter, W.G. 1963. *The Living Brain*. New York: W.W. Norton and Sons.

Warburton, M. February 2020. "Alphabet still facing questions over data use in its Toronto smart city project proposal." *Reuters*. Available at www.reuters.com/article/us-alphabet-sidewalk/alphabet-still-facing-questions-over-data-use-in-its-toronto-smart-city-project-proposal-idUSKCN20L042?il=0

Wessen, R.R., and D. Porter. March 1998. "Market-based approaches for controlling space mission costs: the Cassini Resource Exchange." *Journal of Reducing Space Mission Cost*, pp. 9–25.

World Economic Forum. 2020. *The Global Risk Report 2020*. Insight Report 15th edition. Available at www3.weforum.org/docs/WEF_Global_Risk_Report_2020.pdf

Yano, K. June 2016. "AI For Taking on the Challenges of an Unpredictable Era." *Hitachi Review*, p. 1434. Available at www.hitachi.com/rev/pdf/2016/r2016_06_101.pdf

Zweben, S., and B. Bizot. 2019. *Taulbee Survey 2019*. Pittsburgh, Computer Research Association.

About the Author

Ian Domowitz is former Vice Chairman of Investment Technology Group [NYSE: ITG] and CEO of ITG Solutions Network Inc., a pioneer in the application of machine learning to institutional trading performance. Author of *The Vice Chairman's Doctrine: A Guide to Rocking the Top in Industry 4.0*, he has published more than 100 articles over 19 years in academics and 17 years on Wall Street and holds 12 patents in financial technology. He received a PhD in Economics from the University of California, San Diego and currently serves on the board of directors of McKinley Management LLC.

Index

www.ingramcontent.com/pod-product-compliance
Lightning Source LLC
Chambersburg PA
CBHW061140220326
41599CB00025B/4307